THE PRACTICE OF
Sustainable Development

Douglas R. Porter
Principal Author and Editor

PRIMARY AUTHORS

Rutherford H. Platt
Christopher Leinberger
Edward J. Blakely
Susan Maxman

CONTRIBUTORS

Thomas Cahill
Rolf Sauer
Robert Hotes
Muscoe Martin
Don Prowler
George Brewster

**Urban Land
Institute**

About ULI—the Urban Land Institute

ULI—the Urban Land Institute is a nonprofit education and research institute that is supported and directed by its members. Its mission is to provide responsible leadership in the use of land in order to enhance the total environment.

ULI sponsors education programs and forums to encourage an open international exchange of ideas and sharing of experiences; initiates research that anticipates emerging land use trends and issues and proposes creative solutions based on that research; provides advisory services; and publishes a wide variety of materials to disseminate information on land use and development. Established in 1936, the Institute today has more than 16,000 members and associates from more than 60 countries representing the entire spectrum of the land use and development disciplines.

Richard M. Rosan
President

ULI Project Staff

Rachelle L. Levitt
Senior Vice President, Policy and Practice
Publisher

Gayle Berens
Vice President, Real Estate Development
Practice

Michael Pawlukiewicz
Director of Environmental Land
Use Policy
Project Director

Nancy H. Stewart
Director, Book Program
Managing Editor

Carol E. Soble
Manuscript Editor

Betsy VanBuskirk
Art Director

Jeanne Berger Design
Design and Layout

Meg Batdorff
Graphic Designer
Cover Design

Diann Stanley-Austin
Director, Publishing Operations

Maria-Rose Cain
Word Processor

Recommended bibliographic listing:
Porter, Douglas R., et al. *The Practice of Sustainable Development*. Washington, D.C.: ULI–the Urban Land Institute, 2000.

ULI Catalog Number: P93
International Standard Book Number: 0-87420-831-9

Library of Congress Catalog Card Number: 00-105575

© Copyright 2000 by ULI–the Urban Land Institute
1025 Thomas Jefferson Street, N.W.
Suite 500 West
Washington, D.C. 20007-5201

Cover photograph: Hidden Springs, Idaho

ABOUT THE AUTHORS

Douglas R. Porter

Douglas R. Porter is considered one of the nation's leading authorities on growth management techniques and issues at state, regional, and local levels. In addition to his consulting on growth management issues, he formed the nonprofit Growth Management Institute in 1992 to conduct research and educational efforts in growth management policies and practices. From 1979 to 1991, Porter directed the public policy research program of the Urban Land Institute. He is a Fellow of ULI and has chaired the Maryland Transportation Commission. He has written or contributed to more than 30 books and 100 articles. Porter's recent publications include Managing Growth in America's Communities (Island Press, 1997), Transit-Focused Development: A Synthesis of Transit Practice (National Academy Press, 1997), Profiles in Growth Management (ULI, 1996), Collaborative Planning for Wildlife and Wetlands (Island Press, 1995), and State and Regional Initiatives for Managing Development (ULI, 1992).

Rutherford H. Platt

Rutherford H. Platt is a professor of geography and adjunct professor of regional planning at the University of Massachusetts at Amherst. He holds a B.A. in political science from Yale University and a law degree and PhD in geography from the University of Chicago and is a member of the Illinois Bar. Public policy issues of land and water resources, particularly the management of floodplains, wetland, and coastal zones, have been the focus of his research, teaching, and consulting. He has served on several national panels, including six committies of the National Academy of Sciences/National Research Council. In addition to writing numerous articles and monographs, he wrote Land Use Control (1991, Prentice-Hall) and co-edited The Ecological City (1994, University of Massachusetts Press).

Christopher Leinberger

Christopher Leinberger is a founding partner of Arcadia Land Company, a development company focusing on land stewardship and the commercially successful synthesis of development within and part of the natural environment. For 17 years, Leinberger has been managing director and, until April 2000, co-owner of Robert Charles Lesser & Co., the largest independent real estate advisory firm in the country, which works on over 400 projects a year for developers, corporations, nonprofit entities, and municipalities. He serves on the Board of Directors of Avalon Properties, Inc. (NYSE real estate investment trust), is vice chairman of the Metropolitan Economic Development Council of the Urban Land Institute, and serves on the National Advisory Board of NAIOP. Leinberger is on the National Advisory Board of the Conservation Fund, a national environmental organization, and the American Land Institute, a startup policy organization concerning land use and growth management.

Leinberger has written books and articles running the gamut of economic, social, and environmental implications of land use patterns. Most recently, he coauthored the executive summary chapter of Urban Parks and Open Space, published by ULI and the Trust For Public Land. He is a graduate of Harvard Business School and as an undergraduate attended Swarthmore College, where he majored in urban sociology and politics.

Edward J. Blakely

Edward J. Blakely, PhD, is dean of the Robert J. Milano Graduate School of Management and Urban Policy, the New School University, in New York City. Most recently, he was the Lusk Professor of Planning and Development for the School of Urban Planning and Development at the University of Southern California (1994-1999). Previously, he served as professor and chair of the Department of City and Regional Planning at the University of California at Berkeley (1986-1994). Blakely is an internationally recognized scholar in urban community development, and has also been a successful practitioner in strategic planning, financing, real estate development, and project management. He serves on the National Academy of Sciences Panel on Urban Development and Transportation. He also serves as an adviser to the Organization for Economic Cooperation and Development and to state governments in the United States, Australia, Sweden, and Japan. He is the author of four books and more than 100 scholarly articles. His publications include Fortress America; Separate Societies; Poverty and Inequality in U.S. Cities; Planning Local Economic Development Theory and Practice; and Rural Communities in Advanced Industrial Society.

Susan Maxman

Susan A. Maxman, FAIA, is a nationally recognized advocate and expert on the principles of sustainable design. She has been principal of her own firm, Susan Maxman & Partners, since 1980. Susan Maxman & Partners practices environmentally responsive architecture by designing buildings that fit into their surroundings, are sensitive to user needs, and are in harmony with the community. She has served as the first female president of the American Institute of Architects. Maxman is assistant chair of the Urban Land Institute's Environmental Council. She also has sat on the President's Council on Sustainable Development. A graduate of Smith College and the University of Pennsylvania, she holds numerous awards and honorary degrees.

CONTENTS

FOREWORD

Chattanooga, Tennessee, has positioned itself over the past several years as a center for sustainable development initiatives. We have had successes in downtown redevelopment, inner-city neighborhood planning initiatives, greenway and pedestrian development, and electric bus programs. We have instituted an urban design studio to focus on how we design the built environment and have one of the most successful housing initiatives in the country.

But changing the overall development pattern of our urban area is a complex and difficult process. If one believes, as I do, that our current pattern of outward-spreading development cannot be sustained economically or socially, then we need to understand the factors that encourage development and how to change these forces.

Past development patterns have not been the product of irrational thought. To the contrary, governments, developers, and citizens have followed a logical course that is the result of decades of federal, state, and local policies that encourage the outward expansion of land use while discouraging the redevelopment of urban centers and older suburbs. It will continue to be much more difficult to force people to act in a way that appears to be contrary to their own interests as compared with changing the environment so that market forces result in development patterns that can be sustained.

Before being elected mayor of Chattanooga, I was engaged in real estate development. I had been involved in traditional suburban subdivision development but had also begun to incorporate some new urbanism design into our developments in response to what I perceived to be a change in consumer preferences. As mayor, I became much more knowledgeable of the big picture. In short, changing consumer preferences, particularly an increasing desire for a sense of community, and the growing cost of government services for new development require a new approach.

As we begin to understand that the traditional model of urban development will no longer work for the future, we are still grappling with the difficult task of defining a new model. Some of my fellow developers are concerned that some of the proposed changes will result in the loss of business or substantial increases in cost. Some citizens worry that ideas such as smart growth or sustainable development will constrain personal freedom of choice.

But the existing pattern of development that results in lower densities and greater infrastructure costs will not remain economically feasible for long. And, as to personal choice, the current development model reduces choice. Take transportation, for example. Reduced densities and the greater dispersion of activity centers require use of the automobile for just about all trips. Many of us remember growing up and walking to school or to the store or to the park. "Soccer Moms" are not a reflection of greater participation among children in after-school activities; rather, they point to the need for the automobile to make trips that were previously made by walking, bicycling, or patronizing the local bus system.

Much more analysis and dialogue must take place if we are to develop a new model of development that gains broad support and works with rather than against existing market forces. And this work requires the inclusion of all the actors involved in the development process: government, planners, developers, the business community, and civic groups.

Douglas Porter has taken a major step forward in bringing a sense of coherence and understanding to the complex issue of sustainable development. Through this book, he provides a conceptual model for sustainable development and gives thoughtful examples of the economic feasibility of this new approach. His work continues the process of providing the intellectual underpinnings for the new model of development while providing a connection to the real world of private sector development and political realities.

All of us, government officials, developers, and citizens, owe him a debt of gratitude.

Jon Kinsey
Mayor, Chattanooga, Tennessee

ACKNOWLEDGMENTS

This publication springs from the Urban Land Institute's longstanding commitment to improving the practice of real estate development and to making our cities and towns livable, exciting, civilized places. Institute members' interest in sustainable development has been increasing, but always accompanied by nagging questions about the "what" and "how" of applying the broad principles of sustainability to everyday development practice. Hence this book, which describes applications of sustainable development that are both workable and financially feasible in today's markets and communities. Recognizing our evolving understanding of both the concept of sustainability and the techniques and technologies for achieving it, the Afterword poses questions and issues still to be addressed to make sustainability a real estate reality.

Preparation of this publication was a team effort, although most of the team met only through cyberspace. We tapped the expertise of scholars, market analysts, and professional designers and engineers who understand the technologies and applications of sustainable principles and who are invariably enthusiastic supporters of innovative approaches to development. We also drew ideas and examples from the many publications about sustainability pouring out of publishing houses and from the rich store of materials already available from ULI's *Urban Land* articles, projects profiled in ULI's *Project Reference File* or highlighted in the annual awards for excellence in development, and a working paper entitled "The Ecology of Development" prepared in 1997 for ULI by George Brewster, Marianna Leuschel, and Michael Pawlukiewicz.

As the overall editor, I produced the front matter and the opening chapter. As the member of the authorial team least familiar with specific technical aspects of sustainable development, I grappled in chapter 2 with definitions and components of sustainability, their interrelationships, and issues arising from them. Chapters 3, 4, and 5, which paint a broad background about the environmental, economic, and social concerns of sustainability, were contributed, respectively, by Rutherford H. Platt, Christopher Leinberger, and Edward Blakely. "Rud" Platt is professor of geography and planning law in the Department of Geosciences at the University of Massachusetts, Amherst, Massachusetts, and an eminent scholar of natural resource protection, with many books to his credit. Chris Leinberger, managing director of Robert Charles Lesser & Company in Santa Fe, New Mexico, is well known as a real estate economist, author, and now a developer as well. Edward Blakely is a scholar of community development and a successful practitioner in strategic planning and development. He recently moved from the University of Southern California to become dean of the Milano Graduate School of Management and Urban Policy at The New School University in New York City.

Chapters 6, 7, and 8 were prepared by multiple authors. In chapter 5, on applications of sustainability to development projects, Rolf Sauer, of Rolf Sauer & Partners, Ltd., in Philadelphia, prepared the landscape section, and Thomas Cahill, of Cahill and Associates in West Chester, Pennsylvania, wrote the hydrology section. I contributed some material to both sections and wrote the remainder of the chapter with the help of contributions from Michael Horst at ULI. Susan Maxman, president of Susan Maxman & Partners, an architectural design firm in Philadelphia, oversaw preparation of chapter 7 and wrote the introduction. Don Prowler, of Don Prowler & Associates in Philadelphia, prepared the section on energy efficiency, to which, with Don's help, I added interpretations drawn from the ULI's "Ecology of Development" working paper. Muscoe Martin, AIA, a principal of Susan Maxman & Partners, wrote the building materials section, and Robert Hotes, an associate of Susan Maxman & Partners, prepared the section on adaptive use. I wrote the final chapter with help from George Brewster. In addition, I am grateful for case studies offered by Terry Lassar of Portland, Oregon, a writer on real estate development, and for material on collaborative environmental planning by Lindell Marsh, principal of Siemon, Larsen & Marsh in Irvine, California. I also wrote the Afterword, edited the entire manuscript, and sought out case examples and supplemental material and graphics for most chapters.

The project was launched and overseen by Michael Pawlukiewicz, Gayle Berens, and Rachelle Levitt of the ULI staff, who defined the themes and audience for the book and contributed useful advice along the way. Three ULI members, Anthony Catanese, Wim Wiewel, and Frank Martin, reviewed the first draft and provided helpful comments. Truly a team effort.

I am immensely grateful for the willing assistance of so many experts in so many innovative fields. And, of course, the responsibility for errors is mine.

Douglas R. Porter
President, The Growth Management Institute

chapter 1

INTRODUCTION
SUSTAINABLE
DEVELOPMENT

Douglas R. Porter

"Sustainable development"—a two-word phrase with a thousand meanings. "Sustainable" implies forever, perpetuity, constant rebirth and renewal, an inexhaustible system. "Development" connotes change, growth, expansion, production, movement. Both words speak of time, evolutionary processes, constructive adaptation. But each word modifies the other. Development, to be sustainable, must somehow incorporate renewal that ensures the continuity of matter, resources, populations, cultures. Sustainability, to incorporate development, must allow change and adaptation to new conditions. Today, the two ideas together speak of balancing economic and social forces against the environmental imperatives of resource conservation and renewal for the world of tomorrow.

That linkage between the works of humankind and the surrounding environment was articulated succinctly as early as 1864 when George Perkins Marsh observed, "Man everywhere is a disturbing agent. Wherever he plants his foot, the harmonies of nature are turned to discords."[1] Almost a century later,

Lewis Mumford reaffirmed Marsh's critique, writing that metropolitan growth "is fast absorbing the rural hinterland and threatening to wipe out many of the natural elements favorable to life. . . ."[2]

During the 1960s and 1970s, concerns mounted worldwide over the degradation of fundamental environmental qualities. The global population was expanding explosively, more than tripling in the 20th century. Significant declines in air and water quality and biodiversity were documented in many parts of the world. The alarming destruction of tropical rainforests and the effect of greenhouse gases on the earth's atmosphere were often cited as indicators of the problems at hand. Looking forward, these trends foretold of serious threats to the sustainability of life on the planet.

These anxieties came to a head in 1987 with the work of the Brundtland Commission, which was formed by the United Nations. The commission's report sounded a stern warning about the reality of the reduction in the

earth's capacity to sustain life in the face of overwhelming growth in world population. It called for major initiatives to reverse that decline by recognizing the intertwined relationships of environmental conservation, economic prosperity, and social equity—the essence of sustainable development.

The commission defined sustainable development as "[d]evelopment which meets the needs of the present without compromising the ability of future generations to meet their own needs."[3]

Subsequent international and national conferences and commissions have continued to emphasize the critical importance of attending to this issue. They call for economic development that respects the integrity of natural systems and promotes social advancement. They warn against development that consumes nonrenewable resources such as fossil fuels and poisons the air we breathe and the water we drink.

The ideals of sustainable development are stimulating a rethinking of many facets of our lives, not the least of which is the tremendous growth and geographic spread of our communities. Of particular concern is the rapid expansion of the nation's 284 metropolitan regions into the countryside, converting farmlands and forests into suburban and exurban settlements. The spread of development intensifies pressures on vulnerable land and water resources while frequently leaving behind deteriorating neighborhoods and business centers in central cities and inner suburbs. Since 1940, half of all U.S. metropolitan population growth has occurred in suburban jurisdictions, much of it in forms of low-density development that consume land at a rapid rate and depend on resource-depleting automobiles for mobility. Though the discussion is subject to intense dispute, there seems to be plenty of land and oil to support current patterns of community development; nonetheless, many people are troubled by the downside—the effects of today's development practices on fundamental environmental qualities, the costs of supporting infrastructure systems, the economic vitality of our cities and towns, and the associated social and economic disparities.

Proponents of the "traditional neighborhood development," "new urbanism," and "smart growth" movements respond to these concerns with calls for creating more livable communities. They prescribe forms of development that are designed to maintain and enhance existing neighborhoods, business centers, and infrastructure systems; widen the range of transportation choices; provide a variety of housing and living environments; and conserve natural resources. The aims of these movements, which tend to dwell on the physical elements of community design, comport well with the goals of sustainable development. However, "sustainable" adds a dimension: a deep respect for long-term conservation of

natural resources and concern for economic and social advancement.

Translating the lofty ideals of sustainability into the rough-and-tumble world of everyday development can be a daunting task. Looming large are obstacles such as a business-as-usual mentality, cautions about innovative designs and technologies, regulatory and financial policies, and a marketplace steeped in visions of the low-density American dream. Nonetheless, many developers are already developing projects that exemplify some of the ideals of sustainable development. The innovative technologies of "green building" and resource-conserving forms of development are becoming more widely known and increasingly cost effective. Developers are also listening to advocates of sustainable and "smarter" growth; they understand the benefits of responding to these popular ideas about community development.

In addition, market demands are changing in the direction of more sustainable forms of development. A sizable niche market of consumers apparently values compact, mixed-use development that frees them from maintaining large houses and yards and depending on the automobile. Moreover, not only are households increasingly diverse, desiring a wider array of development products, but the aging of the baby boom segment of the population seems to be generating greater interest in returning to the city, or at least to established neighborhoods, thereby increasing interest in recycling buildings and urban land. Even in suburban locations, tightly knit traditional neighborhoods are attracting consumers.

Guided by its long-established principle of providing "responsible leadership in the use of land in order to enhance the total environment," the Urban Land Institute commissioned this publication to demonstrate the ways that develop-

ers can put into practice the concept of sustainable development. A round-up of the approaches available to developers and builders and described in the following chapters includes these opportunities:

- conserving natural resources by minimizing the consumption of land (through compact development, for example) and maintaining and restoring existing environmental attributes of development sites;

- developing sites and designing buildings to reduce the consumption of energy and nonrenewable materials and the production of waste, toxic emissions, and pollution;

- using existing and renewable urban resources such as underused buildings and sites, infrastructure systems already in place, and historic neighborhoods and structures;

- designing developments to enhance a community's sense of place, livability, and social and economic interaction;

- choosing and designing development sites in ways that increase access to jobs, affordable housing, transportation choices, and recreational facilities; and

- creating developments that expand the diversity, synergism, and use of renewable resources in the operation and output of local economic activities.

This publication explains sustainable development approaches in detail, reviews the issues associated with them, points out the cost differentials that some may pose, and describes numerous examples of developments already in place. It postulates that every developer can apply some elements of sustainability to every project. It also recognizes the corollary premise that no development can hope to achieve the ultimate in sustainability, certainly not in the context of today's economy and society. Much of the responsibility for progressing toward a sustainable future requires national and international attention and impetus. Reducing income and education disparities among peoples, groups, and communities, for example, demands collective, large-scale, long-term changes in society that go far beyond the obligations of individual real estate developers. Nevertheless, the ideas and approaches advocated in the following chapters are based on the belief that every step taken toward more sustainable development is a step toward a sustainable planet.

Chapter 2, which analyzes the purposes, premises, and promises of sustainable development, introduces the discussions in chapters 3 through 5 of the broad environmental, economic, and social dimensions of sustainability that furnish the context for individual projects. Chapter 6 details the techniques and technologies available for siting, designing, and developing a variety of project types, from small- to large-scale developments in locations that range from greenfields to "infields." Chapter 7 describes "green" building techniques, including energy efficiency, materials, and adaptable use. Finally, chapter 8 summarizes a list of "best practices" and outlines proposals for promoting support for those practices by the real estate industry and public agencies.

Through this publication, the Urban Land Institute hopes to influence the quality of future development to achieve the principles of sustainable development.

Endnotes

1 George P. Marsh, *Man and Nature.* D. Lowenthal, ed. (Cambridge: Harvard University Press, 1864/1965), p. 36.

2 Lewis Mumford, "The Natural History of Urbanization," *Man's Role in Changing the Face of the Earth.* W.L. Thomas, Jr., ed. (Chicago: University of Chicago Press, 1956), p. 395.

3 World Commission on Environment and Development, *Our Common Future* (Oxford, UK: Oxford University Press, 1987), p. 43.

DIMENSIONS OF SUSTAINABILITY IN DEVELOPMENT

Douglas R. Porter

The principle of sustainability and the aims of sustainable development have only recently attracted broad public attention. The first international policy statement that pointed out the connection between economic wealth and environmental well-being was advanced in 1987 in the report of the Brundtland Commission. The commission, formally known as the United Nations World Commission on Environment and Development, brought the concept of sustainability to popular attention the world over. The commission's definition of sustainable development remains widely quoted:

> Development which meets the needs of the present without compromising the ability of future generations to meet their own needs.[1]

Expanding on this definition, the commission outlined five key principles of sustainability:

- Needs of the future must not be sacrificed to the demands of the present.

- Humanity's economic future is linked to the integrity of natural systems.

- The present world system is not sustainable because it is not meeting the needs of many, especially the poor.

- Protecting the environment is impossible unless we improve the economic prospects of the earth's poorest peoples.

We must act to preserve as many options as possible for future generations since they have the right to determine their own needs for themselves.[2]

The concept of sustainable development, then, meshes the need for preserving, enhancing, and interrelating economic prosperity, the integrity of natural ecosystems, and social

equity, as depicted in the by-now famous diagram in figure 2-1.

Since the Brundtland Commission's report, a series of international conferences (the 1992 Earth Summit, the 1995 Women's Summit, and the 1996 Habitat II) have explored the concept of sustainability. Today, sustainability is a global concern that focuses on the enormous social, economic, and envi-

The Concept of Sustainable Development 2-1

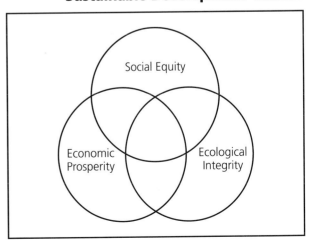

ronmental forces at play throughout all nations. Environmental phenomena such as the potential consequences of global warming, the depletion of the ozone layer, the destruction of tropical rainforests, and the continued decline in biodiversity are the subjects of almost daily news stories. Worrisome social and economic issues also stir debate, including the alarming increase in population, especially in developing countries whose economies can ill afford the stresses of such growth, and the widening gaps between the rich and poor in many nations.

In the United States, President Clinton established the President's Council on Sustainable Development in 1993 to recommend a national action strategy for sustainable development and to raise public awareness of the issues and opportunities associated with achieving sustainable development. In 1996, the council published a blueprint for achieving national sustainability that incorporated a vision statement, ten national goals covering a broad spectrum of topics, recommended policies for implementing these goals, and indicators of progress toward meeting the goals.[3] Goal 6, Sustainable Communities, states that Americans should:

> Encourage people to work together to create healthy communities where natural and historic resources are preserved, jobs are available, sprawl is contained, neighborhoods are secure, education is lifelong, transportation and health care are accessible, and all citizens have opportunities to improve the quality of their lives.[4]

Meanwhile, the cause of sustainability has energized hundreds if not thousands of civic and special interest groups, each with a particular perspective on the issues at stake. Some emphasize close-to-home concerns such as recycling, composting, use of solar energy, and reducing automobile emissions. Others push broad initiatives aimed at conserving forests and farmlands, employing water conservation measures, or preserving biodiversity. Still others promote programs to expand economic opportunities and redress social inequities. All, however, are working within the overarching concept of sustainable development, which places equal weight on the environmental, economic, and social components of sustainability. The concept offers a new way of thinking that stresses the interdependence of global forces, perhaps best explained by this stripped-down version of common ecological principles:

- Everything must go somewhere.

- Everything is connected to everything else.

- There is no free lunch.[5]

The concerns and ideas inherent in sustainable development are motivating a rethinking of our everyday ways of life, the use and abuse of natural and human resources, and, in particular, the forms of development we are creating for the places in which we live and work. The concept of sustainable development challenges how we approach the essential fabric and functioning of our communities.

Cause for Concern: The Case for Sustainable Development

Concerns over the sustainability of development have mounted over recent decades as society has gradually come to recognize that we have populated much of the earth's livable land and depleted much of the earth's resource base. In the process, we have altered fundamental qualities of the global environment. Published in 1962, Rachel Carson's *Silent Spring*[6] docu-mented the harm the industrial age inflicted on air and water and biodiversity. A few years later, highly influential books such as Paul Erlich's *The Population Bomb*[7] and Herman Daly's *Toward a Steady State Economy*[8] warned of the dangers of increasing consumption in a world of limited resources. In recent years, we have heard and read much about the rapid destruction of tropical rainforests, the near-"deaths" of Lake Erie and the Caspian Sea, the drawdown of aquifers that supply water to many growing cities, increases in greenhouse gases that may drive up global temperatures, and rising threats to species diversity.

Meanwhile, the world's population is rising rapidly. Over two millennia, it has risen from about 200 million to 6 billion people. More troubling is the fact that 4 billion of that increase has occurred since 1930; in fact, the global population more than tripled in the 20th century.[9] Most of the population expansion is taking place in metropolitan areas that are growing larger by the minute. The world's urban population multiplied tenfold in the 20th century. Moreover, populations are shifting to coastal regions, where intensive urban growth is increasing pressures on sensitive shoreline ecosystems. All this in a world where only 29 percent of the earth's surface is land, just 16 times the area of the United States.

Is it any wonder, then, that many people are concerned that the pace of human population growth will overwhelm the natural assets and resources that people the world over depend on for sustenance? That even developed nations will find their economies and quality of life diminished by worldwide degradation of basic environmental resources?

These global trends are echoed in communities throughout the United States. The U.S. population is projected to

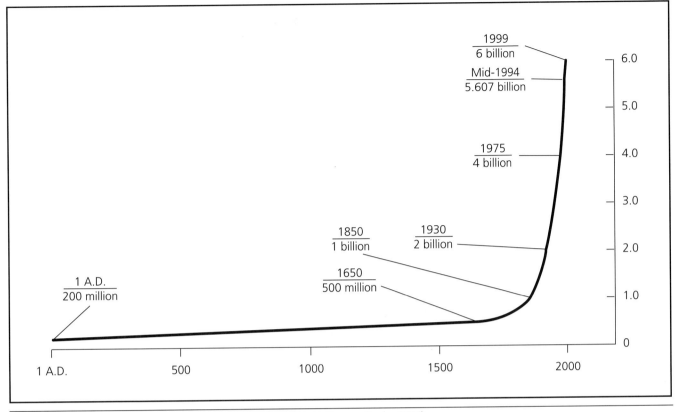

1999
6 billion

Mid-1994
5.607 billion

1975
4 billion

1850
1 billion

1930
2 billion

1650
500 million

1 A.D.
200 million

6.0

5.0

4.0

3.0

2.0

1.0

0

1 A.D.   500   1000   1500   2000

Source: *World Almanac and Book of Facts, 1996* (Mahwah, NJ: World Almanac Books, 1996).

grow from 260 million in 1998 to nearly 400 million by 2050.[10] The nation's 284 metropolitan regions, home to 80 percent of Americans, are pushing development out into hinterlands far from the central cities, converting farmlands and forests to suburban enclaves and exurban estates. Since 1940, half of U.S. metropolitan population growth has occurred in suburbs. From 1991 to 1998, more than 80 percent of new housing construction in the United States occurred in suburban communities.[11] By the early part of the 21st century, more than half of the nation's total population will live in suburbs.[12] And those suburbs are growing outward at an astounding pace. Atlanta's suburbanization, for example, is now occurring 45 to 70 miles north

of downtown, extending toward the South Carolina border.[13]

No matter how carefully development respects natural assets, the spread of urban development intensifies stresses on vulnerable landscapes and brings with it the detritus of urbanization—solid and toxic wastes, exhaust emissions, polluted stormwater runoff, and the like. The most rapid growth is occurring along the nation's coastlines. The 1990 census found half of all Americans living within 50 miles of a coast, a proportion expected to increase to 75 percent by 2010.[14] The population boom along the coasts is affecting beaches, dunes, estuaries, and coastal wetlands and, at the same time, is threatened by periodic storm damage,

shoreline erosion, and declining water quality.

All this comes about because Americans are great consumers. We delight in living in large houses on large lots, relying on individual "auto-mobility" for traveling great distances, and pampering ourselves with high-quality public services in the form of wide streets, grand sites for schools and other public buildings, and expansive parks and recreation areas. It is hardly surprising that our growing communities are consuming land at an unprecedented rate. Christopher Leinberger, a nationally respected real estate economist, predicts that "geometric increases in urbanized land will continue at a rate of at least eight to 12 times faster than the underlying employment and population growth."[15] A recent report by the U.S. Department of Agriculture—its five-year "natural resources inventory"—concluded that the rate at which farmland and forests are lost to development is accelerating. More land was developed between 1992 and 1997, the report says, than in the previous decade—16 million acres in five years versus 13.9 million acres in ten years. And this pattern is occurring in small and medium-sized cities such as Des Moines as much as in the New York metropolitan area.[16]

In the 45 years from 1950 to 1995, for example, the population of the Chicago area grew by 48 percent while land coverage jumped by 165 percent.[17] For the period between 1990 and 1996, the population of the Chicago urbanized area increased by 9 percent while the developed land area grew by 40 percent.[18] The population of the Los Angeles metropolitan area rose by 45 percent from 1970 to 1990 while developed land increased by 300 percent.[19] In the region southeast of Boston, more land has been converted to development in the last 40 years than in the preceding 330 years stretching back to the Pilgrims' landing in 1620—a rate of land consumption two and one-half times the rate of population increase.[20]

To some extent, these startling statistics may be explainable by factors other than the spread of low-density development. In the Chicago area, for example, the Metropolitan Transportation Center (MTC) has tracked population and land trends and observed that the Chicago region's proportion of home-owners compared to renters increased rapidly over the past decade or two. At the same time, household sizes were declining as traditional families gave way to one- and two-person households. In combination, these trends spelled a major increase in home con-

struction, much of it in suburban locations. Recently, says Siim Sööt of the MTC, these changes have moderated, suggesting that the ratio of land consumption per household may be dropping rather than climbing.

In addition, some recent "statistics" may be colored by the ideological stances of the organizations proclaiming them. The recent nationwide report of the Sierra Club, for example, was assembled from information provided by club members based in various metropolitan areas. Perhaps not surprisingly, they found massive increases in land consumption per capita in one region after another. For the Chicago region, the Sierra Club reported that, between 1990 and 1996, the population of the Chicago urbanized area increased by 9 percent while the developed land area grew by 40 percent—certainly a cause for concern. However, statistics analyzed by the Northern Illinois Planning Commission, the region's official producer of metropolitan data, showed that population in the Census-defined metropolitan region had increased by 4.8 percent from 1990 to 1995 while land consumption rose by just 6 percent. Growth trends in other metropolitan areas may present different scenarios, but the Chicago example suggests that current figures on land consumption per capita may not necessarily be reliable.[21]

Americans' love of low-density living brings with it a dependence on the automobile, which consumes gasoline and other nonrenewable resources. With one-twentieth of the world's population, we own over one-third of the world's motor vehicles and drive almost twice the distance per year (12,500 miles on average) as residents of other industrialized countries.[22] The number of motor vehicles is growing more than three times faster than the nation's population. And we are driving more: from 1983 to 1990, as the population increased by 4 percent, the number of

vehicle-miles jumped by 41 percent.[23] Despite the widespread suburbanization of jobs, services, and entertainment during the 1980s, commuting distances lengthened by more than 25 percent, accounting for 38 percent of the growth in vehicle-miles traveled.[24] Furthermore, the United States consumes 13 percent of the world's oil production just to power automobiles.[25] Despite amazing reductions in toxic emissions over the past two decades, the continued rise in vehicle-miles is expected to begin elevating emissions through this decade.[26]

Associated with increased rates of land conversion and travel are other signals of resource consumption, such as drawdowns of aquifers in many metropolitan areas, deteriorating groundwater quality, persistent problems with air pollution, and the destruction of woodlands and wildlife habitats.

Beyond its impacts on natural systems and resources, our contemporary American lifestyle generates impacts on human ecosystems. With metropolitan edges pushing farther out, many central cities and older suburbs lose population and economic vigor as jobs and residents relocate to "greener fields." Jobs continued to move out to suburban locations, even during the robust economy of the 1990s. Four out of five major cities, according to a Brookings Institution analysis, "were not able to stage a 'comeback' relative to their suburbs in one of the most exuberant periods of job growth in the post-war era."[27] Anthony Downs observes that "the dominant growth pattern of American metropolitan areas sets in motion a major process of spatial resource reallocation that drains fiscal and human resources from older core areas and weakens the ability of governments there to provide key services."[28] Even with promising signs of revitalization and renewal in some inner-city neighborhoods and business areas, the out-

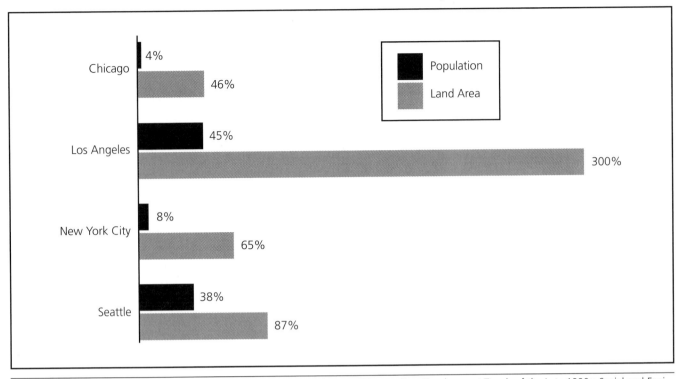

Source: *Planning and Zoning News,* January 1993; Christopher B. Leinberger, "Metropolitan Development Trends of the Late 1990s: Social and Environmental Implications," in Henry L. Diamond and Patrick F. Noonan, *Land Use in America* (Washington, DC: Island Press, 1996).

U.S. Percentage of World Population, Vehicles, and World Oil Production Used by U.S. Vehicles, 1995 2-4

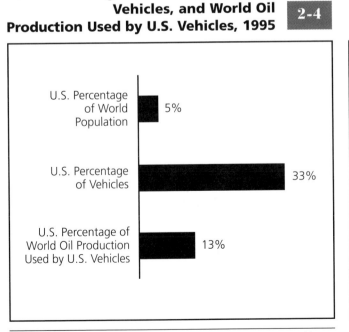

Source: Florida Department of Environmental Protection, *You . . . Your Automobile . . . and Your Environment,* 1996.

U.S. Increase in Population, Vehicle Miles Traveled (VMT), and Commuting Distance, 1983–1990 2-5

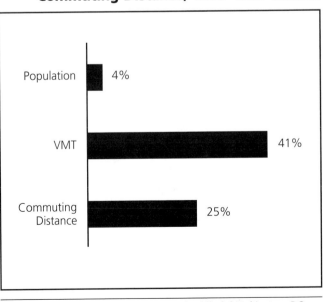

Source: Robert T. Dunphy, *Moving Beyond Gridlock* (Washington, DC: ULI–the Urban Land Institute, 1997).

ward shift of development leaves behind an urban underclass mired in hopeless poverty, beset by crime, poorly nurtured by public services, and increasingly divorced from job opportunities. Abandoned manufacturing sites lie vacant and unusable brownfields require expensive cleanup. The great infrastructure systems that supported intensive urban uses are ill-maintained and prone to the ills of disinvestment (except when they benefit suburban commuters).

Geographer John R. Borchert describes the incredible extent of urban disinvestment occurring in the nation's cities:

> By the end of the 1920s boom the country had [built enough housing] to replace all of the stock that had been built before 1830 . . . . By the 1970s Americans were in a position to abandon the equivalent of all housing built before 1880 [and] . . . . [B]y the turn of the next century we could be abandoning most housing built before the rise of the automobile epoch in the 1920s.[29]

In industrial areas, he says, "railroad-era structures lie as accumulations of architectural solid waste . . . . In this process, the nation is not simply replacing an inventory of buildings . . . , it is also replacing the major part of the fabric three generations have taken for granted as the bedrock geographic pattern of American settlement."[30] The wasted social and economic resources present in once-thriving industrial areas compromise the sustainability of entire metropolitan regions.

The forces responsible for metropolitan growth are powerful and long-standing. They reflect the collective wishes of many American households for privacy, good schools, safe neigh-

borhoods, and unimpeded mobility. Our systems of funding, regulating, designing, and building new living and working areas all support one another to satisfy these wishes. Nevertheless, increasing numbers of people are persuaded that our community development process is not functioning in sustainable ways. They believe that to meet the challenges of sustainable development, we need to modify development practices at all levels— regions, communities, neighborhoods, projects, and even single buildings.

Perspectives on Sustainable Development

Achieving the lofty ideals of sustainable development in the everyday world of community and real estate development may seem fanciful and impractical. Yet, as Timothy Beatley and Kristy Manning point out, "Questions of ecological sustainability are fundamentally and inextricably tied to patterns of human settlement—to metropolitan regions, cities, towns, and villages."[31] The processes of urbanization and community building, they say, can support and help achieve long-term ecological sustainability rather than work against it. Urban places can indeed use land and its resources more wisely, expand the choices associated with housing, jobs, transportation, and other services that meet the needs of *all* the populace, and function economically in ways that generate needed incomes while restoring the integrity of the social and natural environment. Sustainable development means creating "livable, inspiring, enduring, and equitable places . . . where the quality of life and the long-term quality of human existence will be enhanced rather than depleted."[32]

This broad characterization of how sustainable development goals can be achieved still allows for many interpretations. The following prescriptions for community-oriented sustainability illustrate the wide variety of perspec-

tives that inform today's discussion on sustainability.

- "Sustainability implies . . . a vastly reduced energy budget for cities and a smaller, more compact urban pattern interspersed with productive areas to collect energy, grow crops for food, fiber and energy, and recycle wastes . . . ."[33]

- "Sustainable communities acknowledge environmental constraints— from limited groundwater and wetlands to global climate change . . . .

- Sustainable communities work to live within physical and biological limits."[34]

- "A true 'sustainable community' or 'ecological city' is much more than a dense, efficient land-use pattern. It incorporates local food production and waste recycling. Its size is limited to its watershed and its capacity to recycle wastes without damage to the environment. Local economic value created stays largely in the community. Dollars are recycled locally."[35]

The range of concerns reflected in these perspectives indicates that cities, towns, and metropolitan regions should account for all three interlocking circles of sustainability—environment, economy, and society (see figure 2-1). In each of these realms, sustainable approaches can make a difference in community development.

Sorting Out the Terminology. Among the several prescriptions for "good" development, terms and concepts such as "smart growth," "new urbanism," traditional neighborhood development (TND), and "green" development have all entered today's development lexicon. All are subsumed under the heading of sustainable development.

Smart growth seeks to identify a common ground where developers, environmentalists, public officials, citizens, and financiers can find ways to accommodate growth. The smart growth prescription encourages consensus on development decisions through inclusive and participatory processes and, in that sense, is a snappy euphemism for consensus-driven growth management. It promotes compact, mixed-use development that offers a high-quality living and working environment. It encourages choice in travel mode—walking, cycling, and transit—as well as the automobile—by coordinating transportation and land use. It offers a wide variety of housing opportunities and gives priority to maintaining and enhancing existing neighborhoods and business centers. Smart growth protects valued environmental features and resources and makes efficient use of existing infrastructure systems. It stresses regional cooperation and local decision making. Concerns for economic opportunity and social equity are beginning to emerge within the smart growth dialogue, taking it closer to the principles of sustainable development.

New urbanism espouses neighborhood and community design principles that were informally codified as the Ahwahnee Principles by a group of architects in 1991. The 23 principles call for planning "complete and integrated communities" that locate housing, jobs, daily needs, and other activities within easy walking distance of each other and, to the extent feasible, transit stops. New urbanism communities offer a diversity of housing types and jobs; provide a center that combines commercial, civic, cultural, and recreational uses; incorporate public and open spaces designed to encourage use "at all hours of the day and night"; feature well-defined edges and preserve natural terrain wherever possible within parks or greenbelts; provide a system of streets and pathways that fully connect all destinations; and conserve resources, including water and energy, and mini-

mize waste. The principles of the new urbanism urge a regional approach to planning that focuses on a transit rather than highway network, a continuous system of greenbelts and wildlife corridors, concentration of regional institutions and services in a central core, and use of construction materials and methods that reinforce a community identity compatible with a region's history, culture, and climate.[36]

Peter Calthorpe expanded on the Ahwahnee Principles in *The Next American Metropolis*,[37] which lays out systems of urban and neighborhood "transit-oriented developments" (TODs) that largely follow those principles (to which he contributed). Calthorpe's concerns for community design explicitly focus on alternatives to the automobile-oriented urban sprawl that is characteristic of many suburbs and metropolitan fringe areas. His designs emphasize streets as public spaces and walking environments and formal circulation patterns that lead pedestrians to central commercial areas, parks, and transit stops. Calthorpe, however, pays little attention to nonneighborhood forms of development such as downtown cores and densely built employment centers. Both the Ahwahnee Principles and Calthorpe's TODs, like the initial versions of smart growth, give short shrift to the broader goals of sustainable development, particularly those related to economic development and social equity.

Calthorpe's building blocks for his community designs are "traditional neighborhood developments" or the neotraditional neighborhoods espoused by architects such as Andres Duany and Elizabeth Plater-Zyberk. The neighborhoods' well-publicized features include gridiron street patterns, porches and back-alley garages, small lots, and pedestrian-oriented streetscapes, all supposedly harkening back to the small towns of yesteryear. As residential and

neighborhood designs, neotraditional neighborhoods promise more walkable, friendly communities, although most such communities developed to date are located in remote areas inaccessible by transit. Nonetheless, they offer one model for residential development that is more sustainable than the conventional subdivision.

In its concern for resource conservation and sensitivity to the financial and social aspects of real estate development, green development is much closer to sustainable development than the new urbanism and neotraditional neighborhood development. The Rocky Mountain Institute's *Green Development* cites three common elements found in many green development projects: environmental responsiveness, resource efficiency, and community and cultural sensitivity.[38] Green development, it says, "integrates social and environmental goals with financial considerations in projects of every scale and type."[39] While the authors include some green aspects of community development and design—enhanced natural habitats and clustered building patterns, for example—they nonetheless focus largely on specific resource-conserving techniques for developing real estate projects and buildings.

Beyond Buildings, Designs, and Land Use Patterns. As the subsequent chapters of this book demonstrate, sustainable development is all the above development models and more. It is comprehensive and holistic in considering ways in which communities and real estate developments can respond to environmental, social, and economic needs. "Creating sustainable communities," write Beatley and Manning:

> is not simply a matter of avoiding a few wetlands, or saving a few acres of open space, or putting in place a few nonpoint best management practices.

Houses close to the street on small lots, with garages in the rear and trees and sidewalks along the street.

Source: Armando Montero/Geoffrey Ferrell and Suzanne Askew, in *Building Plans and Urban Design Principles for Towns, Cities & Villages in South Florida,* Florida Department of Community Affairs and the Treasure Coast Regional Planning Council, 1999.

Rather, it is a matter of considering ecological limits and environmental impacts at every aspect of community design, from the energy efficiency of buildings to the regional transportation system to how the industrial and commercial sectors go about business.[40]

For developers and builders, moving toward sustainable development means designing projects and buildings in ways that

- conserve energy and natural resources and protect air and water quality by minimizing the consumption of land, the use of other nonrenewable resources, and the production of waste, toxic emissions, and pollution;

- make cost-effective use of existing and renewable resources such as infrastructure systems, underused sites, and historic neighborhoods and structures;

- contribute to community identity, livability, social interaction, and sense of place;

- widen access to jobs, affordable housing, transportation choices, and recreational facilities; and

- expand diversity, synergism, and use of renewable resources in the operation and output of the local economy.

In a white paper prepared for the Urban Land Institute, George Brewster captured these ideas in one pithy statement: Sustainable developments are "designed to integrate natural systems, urban systems, site characteristics, buildings, energy use, economic considerations, and the human community into one permanent, mutually supportive, and economic whole."[41]

Community Development and Environmental Sustainability. In the century and a half since Marsh's and Mumford's observations, environmentalists championing the cause of sustainable development have emphasized the need to rescue and protect environmental resources from the adverse effects of humans' physical, economic, and social pursuits. Indeed, the concept of sustainability has been first and foremost a watchword among environmentalists concerned with forest management, fisheries, water resource management, air quality, biodiversity, and the like. Curiously, however, environmentalists paid little attention to environmental sustainability in cities or, more generally, to the sustainability of human systems. Rutherford Platt notes that Edwin O. Wilson's now-classic tome on biodiversity published in 1988 devoted only six of 496 pages to urban biodiversity.[42] *Agenda 21,* the principal product of the Environmental Summit held in Rio de Janeiro in June 1992, discussed urban issues in only one of 40 chapters and made no reference to urban ecological concerns.[43] Even after the Brundtland Commission broadened the concept of sustainability to embrace economic and social components, environmentalists have generally continued to view the urban realm as essentially a destructive mechanism that overwhelms natural assets and consumes resources such as food, water, and building materials drawn from outside sources. Perhaps most notably, Vice President Al Gore's recent book *Earth in the Balance,* Rutherford Platt observes, "omits any direct discussion of cities and their habitability."[44]

Even when they recognize the significance of sustainability in human communities, particularly urban communities, environmentalists typically focus on the conservation of natural resources. For most environmentalists, communities are sustainable to the extent that they recognize and protect irreplaceable natural assets or, by extension, capitalize on those assets to improve the quality of life for their residents. In chapter 3, Rutherford Platt explains the significance of retaining natural systems as an integral part of the community: hills and ridgelines, rivers and ponds, floodplains and wetlands, species habitats and wildlife corridors, forests and farmlands.

To recognize natural systems in community development, environmentalists invoke approaches such as Ian McHarg's analysis of natural processes in metropolitan areas and the related concept of carrying capacity. McHarg's groundbreaking publication *Design with Nature*, published in 1969, laid out a procedure for identifying and preserving sensitive environmental features:

> Within the metropolitan region natural features will vary, but it is possible to select certain of these that exist throughout and determine the degree to which they allow or discourage contemplated land uses. While these terms are relative, optimally development should occur on valuable or perilous natural-process land only when superior values are created or compensation can be awarded.[45]

The carrying capacity concept builds on McHarg's system and permits an assessment of the levels of development that can be sustained by the capacity of natural systems—soils, geology, water features, and so forth. For example, guided by the notion of carrying capacity, local planning departments can identify areas such as stream valleys, steep slopes, and

This "physiographic expression" of significant landscape features identifies the rivers, the flats (central white space), and the backdrop of hills and summits that guided L'Enfant's layout of the Mall, placement of major government structures, and design of Washington's system of avenues and streets.

Source: Ian L. McHarg, *Design with Nature*, 25th Anniversary Edition (New York: John Wiley & Sons, 1992).

wildlife habitats that should not be developed, areas that may be developed with special care to avoid adverse impacts on natural features, and areas best suited for development.

Many developers incorporate natural resource preservation measures into their projects as a matter of course, prompted in part by local, state, and federal regulations intended to prevent degradation of natural systems and in part by the growing public consciousness of the values of environmental features. Large-scale community builders, in particular, have made giant strides over the past half-century in identifying and protecting natural systems such as erodable hillsides, stream valleys, wetlands, and wildlife habitats and corridors, weaving these features into land

plans in ways that generate amenities for community residents. To limit the effects of erosion, stormwater runoff, and other aspects of development on natural systems, land planners and project designers routinely take account of a site's natural assets in working out development patterns and infrastructure systems. ULI's *Residential Development Handbook* advises designers to "erect a landscape that not only is functional and attractive but also gives the site its character or sense of place. Successful landscape planning and design require an understanding of a site's natural characteristics and the natural processes at work in the local environment."[46]

Taking the next step toward sustainable practices, however, will require even greater efforts to understand

and protect natural systems, that is, to integrate natural and human ecosystems. Orie L. Loucks suggests that as environmentalists focus on sustainability in cities:

> it is no longer useful merely to inventory the ecological resources and processes of the urban environment, or list and summarize what has been ecologically reengineered in the urban system. What we need now is to understand and consider the consequences over long periods of modifications being made in urban ecosystems and urban landscape processes. [We need to focus] attention on regenerative capacities of renewable urban elements such as forests, wetlands, streams, and gardens, and their linkage to urban-rural systems. We need to consider how the physical resources of the urban environment interact over long periods with human society and its institutions and commerce.[47]

Platt's discussion in chapter 3 and Porter's in chapter 6 describe techniques and processes for integrating natural and human ecosystems.

The carrying capacity concept lies at the heart of the great debate over the sustainability of environmental resources in the face of continuing development. On one hand, environmentalists and allied interests assert that the earth's environment has a finite capacity to support the growth of human settlements—the central theme of sustainable development. In fact, local antidevelopment interests frequently seize on the carrying capacity concept and claim that, despite technological advances that can expand capacity or even reduce demands on capacity, natural resources are sacrosanct.[48] As well, population control groups emphasize the limits of the earth's carrying capacity and call for a halt to population growth. Citing classical economists such as John Stuart Mill and Malthus—the latter claimed in 1798 that populations inevitably outrun their food supply—population control groups view growing populations as inimical to preserving essential environmental qualities (as well as responsible for aggravating territorial disputes and creating violent conflict). They regard growth management as a temporary panacea and methods for dealing with environmental effects of development as cosmetic solutions.[49]

On the other side of the debate are economists and others who assert that the adverse effects of development on the environment are either overstated or capable of redress through technological innovations. A case in point is the conversion of farmland by urban or suburban development. While the American Farmland Trust and other groups decry farmland conversion as a threat to the future supply of food,[50] some economists argue that, historically, technological advances have increased crop yields, making restrictions on farmland conversion unnecessary. Professor Tom Daniels, although a supporter of farmland preservation, notes that "the cornucopians, in the tradition of Julian Simon [a well-known critic of the farmland preservation movement], believe there is no shortage of farmland, that the land market is capable of efficiently allocating land resources among competing uses, and that technological advances will continue to generate more food even as human populations increase."[51] Such doubters of farmland "shortages" cite U.S. Department of Agriculture (USDA) statistics indicating that the amount of cropland nationwide is not declining; indeed, cropland acreage in 1992 was the same as in 1945.[52] The figures suggest that croplands are being replaced (apparently from grasslands and forests) as rapidly as they are converted to urban and suburban uses. In addition, farmland prices dropped slightly rather than rising during the 1945–1992 period, attesting to available supply rather than scarcity.[53] Daniels finds that "alarmist claims of impending threats to food supplies appear unwarranted. Food is relatively cheap and abundant. Chronic overproduction and low commodity prices are the main farm problems, even while federal farm programs are idling over 30 million acres."[54]

When measured against sustainability principles, however, the various arguments on both sides of the farmland loss issue are not fully persuasive. For growing metropolitan areas that can boast of prime farmlands at their exurban fringe, the replacement of that acreage with less fertile lands located elsewhere is not necessarily a sustainable practice, particularly when the land is made productive through irrigation, massive applications of nutrients, and other technological "fixes."

In an article entitled "Economics and 'Sustainability,'" Michael Tolman explores the question of whether resource use can be offset by compensatory investments that flow to future generations.[55] He observes that the answer depends on assumptions regarding the substitutability between services provided by natural capital (such as material resources, waste absorption, and aesthetic and cultural values) versus other forms of capital (such as physical plant, equipment, knowledge, and social institutions). Many economists, he says, view all resources as relatively interchangeable sources of well-being, especially if technological progress is sufficient to offset the depletion or degradation of natural resources. Damage to ecosystems such as loss of species diversity is not intrinsically unacceptable if compensatory investments in other forms of capital (such as human knowledge, production techniques, or social organization) are feasible and intended as compensation.

On the other hand, Tolman explains, many ecologists and some economists argue that compensatory investments "often are infeasible as well as ethically indefensible."[56] Resource substitutability is limited by physical laws (such as minimum energy requirements for transforming matter), by the environmental capacity to process wastes, and by the need for the resilience of natural systems against unexpected changes (such as in biodiversity). Technology can do only so much to overcome or substitute for natural forces, as demonstrated by our experience with floods, hurricanes, and other natural disasters. The chair of a National Science Foundation study of natural hazard prevention points out, "One central problem is that many of the accepted methods for coping with hazards have been based on the fantasy that people can use technology to control nature. We will never be totally safe because the world is the way it is."[57] William Rees, the doyen of sustainability, states that the operation of technical advances and market mechanisms may take too long to permit recovery of overused ecological resources. They do not repair pollution damage from waste materials or even recognize some critical resources such as the ozone layer.[58]

Tolman observes that physical scale—local versus global—is important in making judgments about substitutability between natural and capital resources. He comments:

> Sustainability ultimately is intimately wrapped up with human values and institutions, not just ecological functions. An entirely ecological definition of sustainability is inadequate; guidance for social decision making also is required.[59]

Tolman's statement, which reflects the uncertainties inherent in both the scientific method and currently available data, is indicative of the continuing argument over the realities of sustainable development. A return to the farmland issue illustrates the point. *Land Use in America*, the 1996 report of the Sustainable Use of Land Project, cites a set of numbers obtained from the U.S. Soil Conservation Service (SCS) that points to a trend in direct opposition to that disclosed by the aforementioned USDA statistics. The SCS figures show a loss of almost 39 million acres in cropland from 1982 to 1992 as well as a 16 million-acre decline in range and pasture lands.[60] With so much uncertainty about *existing* conditions, how can long-range projections be credible? Mixed in the brew, of course, are tendencies for ideological stances that complicate our understanding and color the public debate.

Tolman advises a middle course that considers tradeoffs among natural and capital resources when potential consequences are small and reversible and a more cautious course when potential consequences become larger and more irreversible.

Economic and Social Dimensions of Sustainability. Internationally, most concerns about economic and social sustainability have focused on developing countries whose burgeoning populations frequently are poorly served by dysfunctional economies and unstable social and political institutions. The Brundtland Commission's pronouncements on sustainable development recognized that protection of environmental resources in developing nations depends on upgrading social and economic conditions. Nevertheless, although better off in relative terms, plenty of communities in the United States have documented the need for economic and social uplift. As a nation,

we are still struggling to equalize opportunities for economic and social advancement and for sharing in the nation's wealth. Recognizing this, many communities have pursued economic development and social welfare programs to improve the well-being of their citizens. Public and private programs have attempted to attract new jobs and broaden and stabilize bases of economic activity. Federal, state, and local governments have established programs that support citizens with special needs and expand opportunities for economic and social improvement, including job training, income assistance, child and senior care, special education, and affordable housing programs.

Increasingly, developers have played significant roles in these efforts. They have joined with public agencies to develop public/private projects that help foster downtown and neighborhood revitalization. One notable example is the Can Company in Baltimore. With substantial financial and other incentives from city and state agencies, developer Struever Bros. Eccles & Rouse renovated an abandoned industrial complex, providing retail and service activities in support of a reviving waterfront neighborhood. In other projects around the country, developers have provided on-site amenities and extended off-site connections to surrounding neighborhoods to benefit area residents; amenities include parks and playgrounds, child care centers, and job training programs. As a condition of project approval, some cities require developers to contribute to affordable housing programs, transit improvements, public open space, and other facilities and amenities.

The tripartite concept of sustainability—interlocking economic, social, and environmental goals—encourages developer involvement that goes beyond the construction of physical improvements and the provision of social services. To be *sustainable*, activities intended to bolster economies and societies require linkages to the protection, restoration, and enhancement of natural resources and environmental attributes. The sustainability concept challenges community economies to function in a way that reduces the consumption of land, energy, ground- and surface water, and other resources; that recycles wastes; and that incorporates farming to produce food, fiber, and energy. At one extreme, some advocates of economic sustainability argue for a return to a sustenance-based local economy. To keep dollars recycling within the community, they lean toward producing food from home and community gardens (rather than importing it over great distances), supporting the growth of local businesses, and even engaging in home-based piece work and crafts instead of mass production.[61] Many communities are promoting local agriculture by reviving moribund farmers' markets and providing public spaces for community gardening.[62] And many are underwriting the establishment of business incubators to stimulate formation of local trades, crafts, and technology.

In these times, however, community economic activities are already interconnected with and even subsumed under regional, national, and global economic systems. Food production is now international in scope and unlikely to return to pre–20th century practices. And although home-based telecommuting is gaining popularity, it is hardly likely to replace corporate workplaces as employment centers. Nevertheless, sustainability calls for local as well as larger-scale initiatives to curb resource consumption and waste.

One means of achieving the goal of sustainability is for communities and developers to invest in the nurture and maintenance of existing business areas and firms, not instead of but in addi-

tion to developing outlying shopping centers and luxurious new office parks lured by lavish tax and subsidy packages. Adding value to existing business areas through economic development makes sense for new and old businesses alike. In Carroll, Iowa, for example, Wal-Mart agreed to locate its new store downtown and to pay half the cost of constructing a new parking lot to serve its store and others, thus strengthening downtown businesses.[63]

The lesson is that developers who want to promote sustainable development can look for opportunities in established areas rather than focusing exclusively on greenfield sites. For example, as developer Charles Shaw was constructing housing in Prairie Crossing, an innovative suburban residential project north of Chicago (described below), he was also engaged in developing Homan Square, about 600 affordable homes, and Orchard Park Townhomes, a 54-unit mixed-income development, both located near Chicago's downtown business district. In addition, developers can and usually do seek out local suppliers of materials and services, thereby helping to keep dollars recycling within the community.

Another approach focuses on cutting back on the use of natural resources through the careful selection of development sites and thoughtful specification of building features and construction processes (see chapter 7). Energy consumption, for example, can be reduced by relying to some extent on solar energy and energy regeneration processes, by specifying designs that cut demand for artificial lighting, heating, and cooling, and by designing development patterns that promote more walking, cycling, and use of transit. All of these energy-reducing techniques illustrate ways that developers can limit resource consumption. In addition, recycling materials helps reduce waste. Each year, for example, a nonprofit

company in Baltimore collects building materials from landfills and then redistributes over $1 million of building supplies.[64] Several communities, some in partnership with developers, are creating industrial parks that bring together companies that can collaborate in cutting consumption of raw materials and energy by exchanging and recycling waste products. Although facing formidable legal and managerial obstacles, waste disposal is a lost opportunity whose benefits are only now beginning to seep into boardroom thinking.[65]

Still another means of connecting economic activity with environmental conservation is recognizing that natural resources are a salable asset. Communities interested in "greening the city" by protecting and restoring important ecological features such as streams and wooded areas can highlight the features' contributions to community livability by making natural assets visible and accessible—and increase property values in the process. Developers long ago came to understand the marketing benefits of retaining significant natural features, providing attractive landscapes, and incorporating greenways and parks into project designs. Communities that embrace nature gain value.

It must be said, however, that the association between local economic functions and the concept of sustainable development has not been fully explored. The gap between sustainability goals and day-to-day economic activities remains wide, and specific steps toward closing that gap, short of a complete reordering of current economic forces, are difficult to define. In chapter 4, Christopher Leinberger sheds some light on new ways of thinking about real estate and public capital financing that can help realize the goals of sustainable development.

So, too, with the social side of sustainable development, particularly on a national scale. The general goal of equal opportunity and equitable sharing in the nation's wealth appears elusive in light of the many past and present attempts to move in that direction. Add the factor of avoiding further degradation of natural systems while attaining that goal and the target seems to recede even further.

At the scale of the community and local real estate development, however, the aims of social sustainability seem more achievable. With community support, there are ways for developers to make more efficient, humane, and equitable use of human resources while creating livable and stimulating environments that contribute to sustainability. Strategies range from reducing or mitigating the undesirable consequences of public and private development on the residents of affected areas, to expanding opportunities for employment, affordable housing, and inexpensive travel, to providing enjoyable and safe neighborhoods. In chapter 5, Edward Blakely emphasizes the scale of the problem in setting forth ten "rules for the new game" for socially conscious development.

NIMBYism plays a large part in most developers' lives but is seldom an impediment when the people affected by proposed developments are poor and relatively powerless. Such is the case with "gentrification," the term that came into use in the 1980s to describe the supposedly desirable makeover of once-slummy neighborhoods into attractive residential areas. Infill and restoration efforts are welcomed as an economic stimulus for aging cities and suburbs; they upgrade existing structures and promise to diminish pressures for outward expansion of urban areas—significant aims of sustainability. And developers and builders make substantial profits on such makeovers, unless they find themselves caught in an economic downturn or stymied by a recalcitrant permitting bureaucracy. Frequently, as well, they rescue from destruction historically or architecturally significant buildings and areas.

But gentrification frequently masks a win/lose scenario in which relatively well-off people displace existing residents unable to afford the newly reno-

vated housing. Displaced people must search for homes in a market already constrained by a limited supply of low-rent units often located in less desirable neighborhoods. At the same time, in almost every metropolitan area, community and neighborhood housing organizations, sometimes with private developer participation, struggle to rehabilitate homes for low- and moderate-income households. Though assisted by public loan and grant programs and nonprofit groups of all kinds, these organizations never come close to meeting demands for affordable, decent housing, especially amid rampant gentrification.

To be sure, developers can contribute to economic and environmental sustainability by restoring existing buildings, but they also can fulfill the social aims of sustainability by supporting or participating in programs that build or rehabilitate affordable housing and stabilize neighborhoods. Struever Bros. Eccles & Rouse, for example, moved on from the Can Company office/retail development in Baltimore (described in chapter 6) to developing The Terraces, a HUD-backed HOPE VI project (a U.S. Department of

The Terraces, Baltimore. On a site formerly occupied by deteriorating public housing, Struever Bros. Eccles & Rouse, Inc., developed 391 housing units and this neighborhood retail-office center in collaboration with city and community agencies.

Housing and Urban Development housing subsidy program). Working with the city's housing authority and community groups, the developers built a new mixed-income community of 203 rental townhomes, 100 for-sale townhomes, an 88-unit seniors' building, a business center, and a community recreation and daycare center on land formerly occupied by ramshackle public housing towers.

In what often proves to be a time-consuming effort, such programs require close collaboration with neighborhood and tenant groups, nonprofit corporations, and public agencies. In fact, developers frequently find themselves responding to demands for upgrading social institutions such as schools, churches, community centers, and even neighborhood retail shops, thus providing the social infrastructure needed for a stable living environment. In addition, residents may need assistance in dealing with or fending off undesirable uses—waste transfer stations, abandoned brownfield sites, unsuitable industries—that often plague low-income neighborhoods. Revitalization efforts may not generate a huge profit or much at all, but they can single out developers as contributors to the civic good, perhaps an asset in securing approval for the next for-profit project.

Another aspect of social sustainability is income-generating employment that involves both physical and educational access to jobs. Employers locating in areas remote from sources of labor seldom give adequate consideration to either employee costs of commuting to work or the economic costs to a business of an inadequate labor supply. Communities can tackle the job/location imbalance by planning and regulating the distribution of employment centers served by public transit corridors. Developers, of course, cannot and should not be expected to counsel their tenants about socially correct locational choices but, as employers themselves,

they can participate in job training programs and equalize any transportation benefits awarded to employees.

To win regulatory approval for many projects, developers have grown accustomed to currying the support of or at least softening outright opposition from neighborhood residents. Typically, developers hold meetings to describe a project's benefits to a community and area and to report on measures for offsetting any potential impacts. They produce flyers and other literature to explain their proposal and, at the same time, allow for neighborhood input into design changes. To further the social aims of sustainable development, developers can expand community participation by involving project neighbors in key design and development decisions and optimizing project benefits for surrounding areas. Although a risky process—neighbors often do not speak with one voice—a skillfully planned citizen involvement program can result in a development that is carefully woven into the physical and social fabric of the surrounding community, a plus for both project and neighborhood value. For example, the designers of the Village Green residential infill development (profiled in chapter 7) designed homes similar in scale and appearance to those in the adjoining neighborhood.

Developers can derive satisfaction from developing projects that fit compatibly into their surroundings and contribute to positive social interaction and a sense of place—mixed-use centers that provide convenient and attractive places for working, shopping, living, and recreation; residential and business projects that are designed to be compatible with and connected to surrounding development; housing that serves a range of household types and income levels; designs that recognize local cultural symbols and values; and public amenities that provide benefits such as child care, civic spaces, streetscapes, facilities,

and art for public enjoyment. Chapter 5 describes some of the ways sustainable projects can help achieve communities' social objectives.

Practical Considerations

Although the aims and techniques of sustainable development make sense in concept, their application to the practice of community and real estate development remains problematic in several respects. First, the all-encompassing nature of the concept itself tends to foster confusion and stasis concerning needs and responsibilities. Most people find it difficult to grasp the significance of the interrelationships of the vast global forces at work, much less perceive how individual actions affect those forces. When we turn to science for assistance in understanding science-related forces, we encounter disagreements among experts as to the reality, causes, or consequences of, for example, global warming or decreasing biodiversity.

Even at the regional or community level, most of us balk at making the connection between starting the car in the morning or lighting a wood fire at night and the declining quality of air across a metropolitan area. We refuse to believe that the septic tank on our two-acre lot may threaten groundwater quality in years to come. And although large-scale or long-term effects may concern us, we are wary of acknowledging that our individual, incremental actions contribute to undesirable environmental effects.

Through experience, moreover, we understand the intractability of the many social and economic forces that buffet our communities and neighborhoods—the difficulties inherent in maintaining or restoring decent school systems, livable neighborhoods, thriving business centers, and crime-free parks and streets. In other words, the long-term, large-scale nature of sustainability itself poses obstacles to

Development-Related Priorities for Consumer Actions Recommended by the Union of Concerned Scientists

1. Choose a place to live that reduces the need to drive.
2. Think twice before purchasing another car.
3. Choose a fuel-efficient, low-polluting car.
4. Set concrete goals for reducing your travel.
5. Whenever practical, walk, bicycle, or take public transportation.
6. Choose your home carefully.
7. Reduce the environmental costs of heating and hot water.
8. Install efficient lighting and appliances.

Source: Michael Brower and Warren Leon, *The Consumer's Guide to Effective Environmental Choices*. Published for the Union of Concerned Scientists (New York: Three Rivers Press, 1999).

taking short-term, small-scale actions toward its fulfillment.

A second hurdle is the inertia built into the present development process. We have constructed transactional systems of finance, construction, public regulation, and consumer expectations that generate conventional projects satisfying many of our wants. Developers and builders have gained considerable experience in delivering products that appeal to the marketplace while consumers have developed a set of expectations and values that are expressed as marketplace demands. Bankers and carpenters and appraisers know their jobs and understand their roles in the current process of community building. Lenders cringe at the prospect of financing anything out of the ordinary; they base construction loans on appraisals by appraisers who reduce comparable developments to a price per square foot regardless of real value. Building officials adopt progressively more stringent and inflexible standards that increase resource consumption. Contractors base construction bids on known or least-risk materials and techniques.

Altering or redirecting these complex economic and social structures and interrelationships is an enormous task. It requires changes in the way we recognize and measure costs and benefits of development and its associated effects.

It also means overcoming the sometimes higher initial costs of innovative technologies and unfamiliar procedures and bridging gaps between the long- and short-term beneficiaries of the development process. For example, despite decades of technical development of solar energy systems, developers and builders know that the increased cost of installing residential solar energy systems requires several years for payback in the form of lower heating and cooling expenses. They also know that consumers resist higher front-end costs and discount the value of long-term reductions in operating costs, especially for what many perceive as untried or unproven technologies.

Technological advances, capital cost accounting methods, consumer education, oil price levels and trends, tax incentives and disincentives, and other concerns affect decisions on sustainable products and practices. Even passive solar design, for which initial cost margins are relatively minor, generally goes ignored as a marketable feature. As a result, developers create site plans without regard to the potential solar orientation of buildings, public planners approve such plans according to conventional layout requirements, and builders acquire finished lots that may or may not optimize opportunities for solar design. Frequently, developers' and builders' lack of familiarity with solar

energy technology and energy-efficient home design either forecloses consideration of energy-saving options or heightens the perception of associated risk.

Another example concerns septic tanks. Almost automatically a symbol of sprawl, septic tanks are widely used for low-density development where the extension of sewer service is deemed too expensive. In fact, the United States now counts 22 million septic systems that introduce over 1 trillion gallons of effluent annually into subsurface aquifers. The nitrogen, phosphorous, bacteria, viruses, detergents, solvents, and other chemicals in the effluent can contaminate groundwater and affect water quality in nearby lakes, rivers, and ponds. Even though standards for drain field percolation and size have grown more rigorous in many areas, the effectiveness of underground filtering on effluent quality is seldom monitored or controlled—short of a backup in the house—while impacts on aquifers are difficult to trace. Often, however, alternatives to individual septic systems run into massive opposition. Although much more conducive to effective management than individual systems, so-called package plants that treat sewage from development in small areas have earned nothing but scorn from many health departments and local public works departments. Moreover, public officials rarely acknowledge much less evaluate alternative approaches such as constructed wetlands and solar aquatic systems that purify pollutants through physical, biological, and chemical processes.

Even sophisticated technology with proven effectiveness can be waylaid by consumer skepticism. One developer recently described an innovative system of heating and cooling controls installed at some additional cost in a new office building. The controls permitted the tenants themselves to fine-tune temperatures among zoned spaces, thereby achieving significant energy savings and presumably improving occupant comfort. As new tenants signed leases, however, they uniformly rejected the controls in favor of conventional systems that are off limits to employees.

As the various examples demonstrate, putting sustainable principles into practice may seem like swimming upstream. Nevertheless, process and product barriers are being whittled away, and lenders and public officials and consumers are growing more sensitive to the long-term rather than just short-term benefits of sustainable practices. Furthermore, as spelled out in chapters 6 and 7, developers can enhance their bottom line by approaching project and building development through whole-systems thinking, understanding the ways sustainable practices can be mutually supportive. More efficient office lighting, for example, reduces heating and cooling loads and thus reduces the requirements for heating, ventilating, and cooling systems and lowers construction and operating costs. The ripple effect at the community level is a reduction in electric power generation and its impact on air and water quality. Compared with standard lighting, a single compact fluorescent light bulb in a New York City office building can, over its life, keep three-quarters of a ton of carbon dioxide out of the earth's atmosphere.[66]

Experience has shown that developers can produce profitable developments by following principles of sustainability. Designers of Prairie Crossing, a 667-acre residential development north of Chicago, mitigated the project's environmental impacts by planning narrower streets and minimizing the area devoted to sidewalks, thus reducing stormwater runoff and allowing the use of vegetated swales and detention basins—rather than conventional storm sewers—for stormwater filtration. The infrastructure cost savings helped finance landscaping and

other project amenities.[67] The development demonstrates that integrated planning and design can yield multiple benefits from individual changes.

The public/private team developing the Civano community in Tucson, Arizona, has quantified many of the financial benefits associated with Civano's sustainable features. The development incorporates passive solar design, high-efficiency windows and HVAC (heating, ventilating, and air conditioning) equipment, options for walking, cycling, and alternative-

fuel vehicles, use of harvested and reclaimed water for irrigation, enhanced recycling and composting of waste, and the creation of nearby jobs and telecommuting opportunities. The community is designed with higher densities and narrower streets than conventional development, saving open space and reducing travel demands. Some of the financial benefits include the following:

- $500,000 in annual savings for city services (for water, landfills, and road construction and maintenance);

Stormwater drainage swales in Prairie Crossing, Grayslake, Illinois.

- $250,000 in annual community health benefits from improved air quality;

- $37 per month in savings to households from lower utility costs, which permits a $5,000 increase in a mortgage loan;

- $6,000 lower home cost (for a 100-square-foot reduction in home size) that offsets costs of generous amenities not usually available in conventional development; and

- a projected 23 percent internal rate of return to the city on its initial $3 million cash investment, repaid within six years.

To these savings should be added environmental benefits from reductions in land and water use, air pollution, and energy consumption.

Less quantifiable but highly marketable benefits derive from Civano's sense of community. Surveys of the first home-buyers indicate that they value the community's quality of place and neighborliness as much as its respect for the environment. Buyers appear much less price-sensitive than is typical for production housing in Tucson, as evidenced by the number of upgrades purchased. The community stability implied by homeowner responses should also reduce demand for police and social services. In Civano, the city, developer, and residents all come out ahead.[68]

Achieving Sustainability

One product of the Earth Summit in Rio de Janeiro in 1992 was the *Agenda 21* action plan for pursuing worldwide sustainable development through global, national, and local government actions. Subsequently, a group of researchers published a report on progress toward sustainability. The book established a set of criteria for measuring achievements in applying sustainability ideals to everyday activities. Although addressed mostly to public officials, the criteria suggest how developers can respond to those ideals when considering where, how, and what to develop. The criteria urge:

1. A more conscious attempt to relate environmental effects to underlying economic and political *pressures* (which in turn derive from political decisions, non-decisions, and markets.)

2. A more active effort to relate local issues, decisions, and dispositions to *global impacts*, both environmentally and with respect to global solidarity and justice.

3. A more focused policy for achieving *cross-sector integration* of environment-and-development concerns, values and goals in planning, decision-making and policy implementation.

4. Greater efforts to increase *community involvement*, i.e., to bring both average

Neighborhood center in Civano, Tucson, Arizona. The center incorporates passive solar design and active solar systems, recycled materials, and other environmentally friendly features. Photo by Haskell Photography, Tucson, Arizona.

citizens and major stakeholder groups, particularly business and labor unions, into the planning and implementation process with respect to environment-and-development issues.

5. A commitment to define and work with local problems within: (a) a broader ecological and regional framework, as well as (b) a greatly expanded time frame (i.e., over three or more generations).[69]

The operative notion in each statement describes movement toward an objective, not an absolute or immediate outcome. Developers who specialize in major, long-term, multiphase developments, in which they have a long-term stake in maintaining value, are probably already putting into practice many elements of sustainability. Other developers embarking on smaller projects, however, can adopt designs and techniques that embody sustainability principles.

The vision of sustainable development reflected in this book aims at creating and nurturing sustainable communities through sustainable development practices that make sense economically, socially, and environmentally. The next six chapters describe the types of approaches and techniques that developers can adapt and apply to their developments.

As an overview of the remainder of the book, the following points summarize practices appropriate for entire communities, individual developments, and buildings.

At the *community* level, as further discussed in chapters 3, 4, and 5, it makes sense to

- use land wisely and reduce the risks of adversely affecting natural resources by taking a conservative approach when converting land to urban uses, maintaining the integrity of natural

systems in urban settings, and protecting and restoring valued natural resources, features, and qualities;

- maintain, recycle, and build on existing urban structures and systems by leveraging previous investments to optimize locational efficiencies, enhancing and restoring place-making historic and architectural qualities, and integrating new with existing development;

- expand the range of and increase access to economic and social opportunities by recognizing the increasing diversity of needs, stimulating interaction within the community, and connecting to existing communities and neighborhoods; and

- integrate development with transportation and other infrastructure systems by expanding travel options and access to them, recognizing the need for expanding public facility capacities as development occurs, and focusing on public facility investments that promote compact forms of development.

At the *project* level, as further discussed in chapter 6, it makes sense to

- take advantage of a site's natural systems and assets by preserving and restoring natural systems as an essential component of development, maintaining and restoring natural systems to reduce runoff and pollution, maintaining and restoring native vegetation and landforms, and maintaining and restoring landscapes to enhance associated development;

- design infrastructure systems to optimize efficient use by reusing or connecting to existing systems when feasible, minimizing impermeable surfaces and site disturbance, and planning for walking,

cycling, and transit as well as for cars;

- recycle urban land through infill and redevelopment; and

- plan for diverse and adaptable neighborhoods and business centers by providing a mix of uses and a broad range of housing choices, allowing for individual expression and change, promoting the evolution of a unique character or sense of place, and providing beneficial economic and social connections and interaction.

For *individual buildings*, as described in chapter 7, it makes sense to

- minimize the impact of buildings on their sites by limiting the building "footprint," retaining trees and natural landforms, and minimizing paving and use of permeable materials; and

- design buildings for resource efficiency by recycling materials and using local materials whenever possible, adapting and reusing existing buildings, maximizing opportunities for using solar energy, using water-conserving fixtures, appliances, and landscaping, and minimizing or recycling waste during construction.

In *conceiving and designing development*, as discussed in chapter 8, it makes sense to

- select sites that balance use of land and other nonrenewable resources with expanding social and economic opportunities;

- connect new developments and on-site systems to surrounding developments and sites;

- tailor site and building designs to add value to surrounding uses;

design and use natural and built systems in a holistic manner that considers interactions and tradeoffs; and

■ plan in coordination with communitywide and neighborhood expectations and values.

The Practice of Sustainable Development describes how these concepts and approaches to sustainable development can be feasibly applied in the here-and-now, how they can make bottom-line sense for developers and builders, and, at the same time, how they can make a significant contribution to community and global sustainability.

Like Ebenezer Scrooge, we have seen the ghost of things to come. However, we have the opportunity to change the present before it becomes the immutable past. There is a better way to build that recognizes stewardship of the land and its resources. As stated in the Urban Land Institute's Code of Ethics, development efforts "will be judged by the integrity and permanence of my developments, which will survive my lifetime . . . . "

Endnotes

1 World Commission on Environment and Development, *Our Common Future* (Oxford, UK: Oxford University Press, 1987), p. 43.

2 Ibid., p. 45.

3 President's Council on Sustainable Development, *Sustainable America: A New Consensus* (Washington, DC: Author, 1996). Annual updates also have been published.

4 Ibid.

5 Kevin J. Krizek and Joe Power, *A Planner's Guide to Sustainable Development*. Planning Advisory Service Report, No. 467 (Chicago: American Planning Association, 1996), p. 17.

6 Rachel Carson, *Silent Spring* (Boston: Houghton Mifflin Co., 1962).

7 Paul Erlich, *The Population Bomb* (New York: Ballantine Books, 1968).

8 Herman Daly, *Toward a Steady State Economy* (San Francisco: W. H. Freemen and Co., 1972).

9 *World Almanac and Book of Facts* (Mahwah, NJ: World Almanac Books, 1996).

10 Leon F. Bouvier and Lindsey Grant, *How Many Americans? Population, Immigration and the Environment* (San Francisco: Sierra Club Books, 1994).

11 Alexander von Hoffman, "Housing Heats Up: Home Building Patterns in Metropolitan Areas," *The Brookings Institution Center on Urban & Metropolitan Policy Survey Series* (December 1999), p. 1.

12 Bureau of the Census, "Metropolitan Areas and Cities," *1990 Census Profile*, No. 3, September 1991, p. 1.

13 Christopher B. Leinberger, "The Changing Location of Development & Investment Opportunities," *Black's Guide* (1996), p. 22.

14 Marya Morris, "The Rising Tide," *EPA Journal*, Vol. 18, No. 4., September/October 1992, p. 39.

15 Christopher B. Leinberger, "Metropolitan Development Trends of the Late 1990s: Social and Environmental Implications," in Henry L. Diamond and Patrick F. Noonan, *Land Use in America* (Washington, DC: Island Press, 1996), p. 220.

16 Reported by William K. Stevens, "Sprawl Quickens Its Attack on Forests," *New York Times*, December 7, 1999, p. D6.

17 See *Losing Ground: Land Consumption in the Chicago Region, 1900–1998* (Chicago: Openlands Project, 1998), p. 19.

18 Sierra Club, *The Dark Side of the American Dream: The Costs and Consequences of Suburban Sprawl* (San Francisco: Sierra Club, 1998).

19 Ibid.

20 *Southeastern Mass: Vision 2020 An Agenda for the Future.* Report of the Southeastern Massachusetts Vision 2020 Project (Taunton, MA: Southeastern Regional Planning and Economic Development District, 1999), p. 2.

21 Preliminary conclusions from a current (Spring 2000) Brookings Institution study of housing development and land consumption in metropolitan areas suggest that although urban densities have dropped significantly across the nation, trends vary among the areas. In some metropolitan areas, average densities have either remained fairly constant or actually increased, while in others, densities are declining, particularly in outer counties. It is also possible that counties just beyond the census-defined metropolitan area are experiencing very low-density growth that would color average densities if included in overall development trends.

22 See Florida Department of Environmental Protection, *You . . . Your Automobile . . . and Your Environment* (Tallahasee: Florida DEP, 1996), p. 12.

23 Robert T. Dunphy, *Moving Beyond Gridlock* (Washington, DC: Urban Land Institute, 1997), p. 4.

24 Ibid.

25 Florida Department of Environmental Protection, p. 12.

26 U.S. Department of Transportation, *1995 Status of the Nation's Surface Transportation System: Conditions and Performance* (Washington, DC: US DOT, 1995), p. 149.

27 John Brennan and Edward W. Hill, "Where Are the Jobs?: Cities, Suburbs, and the Competition for Employment," *The Brookings Institution Center on Urban & Metropolitan Policy Survey Series*, November 1999, p. 8.

28 Anthony Downs, "The Challenge of Our Declining Big Cities," *Housing Policy Debate*, Vol. 8, Issue 2, 1997, p. 383.

29 John R. Borchert, "Futures of American Cities," *Our Changing Cities*. John Fraser Hart, ed. (Baltimore: Johns Hopkins University Press, 1991), p. 233.

30 Ibid, p. 295.

31 Timothy Beatley and Kristy Manning, *The Ecology of Place* (Washington, DC: Island Press, 1997), p. 2.

32 Ibid.

33 Sym Van der Ryn and Peter Calthorpe, *Sustainable Communities* (San Francisco: Sierra Club Books, 1986), p. ix.

34 Timothy Beatley, David J. Brower, and Ruth Knack, "Sustainability Comes to Main Street: Ecological Community Planning," *Planning*, May 1993, Vol. 59, No. 5, p. 16.

35 Bob Walter, Lois Arkin, and Richard Crenshaw, eds., *Sustainable Cities—Concepts and Strategies for Eco-City Development* (Los Angeles: Eco-Home Media, 1992), p. 68.

36 Judith Corbett and Joe Velasquez, "The Ahwahnee Principles: Toward More Livable Communities," *Western City*, September 1994. Reprinted and disseminated by The Center for Livable Communities, Sacramento, California.

37 Peter Calthorpe, *The Next American Metropolis* (New York: Princeton Architectural Press), 1993.

38 Alex Wilson et al., *Green Development: Integrating Ecology and Real Estate* (New York: John Wiley & Sons, Inc., 1998).

39 Ibid., 4.

40 Beatley and Manning, p. 28.

41 George B. Brewster, *The Ecology of Development: Integrating the Built and Natural Environments*. Working Paper No. 649 (Washington, DC: Urban Land Institute, 1997), p. 17.

42 Rutherford H. Platt, "Introduction and Overview," in Rutherford H. Platt, Rowan A. Rowntree, and Pamela C. Muick, eds., *The Ecological City* (Amherst, MA: The University of Massachusetts Press, 1994), p. 9.

43 Ibid., p. 10.

44 Ibid.

45 Ian L. McHarg, *Design with Nature* (New York: John Wiley & Sons, 1992), p. 57. Originally published for the American Museum of Natural History by the Natural History Press, Garden City, NY, 1969.

46 Lloyd N. Bookout, Jr., *Residential Development Handbook* (Washington, DC: Urban Land Institute, 1990), p. 231.

47 Orie L. Loucks, "Sustainability in Urban Ecosystems: Beyond an Object of Study," in Platt, Rowntree, and Muick, eds., *The Ecological City*, p. 49.

48 See Rice Odell, "Carrying Capacity Analysis: Useful but Limited," in Randall W. Scott, ed., *Management and Control of Growth*, Vol. 3 (Washington, DC: Urban Land Institute, 1975), pp. 22-28.

49 See, for example, David F. Durham, "Carrying Capacity Perspectives," *Focus* (a publication of the Carrying Capacity Network), Vol. 1, No. 2, Winter 1992, pp. 2-4. In the same issue, there is an excellent overview of the literature on this subject, both pro and con, by Nathan Keyfitz, "Population and Development Within the Ecosphere: One View of the Literature."

50 For the position of the trust, see "Preserving Farmland; The American Farmland Trust and Its Partners," in Eve Endicott, ed., *Land Conservation through Public/Private Partnerships* (Washington, DC: Island Press, 1994), p. 44.

51 Tom Daniels, "A Cautionary Reply for Farmland Preservation," *Planning & Markets*, Vol. 2, Issue 1, 1999, taken from the Internet at www-pam.usc.edu.

52 James D. Riggle and Jonathan Tolman, "Land Development Not a Threat to America's Farmland," *Land Development* (Washington, DC: National Association of Home Builders, Winter 1999), p. 21.

53 Ibid.

54 Daniels, "A Cautionary Reply . . ."

55 Michael A. Tolman, "Economics and 'Sustainability': Balancing Trade-offs and Imperatives," *Land Economics*, Vol. 70, No. 4, November 1994, pp. 399-413.

56 Ibid., p. 404.

57 Dennis Mileti, quoted by Guy Gugliotta, "Cost of Natural Disasters Growing," *Washington Post*, May 20, 1999, p. 18.

58 William E. Rees, *Sustainable Development and the Biosphere* (Chambersburg, PA: ANIMA Books, 1990), p.10.

59 Tolman, "Economics and 'Sustainability'," p. 409.

60 Henry L. Diamond and Patrick F. Noonan, *Land Use in America* (Washington, DC: Island Press and the Lincoln Institute of Land Policy, 1996), p. 2.

61 For an excellent roundup of methods for increasing local food production, see Beatley and Manning, *The Ecology of Place*, pp. 92-93 and 150-152.

62 An interesting example is the political war in New York City over Mayor Rudy Giuliani's attempt to raise funds by selling scattered public land parcels, many of which have been used for years as community gardening sites. As reported in the *New York Times*, May 9, 2000, neighborhood uprisings of angry gardeners and funding from nonprofit sources changed Giuliani's mind.

63 Constance E. Beaumont, *How Superstore Sprawl Can Harm Communities, and What Citizens Can Do About It* (Washington, DC: National Trust for Historic Preservation, 1994).

64 Public Technology, Inc., *Sustainable Building Technical Manual* (Washington, DC: PTI, 1996), p. 1.10.

65 David Salvesen, "Making Industrial Parks Sustainable," *Urban Land*, February 1996, pp. 29-32.

66 RMI, *Green Development*, p. 10.

67 Ibid.

68 Information provided to the author by John Laswick, manager of the city of Tucson's Sustainable Communities Program, on January 6, 2000.

69 William M. Lafferty and Katarina Eckerberg, eds., *From the Earth Summit to Local Agenda 21* (London: Earthscan Publications Limited, 1998), pp. 5, 6.

chapter 3

ECOLOGY AND LAND DEVELOPMENT
PAST APPROACHES AND NEW DIRECTIONS

Rutherford H. Platt

The view from any metropolitan highway tells the story: American cities continue to expand outward into the hinterlands while filling in patches of remaining "countryside" skipped by earlier waves of development. The process of ongoing urban development consumes forests and farms, wetlands and floodplains, riparian habitat, scenic views, and ecological habitats even as it provides homes, jobs, transportation, schools, medical facilities, and infrastructure. The latter are needed; but in the absence of the former, urban communities are oppressive, monotonous, uninspiring, and unhealthy. To promote sustainability, the challenge is to design new urban developments that incorporate, rather than obliterate, elements of natural ecosystems, visual diversity, and green space for rest and recreation. That is the subject of this chapter.

We begin with a brief statistical review of the problem, namely, the prospect of a wave of new development over the next 50 years that will rival what has been built since World War II, with even greater demand for land per new home. The sec-

ond part of the chapter summarizes the heritage of past approaches to preserving open space for diverse purposes. The legacy of past approaches is the "green capital" of today's metropolitan regions. Next, we examine the nation's present metropolitan landscape as a function of changing laws and institutions that influence the unfolding of the city. Recent years have witnessed a significant expansion in the reach of federal, state, and local environmental laws, a stronger role for various types of nongovernmental organizations, and a new emphasis on "partnering" among public and private interests. In particular, several types of open-space initiatives have adopted a decidedly regional focus and depend on an unprecedented level of public/private collaboration. These are the forces that are placing new emphasis on the long-term protection of natural resources as a fundamental aspect of sustainable development.

The Next Wave of Development: The Vanishing Landscape

Over the past 50 years, the American home building industry has built nearly

75 million new homes and apartment units, or three out of four of all housing units in the current U.S. housing inventory.[1] During the same period, the nation's population grew by 120 million or 77 percent—from 152 million in 1950 to over 270 million in 1999. In the next 50 years, the Bureau of the Census projects that the nation will add another 120 million inhabitants to reach a total population of 391 million.[2] Assuming the same (or higher) rate of obsolescence of older housing, the projected population increase would suggest the need to build at least another 75 million units over the next half-century.

Even greater numbers of new units may be needed to accommodate the rising number of smaller, average-sized households. With more elderly and other persons living alone and increasing numbers of single-parent families, average household size shrank from 3.33 persons in 1960 to 2.67 persons in 1994.[3] Smaller household sizes, it might be thought, should be reflected in compact development—in the form of apartments, townhouses, and condominiums—but the trend toward ever-larger single-family homes and lots at the suburban fringe continues unabated. Floor area per capita in new single-family homes has tripled over the last 50 years, and average lot sizes have grown correspondingly.[4]

Moreover, new urban development patterns continue to be more land-extensive than ever before. As noted in chapter 1, the land area embraced by many metropolitan areas is expanding much faster than the increase in population. Even for metropolitan regions experiencing little or no population growth, additional land is devoted to highways, parking, office parks, water and sewage treatment facilities, schools, shopping centers, and other types of nonresidential development.

It is clear, then, that population growth and replacement of older housing over the next 50 years will require at least as many new homes as were built over the last half-century. Further, the experience of the 1990s suggests that about 80 percent of those units will be single-family homes; the remainder will be in multifamily developments. Most new homes of both types will be located at or near the ever-expanding metropolitan fringe. The potential impact on farmland, forests, wetlands, and other natural habitat will be dramatic and rapid. For example, the Chicago Openlands Project estimates that, by 2020, the greater Chicago region will experience population growth of 25 percent and a probable 55 percent increase in its developed land.[5] Figure 3-1 summarizes the potential change in land use in three Chicago-area fringe counties over the next 30 years. While the analysis is perhaps overly pessimistic in projecting no increase in preserved open space, a massive conversion of rural to urban land use seems inevitable.

Of course, not all new construction will occur at the periphery; the infill of exist-

Present and Estimated Future Land Use in Three Chicago-Area Counties 3-1

County	Developed Land	Preserved Open Space	Agricultural or Other Rural Land
Kane County, Illinois			
1998	16.4 percent	4.0 percent	78.8 percent
2028	52.4 percent	4.0 percent	42.8 percent
Will County, Illinois			
1998	12.7 percent	9.0 percent	76.8 percent
2028	63.1 percent	9.0 percent	26.4 percent
Kenosha County, Wisconsin			
1998	9.8 percent	14.5 percent	74.3 percent
2028	46.8 percent	14.5 percent	37.2 percent

Source: Adapted from *Under Pressure: Land Consumption in the Chicago Region, 1998–2028* (Chicago: Openlands Project, 1999), p. 5.

ing metropolitan areas is also expected. The National Association of Home Builders and U.S. Conference of Mayors recently pledged to construct 1 million additional market-rate housing units in the nation's cities and inner-ring suburbs over the next ten years.[6] Infill housing will provide convenient and affordable new homes without encroaching on rural land at the urban fringe. But infill development also involves the loss of many odds and ends of natural or agricultural land skipped over in earlier waves of development; some of that land represents locally important "incidental open spaces."

Thus, a critical challenge associated with both peripheral and infill urban growth is how to plan new development that minimizes loss of the ecological functions and amenities of undeveloped open space both within and outside metropolitan areas. The quest is an old one, dating back at least to Queen Elizabeth I's famous (and ignored) proclamation of 1580 that ordered "all manner of persons, . . . to desist and forbear from any new building of any house or tenement within three miles from any of the gates of the said city of London. . . ."[7] The queen's decree was a far cry from today's arsenal of growth management ordinances, policies, and techniques, which, it could be argued, have been no more effective than the Elizabethan fiat.

While stopping urban sprawl is infeasible, efforts have long been underway to temper the impacts of unchecked growth by carving out open areas, some of them artificially designed for human uses and others relatively "natural" in character and purpose. Older American cities are blessed by a legacy of a wide variety of protected spaces that were set aside for various purposes over the course of the nation's history. Imagine New York City without Central Park; Boston without the Boston Public Garden; Chicago without its lakefront parks; San Antonio without the Riverwalk; Portland, Oregon, without its Forty-Mile Loop. These and countless other preserved green spaces within our older cities and suburbs did not simply happen. They required the same vision, talent, energy, political skills, and sheer persistence that are essential in creating today's greenways, cycle paths, ecological refuges, or river corridors. The objectives, the means, the vocabulary, and the geographic scale have changed, but today's quest for livable cities and suburbs draws its inspiration from past successes and failures.

From Town Commons to New Urban Commons: The Open Space Evolution from 1630 to 2000

As stated above, the growth and evolution of American cities have been accompanied by successive waves of efforts to set aside certain areas as open space for various purposes. Over the course of the nation's history, the perspective on urban open space has in fact come full circle—"from commons to commons."[8] The process that began with the colonial New England town common has now led to the "new urban common"—the fortuitous survival, through deliberate action or happenstance, of bits and patches of relatively underused land in metropolitan areas regardless of size, ownership, or type of management. These spaces within urbanized and urbanizing areas form the urban counterpart to the farmlands, natural features, and environmentally sensitive lands that are preserved in the rural countryside outside metropolitan areas. The current emphasis in regional planning calls for incorporating such spaces into a larger framework of preserved and informal spaces that collectively serve a variety of human and ecological functions.

The evolution of urban open space outlined below is indicative of a complex history. Chronologically, one phase blends into the next, and a given site may reflect multiple perspectives, e.g., recreation and visual amenity. A site may evolve in its use from one purpose to others as in the case of military lands converted to parks or water supply lands that later support recreational uses. Geographically, the legacies of different phases may coexist side by side, e.g., the Boston Common and

the Boston Public Garden, in the mosaic of the contemporary urban landscape.

The Colonial Era. Certain types of open spaces sprang into existence with the first colonies, including town commons fashioned after the communal open spaces preserved in many English settlements, open lands platted by early town planners, and lands initially dedicated to military use.

Town commons. From the outset of New England settlement in the 17th century, town founders—whether ecclesiastic congregations or individual grantees—often designated spaces for communal use. The practice grew out of the declining English tradition of holding feudal land in common tenure as opposed to individual freehold ownership. Town commons served diverse purposes such as livestock pasturage, burial grounds, sources of timber, fields for recreation, militia training grounds, and sites for public ceremonies.

The allocation and use of lands within early colonial towns was ecologically based. In coastal settlements, for example, a town's inhabitants valued tidal salt marshes as common resources for livestock pasturage. According to John Stilgoe, "The practice of grazing livestock on common pasture endured for centuries in New England. It lasted the longest where it first began, in the coastal towns because the great salt marshes and grass-covered dunes made perfect, easily accessible pastures."[9] Other common rights pertained to a variety of natural resources found in the surrounding countryside: fish, firewood, timber, peat, sand, limestone, and so forth. The allocation of common rights was town-based; in other words, outsiders were denied access to resources within the town limits as roughly surveyed. This practice protected the "carrying capacity" of local resources in relation to the needs of the local population. When

that population became too large for the resource base, groups of emigrants moved elsewhere to found new towns in the hinterlands.

The ecological basis for common resources in colonial New England was not formalized in any plan as such but rather was determined by customary usage. Far from the lavishly designed urban parks of the 19th century, the colonial common was an organic or vernacular landscape feature. It simply happened because it was needed, and the appropriate land for each purpose was identified not by planning but by the common sense of the original proprietors and inhabitants. The size, shape, and functions of commons were determined more by contemporary socioeconomic conditions than by a preconceived plan.

Areas such as the Boston Common were literally held and used in common by town inhabitants. Later, they survived as municipal public spaces that, though diminished in size, embellish the centers of New England towns with their elm trees, war memorials, and bandstands. Even when degraded by parking meters, street encroachments, incompatible signage, and inappropriate plantings, they continue to provide a sense of common identity and, on occasion, a locus for community festivities.[10]

Platted open spaces. In contrast with the organic, unplanned commons typified by the Boston Common, platted squares or small parks appeared in communities whose settlement was guided by a preconceived land use plan for streets, house lots, and open spaces. A well-known example in New England is the Green in New Haven, Connecticut. That space originated as the central block of a nine-block grid plan that was drawn up before New Haven's 1638 settlement. The central open space was reserved for a marketplace and used as the site of the meetinghouse, jail, grammar school, park, and "front yard" for Yale University.[11]

Platted open spaces were integral to William Penn's famous 1683 plan for Philadelphia. Under a grant from the Crown, Penn laid out Philadelphia as an entirely new city to serve as a refuge for Quakers fleeing persecution in England. Penn personally selected the new city's site on the Delaware River (to be "navigable, high, dry, and healthy") and drew up its land use plan. Following the model of public open areas in London, Penn provided for a central ten-acre market square and for four eight-acre squares conveniently situated in residential districts—all encompassed within a grid pattern of streets and house lots extending two miles from the Delaware River to the Schuylkill River.[12]

In New York City, the 1811 Plan of the Commissioners of Streets and Roads mapped the grid of future streets and avenues that today characterize Manhattan. The commissioners platted small parks at the intersections of the existing diagonal "Broadway" and the planned north/south avenues; these odd-shaped spaces became Union, Madison, Herald, Times squares, and so on. Gramercy Park in central Manhattan was laid out in 1832, modeled on the private parks of London's West End; as with the West End parks, use of Gramercy Park was limited to the occupants of surrounding townhouses and apartments. Similarly, Boston's Louisburg Square was laid out in 1826 as a private park in the original development plan for Beacon Hill. Such squares, though closed to the general public, are still green oases within their respective cities.

Military fortifications. Lands set aside for military use are another colonial-era contribution to today's urban open spaces. Especially notable

are the "batteries" at the tip of Manhattan Island and the end of the peninsula in Charleston, South Carolina. The Plâce d'Armes (later Jackson Square) formed the core of the French colonial plan for New Orleans. Originally used for military parades, the square is now the heart of the French Quarter, awash in tourists, flowers, music, and outdoor amusements. San Francisco's superb Presidio, a military post overlooking the Golden Gate, is now located partly within the Golden Gate National Recreation Area. The Spanish colonial pueblos at Los Angeles, Santa Fe, and elsewhere in the Southwest were once central plazas that accommodated markets, parades, religious festivals, and evening socializing.[13]

Designed Urban Parks. In the early 19th century, America's newly wealthy, leisured upper class demanded elegance in its urban surroundings, country estates, and cemeteries. It drew its inspiration from Europe: the formal gardens of Versailles and Paris and the "picturesque" vistas of English estates and parks, particularly John Nash's 1811 design for Regent's Park in London. These designed landscapes were lavish, colorful, and eclectic but bore little or no resemblance to the natural ecology of their respective sites.

Among the earliest landscaped parks in America was the Boston Public Garden of the 1840s; the garden's manicured lawns, gaudy but geometric flower beds, colorful foliage, pathways, and pond with its trademark swanboats "irresistibly recall a French park of the Second Empire."[14] The Boston Public Garden was and is the antithesis of a natural habitat. Its lush botanical landscape blends varieties of exotic plants selected for ornamental effect rather than for ecological integrity. Indeed, the public garden was created on a site newly reclaimed from a swamp, which, at the time, was considered a wasteland.

Despite our heightened appreciation of natural ecosystems, it is hard to deny the appeal of an artificially created landscape (see photo on page 29).

In the 1830s and 1840s, the influential landscape architect Andrew Jackson Downing crusaded for the creation of new urban parks to give the general public access to "picturesque" surroundings previously enjoyed only by the wealthy.[15] Together with New York poet and editor William Cullen Bryant, Downing recognized the need for the creation of a large "central park" in Manhattan in advance of the island's development. In 1853, the New York state legislature authorized the city to acquire a 770-acre site and proceed with the construction of Central Park. A picturesque-style landscape design (the Greensward Plan) created by Frederick Law Olmsted and Calvert Vaux was selected in a design competition. The design featured contrasting areas of open meadow, water, and groves of woods and the separation of roadways for different forms of traffic and recreation.[16] The park incorporated the site's physical features such as hills and rock outcrops but otherwise created an entirely artificial "rus" within the "urbs" (countryside within the city).

Central Park and later Olmsted parks in other cities not only served the wealthy but also promoted the public health and morality of lower-class immigrants and factory workers. Victorian reformers referred to parks as the "green lungs of the city." Olmsted himself wrote in 1881, "How could New York have got on without the park? Twelve million visits are made to it every year. The poor and the rich come together in it in larger numbers than anywhere else, and enjoy what they find in it in more complete sympathy than they enjoy anything else together. . . ."[17] Olmsted could also justly boast that Central Park soon paid for itself through enhanced property values and taxation of adjoining real estate.

The Boston Public Garden. A view looking toward the Boston Common and the Massachusetts State House dome. Photo by R.H. Platt.

The "City Beautiful." The Chicago Columbian Exposition of 1893 hailed another era of open-space design. Located on the edge of Lake Michigan, the exposition (world's fair) assembled a great collection of pseudo-classical pavilions set amid reflecting pools, fountains, and statuary, the so-called White City. Nearby was a more rustic landscape designed by Olmsted; in fact, it survives to the present day as Jackson Park. But the fair's legacy is the influence of the White City on American civic design, launching what would become the City Beautiful movement in architecture and city planning. The City Beautiful movement, like the picturesque style that preceded it, mimicked European fashion, especially Paris as redeveloped by Georges Haussmann beginning in the 1850s.

The City Beautiful style used open space as a stage set for great public buildings and monuments. The spaces were often wind-swept, endless expanses of pavement (icy in winter, scorching in summer) embellished with flower beds and lawns (to which access was forbidden), statues of unknown heroes, and intermittently operating fountains. From Washington, D.C., to Denver, to San Francisco, to Seattle, the efforts of local leaders to emulate the capitals of Europe dominated central-city planning and civic architecture during the mid-19th century. The urban historian Lewis Mumford wrote scornfully, "Our imperial architecture is an architecture of compensation: It provides grandiloquent stones for people who have been deprived of bread and sunlight."[18] It also lacks any sense of the ecological character of a city's location. Where sensitively designed, however, City Beautiful civic architecture has proven versatile and adaptable to the changing needs of the populace as with the Washington, D.C., Mall (see figure 3-2) and Chicago's Grant Park. Grant Park is Chicago's "front yard" on Lake Michigan, with playing fields, flower gardens, a band shell, yacht harbor, and the Chicago Art Institute.

Metropolitan and Regional Plans. In the 1880s, Frederick Law Olmsted formulated a plan known as the "Emerald Necklace" for the Boston park system (see figure 3-3). The "necklace" is a series of loosely connected open spaces anchored at one end by the Boston Common and Boston Public Garden and at the other by Franklin Park

29

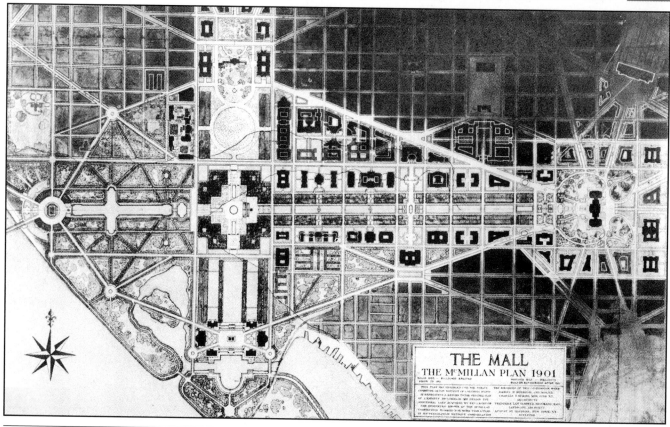

Note the major axis extending from the Capitol at the right to the (future) Washington Monument and Lincoln Memorial, and the minor axis extending from the White House at top left to the (future) Jefferson Memorial at the bottom.

Source: National Capital Planning Commission.

Boston's Emerald Necklace

3-3

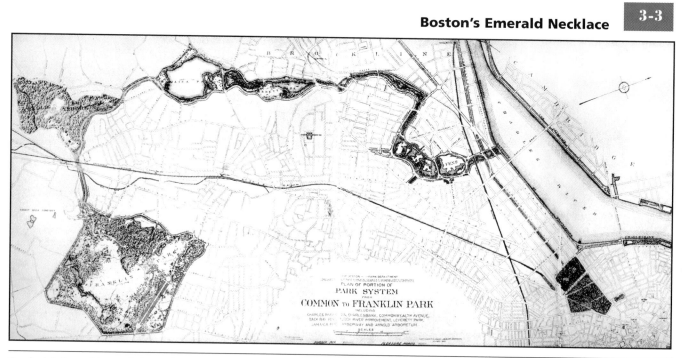

Frederick Law Olmsted drew the plan for the Boston park system.

(another Olmsted creation). The anchors were linked by Commonwealth Avenue (a new Parisian-style boulevard through Back Bay), the "fens" along the Muddy River, Jamaica Pond, and the Arnold Arboretum. The goal was to provide a linear system of green spaces for horse-back riding, cycling, and strolling that would also serve as a buffer between adjoining urban neighborhoods. Thus, the necklace would at once connect and separate.

An important element of the Emerald Necklace was the protection of existing habitat along the Muddy River to alleviate future flood losses. The plan proposed interceptor sewers to reduce public health hazards and a parkway to provide carriage, horse, and pedestrian connections with the rest of the park system. The Emerald Necklace was, in essence, the first explicit American proposal for a "greenway," an open-space concept a century ahead of its time. It also represented an early recognition that perhaps the "natural ecology" of an area is preferable to a totally redesigned landscape.

Garden cities and greenbelts. In 1899, the English urban reformer Ebenezer Howard published his proposal for the construction of "garden cities" that would function as a middle ground between the crowded, unhealthy industrial city and the bucolic but boring rural village.[19] The garden city was to be a new type of suburb, offering a range of housing types and jobs. It would be connected to a larger city by train (and later highways) but would offer social, educational, cultural, and recreational activities locally.

Open spaces of several types were integral to the garden city, as realized in Howard's prototype Letchworth Garden City (established 1905). Howard and his disciples eschewed both the grandiose plazas of the City Beautiful movement and the artificial landscapes

of the English picturesque style in favor of informal, functional types of open land reminiscent of colonial commons. These spaces included useful, unpretentious community parks and individual garden plots scattered throughout Letchworth's residential core. The defining element of Howard's model was to be a circumferential "greenbelt" of rural land separating the garden city from its neighbors.[20]

Howard directly inspired the construction of two demonstration communities near London and later Radburn, New Jersey, near New York City. But his influence was vastly magnified as the scale of planning shifted from the local to the regional level under the guidance of Patrick Geddes in Edinburgh, Lewis Mumford in America, and Howard's successor, Frederic Osborn. The Garden City/greenbelt formulation became a defining element of Patrick Abercrombie's 1944 Plan for Greater London, the blueprint for the postwar development of the British New Town and metropolitan greenbelt system.[21]

Aside from Radburn and a few other model developments, Howard's thinking bore little fruit in the United States, where private property rights were held sacred and regional planning was considered radical. But a home-grown American regional concept proved too attractive to be ignored, namely, Benton MacKaye's 1922 proposal for an Appalachian Trail that would extend 2,100 miles from Georgia to Maine. The trail, in time, was established through the combined efforts of the Appalachian Mountain Club, the National Park Service, and a host of other public and private sponsors. It has served as the model for countless other cross-country trail systems, including the Pacific Crest, Santa Fe, Oregon, and Mormon trails and the Natchez Trace.

Ecology and bioregionalism. In his 1928 book *The New Exploration,* Benton

MacKaye voiced concern over what he viewed as the "flooding" of rural communities by metropolitan growth, perhaps the first articulation of the problem later referred to as urban sprawl. His mentor and friend Lewis Mumford later described MacKaye as confronting "the problem of how to use the natural and cultural resources we have at hand today without defacing the landscape, polluting the atmosphere, disrupting the complex associations of animal and plant species upon which all higher life depends . . . ."[22] MacKaye was, in other words, a proto-environmentalist about four decades ahead of his time.

In a prescient 1956 essay, Mumford himself, America's preeminent critic of metropolitan growth,[23] deplored "a tendency to loosen the bonds that connect [the city's] inhabitants with nature and to transform, eliminate, or replace its earth-bound aspects covering the natural site with an artificial environment that enhances the dominance of man and encourages an illusion of complete independence from nature."[24] In his concluding paragraph, Mumford calls for urban patterns that are "stable, *self-sustaining,* and self-renewing" and that restore "the *ecological balance* that originally prevailed between city and country . . . ."[25] These early references to "sustainability" and "ecology" presage a sea change in thinking about urban land use, namely, a shift from mechanistic and technological approaches to "solving urban problems" toward increasing recognition that cities must conform to their natural environments rather than vice versa. In other words, "Nature bats last."

In his formulation of a "land ethic," Aldo Leopold clearly articulated the role of ecology as a constraint on human settlements and land:

> Quit thinking about decent land-use as solely an economic

problem. Examine each question in terms of what is ethically and aesthetically right as well as what is economically expedient. A thing is right when it tends to preserve the integrity, stability, and beauty of the biotic community. It is wrong when it tends otherwise.[26]

As with MacKaye's *The New Exploration*, Leopold's plea for the biosphere resonated with subsequent generations and would become holy scripture for the environmental movement that emerged in the 1960s.

Some of the earliest research in the field of ecology was conducted by University of Chicago botanist Henry Cowles. He studied the succession of plant communities in relation to time and environmental stresses at the Indiana Dunes at the southern end of Lake Michigan.[27] That location would in fact not only become the "birthplace of ecology" but also the focus of an archetypal environmental conflict over the fate of the dunes, a landscape typified by ever-shifting sand hills, forests, and wetlands near Chicago. The dunes region was attractive to the steel industry as an ideal site for new steel mills, but Chicago-area artists, naturalists, poets, and hedonists treasured the region as a place of superb natural beauty, tranquillity, and privacy. Poet Carl Sandburg, landscape architect Jens Jenson, and Illinois Senator Paul Douglas were among those who championed the cause of saving the dunes from total destruction.

J. Ronald Engel described the long struggle as "a fusion of *ecology and spirituality* as directed to the preservation of a symbol-laden landscape."[28] The battle lasted over 50 years, culminating in 1966 when Congress established the Indiana Dunes National Seashore.[29] Today, the National Park Service seeks to protect, restore, and interpret the natural ecosystems of the Indiana

Dunes in the midst of a complex of steel mills and the outward sprawl of metropolitan Chicago. Thus, what began as a quest to protect a quietly spectacular landscape and habitat far beyond the city now promises to become an oasis of natural beauty and ecological process within the expanding urban region—a "bioregional Central Park" for the 21st century.

Outdoor Recreation. Postwar suburbanization and the launch of the interstate highway program in the 1950s began to attract growing public concern about the loss of open space and recreation opportunities in and around metropolitan areas. Among the diverse publications addressing the problem at the time were *Fortune* magazine's *The Exploding Metropolis* (1958),[30] Edward Higbee's *The Squeeze: Cities without Space* (1960),[31] *The Race for Open Space* (1960)[32] by the New York Regional Plan Association, and geographer Jean Gottman's epic study *Megalopolis* (1961).[33] The collective message of these and other writings was that urbanization was needlessly causing the loss of farmland, forestland, and recreation areas in and around the nation's metropolitan areas.

In 1958, Congress established the Outdoor Recreation Resources Review Commission (ORRRC) to survey the nation's need for additional public open space. Chaired by Laurence Rockefeller, the commission reported a growing shortage of accessible, usable recreational open space, particularly in suburban areas. It documented the rising popularity of outdoor activities such as swimming, fishing, skiing, hiking, and camping despite a relatively static supply of public areas to serve such needs. Indoor sports facilities and inner-city parks attracted less attention than outdoor recreation and conservation sites in and beyond the suburbs. (The report gave little attention to inner-city or minority needs, as reflected in the several photographs of smiling, white sub-

urban families in their Fords and Chevrolets.)

Federal open-space funding. The ORRRC report led to passage of the Land and Water Conservation Fund Act of 1965 (LWCF), which, for two decades, was the primary source of federal funds for public open space. By the 1990s, the act had made available over $3 billion to state and local governments—on a 50-50 matching basis—for the acquisition and design of outdoor recreation facilities. In place of the manicured lawns and gravel paths of the older urban parks and the cement plazas of the City Beautiful era, the LWCF ushered in a new age of wooden boardwalks spanning salt marshes and freshwater wetlands. Appreciation of nature as it exists, rather than as transformed by human intervention, took root in the 1960s.

Housing projects. Between the 1930s and the 1960s, the federal government encouraged local housing authorities to construct high-rise rental apartment "projects" for low- to moderate-income households. Some projects were built and operated by public housing agencies; others were undertaken by non-profit or conventional developers under federal subsidy programs. These ill-fated experiments in housing the poor were modeled on the Radiant City, a design concept pioneered by the French architect Le Corbusier that featured tall, monolithic apartment towers set amid verdant common open spaces. While the Radiant City model found widespread application in postwar urban construction around the world (e.g., France, Scandinavia, Russia, China, and Hong Kong), it was poorly suited to low-income housing in America's inner cities. Well-intended playgrounds and "green" spaces were soon covered with pavement, junk cars, litter, and other detritus and proved menacing to the inhabitants of nearby buildings. In her classic critique of urban renewal, Jane

Jacobs deplored the loss of traditional streets in favor of anonymous, threatening spaces between buildings in housing projects.[34] By the start of the 21st century, many of these high-rise ghettos had been abandoned and razed.

Recreation on federal lands. In 1960 and 1964, Congress adopted multiple-use planning acts that required federal land agencies to reassess their holdings to determine what lands should be protected for natural habitat values and recreation rather than licensed for forestry, mining, or other economic operations. The Wilderness Act of 1964 strengthened federal protection of federal lands classified as wilderness areas. In addition, during the 1960s, Congress designated nine national seashores and four national lakeshores, including those along Cape Cod and the Indiana Dunes. And the LWCF provided billions of dollars over the next four decades to acquire additional land for many federal parks, national forests, and wildlife refuges.

Development Regulations. Since the advent of land use planning and zoning in the 1920s, governments have dictated how landowners and developers may use their land. Most familiar are the dimensional requirements specified by traditional zoning laws to establish minimum lot size, frontage, and widths of front, side, and rear yards as well as a maximum percent of lot coverage. Minimum street setbacks (front yards) are commonplace in single-family neighborhoods; setbacks remain in private ownership but, when landscaped, serve as quasi-public space in terms of visual amenity. As for subdivisions, local regulations typically require "dedications" (contributions) of streets, drainage, and utility easements and other internal linkages that function secondarily as open spaces.

Exactions. Many communities have expanded the reach of their subdivision ordinances to require the reservation or dedication of sites for local schools, playgrounds, small parks, and environmentally sensitive lands. (In addition, some developers, particularly those engaged in large multiuse communities, expect to incorporate community-serving sites and even facilities into their plans to increase the market appeal of their projects.) State courts have validated the constitutionality of expanded subdivision requirements, especially when the need for public amenities and facilities is attributable to a specific development.[35] Where facilities and sites are not needed within a particular subdivision, local government frequently requires the developer to pay a monetary fee in lieu of land dedication.[36] Many states have authorized the imposition of impact fees on new development of any type to help defray the cost of providing additional public services such as public roads, sewer and water infrastructure, and schools. Some local governments levy impact fees for parks and open space.[37]

In 1994, the U.S. Supreme Court issued a landmark decision involving development exactions. In *Dolan* v. *City of Tigard* (Oregon),[38] the owner of a business property sought permission to expand her building; the city, however, required the owner to dedicate to the city that portion of her property that lay within the 100-year floodplain plus an additional strip of land to be used as part of a public bikeway system. The majority opinion by Chief Justice Rehnquist held that to require such public access without compensation violated the "takings clause" of the Fifth Amendment of the U.S. Constitution. "Nor shall private property be taken for public use without just compensation." The opinion generally approved of the need for regional open space but concluded that the property owner was unfairly burdened. The decision called for evidence of "rough proportionality" between the burden to a property owner and public benefit.[39]

Cluster zoning. Familiar to most readers of this book, incentives such as cluster zoning and planned unit development (PUD) encourage developers to protect open space in exchange for relaxation of applicable zoning requirements. Pursuant to a negotiated agreement between a developer and local government, a developer may agree to retain specific sites in permanent open spaces that will be held by a public entity, homeowners' association, or conservation organization. Preserved areas contribute to ecosystem protection while enhancing property values.[40]

Urban growth boundaries. Hundreds of communities, particularly in the West, have established urban growth boundaries. Where permitted by state law, such boundaries are intended to demarcate areas expected to undergo development, distinguishing them from areas in which development is considered undesirable.[41] Boundaries are frequently set to accommodate foreseeable (or desired) future levels of growth, thereby encouraging development to occur in proximity to an existing urban area. Restrictions on extensions of urban services such as roads and water and sewer lines and limits on zoning densities maintain the integrity of the urban growth boundary. To the extent that various restrictions enable a local community to control development outside the boundary, farmlands, forests, and other open spaces can be preserved until additional land is required for development.

Environmental Planning and Activism. The 1960s proved to be a time of ferment and change on several fronts: civil rights, the feminist movement, the antiwar movement, and the environment. Urban land development was among the several aspects of

American society to be challenged by new thinking. In 1968, three landmark publications influenced how land in the United States would thereafter be perceived, planned, and used. Biologist Garrett Hardin's essay "The Tragedy of the Commons"[42] argued that ecological "commons" requires the acceptance of restraints on our actions for the protection of all; if not, "freedom in a commons brings ruin to all." Landscape architect Ian McHarg's *Design with Nature*[43] made the case that land development must be guided by the natural qualities and limitations of a development site. William H. Whyte's *The Last Landscape*[44] considered how public laws and policies can achieve more desirable patterns of land use and nonuse. By implication, Whyte built on Hardin's principle of "mutual coercion mutually agreed upon" to summarize how land development could be improved through a blend of coercion and incentives.

Hardin, McHarg, and Whyte joined the larger 1960s "chorus of dissent" that was led by Rachel Carson's *Silent Spring* and included the voices of David Brower, Ralph Nader, Paul Erlich, Barry Commoner, Edward Abbey, William O. Douglas, Henry "Scoop" Jackson, Wendell Berry, and the grassroots activists who sprang into action in localities across the nation.[45] From the ferment emerged four federal environmental laws—the National Environmental Policy Act, the Clean Water Act, the Safe Drinking Water Act, and the Endangered Species Act (discussed later in this chapter)—all of which continue to influence metropolitan growth.

At regional and local levels across the country, new forms of multifunction open-space corridors and areas came under government protection. Some of these open spaces are protected through the types of regulatory restrictions described above; other open spaces are preserved through zoning and restrictions

often used to protect agricultural lands or highly valued natural areas such as the Chesapeake Bay and the New Jersey Pinelands. In addition, many types of conservation groups, including conservancies and land trusts, remain active in securing easements and ownerships for the protection of rural areas and natural landscapes.

Farmland protection. Nearly every state has adopted agricultural preservation laws that allow farmers to join districts that protect their lands against tax increases propelled by rising land prices and protect their "right to farm" against attempts to restrict farming practices. Several local governments, many of them counties, also preserve farmland through large-lot zoning requirements that discourage development. Most important, perhaps, are the 19 states and many local governments that have spent nearly $1 billion to purchase the development rights to over 590,000 acres of farmland.[46] Increasingly, voters are willing to pay for farmland preservation; in 1998, the electorate passed 172 ballot measures authorizing the expenditure of $7.5 billion for parks, recreation, and land preservation projects.[47]

Greenways. Beginning in the 1970s and 1980s with the decline of federal funding and rising urban land values, a new approach to providing urban space found widespread application, namely, multipurpose "greenways." Like Olmsted's Emerald Necklace plan for the Boston park system of a century earlier, the greenway approach seeks to connect diverse patches of open space in a more or less continuous linear system. Greenways, however, involve the use of creative legal arrangements that affect both public and privately owned lands. Nonetheless, hundreds of cities and metropolitan regions have engaged in some form of greenway or urban trail development. Most greenways provide a variety of public benefits such as

flood damage reduction, wetlands habitat protection, recreation, and visual amenity.[48]

One form of greenway is the rail trail, a new form of open space in settings ranging from historic industrial areas (once served by rail lines) to relatively natural landscapes. Examples include Prairie Path in the Chicago suburbs and the Rail Trail on Cape Cod. Today, the trails movement embraces not only long-distance trails but also hundreds of urban trails for hiking, cycling, skateboarding, cross-country skiing, dog walking, and other nonmotorized enjoyment. Urban and metropolitan trails follow shorelines, river banks, utility rights-of-way, or other linear features. Most involve public and private cooperation to ensure access to private land, maintenance, signage, litter control, and other management needs.

"Greenline parks." Modeled on the English national parks, connected parks are another form of multipurpose, collaborative open space. Among many examples in the United States, one of the most notable is the Illinois-Michigan Canal Corridor (I & M Canal) that extends for over 100 miles from Chicago southwest to the Illinois River at LaSalle and Peru, Illinois. The I & M Canal, constructed during the 1830s in the same era as the Erie Canal in New York state and the Chesapeake and Ohio Canal in Maryland, established an all-water route between the Midwest heartland and the East Coast and boosted the fortunes of Chicago. (The railroads, of course, reinforced Chicago's hegemony in the Midwest.[49])

By the 1970s, the I & M had fallen into dereliction; it became a disconnected series of stoneworks, stagnant water, humble buildings, and other relics. Through the persistence of local historians and recreation activists led by Gerald Adelmann, Congress designated the

Illinois & Michigan National Heritage Corridor in 1984, the first of several such corridors to be established. The federal designation involved no significant funding but helped put the canal "back on the map" and stimulated further state, local, and private efforts to reassemble as much of the physical canal and its historical context as possible. A 61.5-mile I & M State Canal Trail was established in the 1980s.[50]

Urban rivers. Historically, rivers have served as arteries of commerce. In the United States, rivers were usually bordered by railroads and industries and thus became heavily polluted. But increasingly, cities are reclaiming their rivers and riverfronts for recreational open space. All across the nation, large cities such as Chicago and Minneapolis and small cities such as Hartford and Lansing, Michigan, are creating pathways, parks, and other open spaces along their rivers. At the same time, nearby development is turning toward rather than away from riverscapes. Combined with massive water cleanup efforts mandated by the Clean Water Act, urban rivers are becoming important components of metropolitan open-space and park systems.[51]

The "New Urban Commons." We seemingly have run out of new ideas, opportunities, and funds to secure further urban open spaces on the scale of a Central Park, Balboa Park in San Diego, or the Cook County, Illinois, Forest Preserves. Large blocks of undisturbed land close to or within urban areas are rare except in the case of defense base closures.[52] When well-located open land is available in or near metropolitan areas, it now costs hundreds of thousands of dollars per acre, even as the federal government has starved the Land and Water Conservation Fund and other sources of open-space funding (although, in 1998, the Clinton Administration proposed a new Better America initiative to lever-

age $10 billion in state and local open-space expenditures).[53] Despite the recent groundswell in voter approval of ballot measures to save open space, it is difficult to assess the impact of the referenda on the outward tide of urban growth forecast for the next 50 years. In many cases, the available funding may neither be directed specifically to nor adequate for preserving regionally significant open spaces around metropolitan areas.

Meanwhile, prospects for using land use controls to achieve open-space preservation are uncertain. As it gains momentum, the property rights movement is seeking to enlarge the scope of the Fifth Amendment to the U.S. Constitution, requiring compensation to owners whose property is "devalued" by public regulations regardless of regulatory rationale. In particular, the 1992 U.S. Supreme Court decision in *Lucas* v. *South Carolina Coastal Council* intimidated public officials from advocating noncompensatory land use regulations out of concern that a "takings" suit would be filed by the aggrieved landowners.[54] While long-standing zoning and subdivision doctrines remain in effect, many local elected officials are leery of further restricting development to retain open space.

Certainly, there is some cause for concern, but not despair, about the balance between developed and open land in metropolitan America. Strangely, even as cities encroach further into the hinterlands, the "country" is infiltrating the city. "The distinction between *urbs* and *rus* has become increasingly blurred."[55] Sometimes natural areas are woven into suburban developments and produce plentiful parks, school grounds, and other public open spaces and sizable lots. Other natural areas find use as individual and community gardens. Many communities practice conservation and replanting of trees—in some subdivisions, more trees exist today than when the land was farmed,

although other developments have cleared extensive woodlands.[56]

But there is a growing appreciation of smaller, more intimate patches and clusters of natural areas woven into the fabric of urbanization. A closer look at today's metropolitan areas reveals a surprising abundance of relatively undisturbed and underused bits and pieces of land. Some are owned by public agencies, some by private institutions, some by individuals, some perhaps by no one. Such spaces are not necessarily scenic, biodiverse, or even safe. Some may have been devoted to purposes now discontinued or inactive, such as rail rights-of-way (beyond those already converted to urban cycle paths), old cemeteries, and the margins of hospital grounds, college campuses, golf courses, or other large holdings. Others may be fragments left unused because of poor soil, steep slopes, wetness, or lack of access when development passed through the area. Here and there are the remnants of an old farmstead whose feisty owner resisted selling out to a developer. There are the monotonous mowed areas along interstate highways and in cloverleaf intersections that in some locales have recently been planted with native flora or wildflowers. And there are the nondescript vacant lots, often tax-delinquent, littered with trash, beer bottles, junk cars, and other unhealthy debris (see photo on page 36).

Is there a "resource" to be recognized in this hodge-podge of miscellaneous open patches? Michael Hough has termed the hodge-podge assortments of open patches a "fortuitous landscape";[57] Richard Mabey has called them "unofficial countryside."[58] In the most detailed treatment of the subject, David Nicholson-Lord has noted that mundane and ignored patches of underused land may yield ecological surprises. "The picture that emerges is thus one of discovery, of an urban society beginning to look at its immediate surroundings with fresh

35

An "incidental urban commons." Vacant land in Chicago waiting for a little attention. Photo by R.H. Platt.

eyes, seeing new possibilities in old things. A radical change in perception is involved."[59] It may also be called a "new urban commons."[60]

Clearly, our traditional open-space planning practices do not fit these humble odds and ends of land. These lands are not likely to be picturesque, monumental, urban-defining, or even scenic. They may, however, prove to be of hydrologic value as water storage areas or of ecologic value as habitat for vigorous "weeds," colorful butterflies, odd insects, birds, and other small fauna. Some may be suitable in size, character, and ownership for urban gardening plots. Some may be natural sites for environmental education when rights of access can be secured. While scarcely a greenbelt, they may even soften the harshness of a highway

corridor, provide shade for a bus shelter, or relieve the monotony of tract subdivisions. They may be places to enjoy visually from a public way or, when possible, to explore up close. They may provide a dark place at night from which to view the Milky Way. Even a solitary ancient tree may offer, to paraphrase Carl Sandburg, "a signature of time and eternity" against the evening sky.

Among the various open-space paradigms discussed earlier and summarized in figure 3-4, perhaps the closest analogue to today's odds-and-ends spaces is the town commons, an unplanned area of mundane but practical utility to the inhabitants of the surrounding area. Today's metropolitan areas are strewn with incidental open spaces that, while not literally held in common tenure, nev-

ertheless provide common benefits to the nearby populace. They are also the source of negative externalities—litter, rats, fire hazards, ragweed, and so forth. The problem is to recognize the various lands' benefits while reducing the associated detriments through efforts to provide minimum levels of management consistent with the form of ownership involved. Obviously, the approaches to hodge-podge lands must vary greatly depending on the location, size, and character of the area(s) under consideration.

From Mandates to Collaboration: The Federal Role in Ecosystem Protection
As already noted, water quality, wildlife habitats, wetlands, and other vital natural resources are subject to protection

Approximate Period	Type of Open Space	Functions	Examples
17th to 18th Century	Town commons	Pasturage, militia training, burial grounds, recreation	Boston Common
17th to 19th Century	Platted squares	Marketplace, church grounds, residential amenity	New Haven Green Penn Plan for Philadelphia Gramercy Park (New York City)
Late 18th to 19th Century	Designed landscapes ■ Formal ■ "Picturesque"	Private estates, cemeteries, urban parks	Downing landscapes Mt. Auburn Cemetery (Cambridge, Mass.) Boston Public Garden
Mid-19th Century to 1920s	Large urban parks	"Rus in urbs," recreation, public health	Central Park Franklin Park (Boston) Lincoln Park (Chicago)
1880s to Present	Linked green spaces ■ Greenbelts ■ Greenways	Urban separation, community definition, recreation, traffic circulation	Emerald Necklace (Boston) Bay Circuit (Boston) Parkways (New York) Lakefront parks (Chicago)
1880s to Present	Natural preserves	Ecological habitat, sense of place/region, spiritual values, ecological research	Adirondack Park Preserve Indiana Dunes Muir Woods (California) Cape Cod National Seashore
1890s to 1960s	Civic malls and plazas ■ City Beautiful	Monumental setting, civic pride, recreation and festivals	Washington, D.C., Mall Grant Park (Chicago)
1920s to Present	Development requirements, exactions, impact fees, cluster zoning	Small natural areas and corridors within subdivisions	Various
1930s to 1960s	Open areas between high-rise buildings	Green setting, recreation, parking	Co-op City (New York City) Public housing Urban renewal projects
1960s to Present	Suburban green areas, trails, and corridors	Outdoor recreation, watershed protection, floodplain and wetlands, environmental education	Local conservation areas Portland Forty-Mile Loop (Oregon) Forest Preserves (Illinois) I & M Canal Corridor
1970s to Present	"Incidental urban commons"	Biodiversity, recreation, visual amenity, environmental education, community pride	Woodlots, prairie remnants Urban garden projects Small-scale nature areas Vacant lot reclamation Highway medians/borders

under four major federal laws that grew out of the environmental ferment of the 1960s: the National Environmental Policy Act, the Clean Water Act, the Safe Drinking Water Act, and the Endangered Species Act. The acts and their accompanying regulatory requirements stirred controversy from the moment of their enactment. For example, some property owners, developers, and local elected officials have criticized federal influence over local land use decisions, the government's reduction of private property values, and poorly informed administrative decisions.

At the same time, though, the laws have succeeded in protecting valuable resources for the sustenance and enjoyment of future generations. An unexpected byproduct of the federal environmental laws is the infusion of ecology into urban land development. While Congress still purports to defer to states and local governments concerning the use of land, federal environmental laws are continuing to help—albeit indirectly—shape "greener" urban and metropolitan landscapes.[61] And, over the years, the parties on both sides—all sides—of environmental controversies have begun to learn the value of collaboration in achieving the aims of both development and environmental protection, a necessary outcome for sustainable development. The following four "stories" describe how potentially divisive events were transformed through collaborative (and often nerve-wracking) efforts.

Thorn Creek Woods in Metropolitan Chicago. How Thorn Creek Woods, an obscure piece of real estate in the south suburbs of Chicago, came to be the subject of a *Wall Street Journal* front-page article illustrates the emergence of a new sensitivity to ecologic concerns in land development. According to the article, the mature Thorn Creek Woods offered "a rare reminder in 1970 of how many parts of Mid-America looked when Abe Lincoln was a boy. Century-old oaks and hickories shade the steep hillsides above the creek. Deer, raccoon, and the great horned owl are among the 150 wildlife species found in its 800 acres. The forest also [happened] to be a choice piece of real estate directly in the path of Chicago suburbia . . . ."[62] In fact, it was part of a planned new community to be developed by Park Forest South Developers, Inc. And that, in a hickory nutshell, was the problem. Like the postwar suburban village of Park Forest just to the north, Park Forest South (PFS) was envisioned as a large-scale new development that would provide affordable housing within easy reach of Chicago by rail or highway. But unlike its parent community, PFS eschewed 1950s tract development in favor of mixed uses and housing types. It was sufficiently innovative to be designated by the U.S. Department of Housing and Urban Development

(HUD) as one of the first "new communities" to be eligible for federal loan guarantees under the Housing and Urban Development Act of 1968.

The writer, at the time an attorney with the Chicago Open Lands Project, characterized the woods as:

> . . . a pocket wilderness. Though small in area, its steep terrain, dense understory and overhead canopy contribute to a perceptual sense of removal from the surrounding communities. Relict farm clearings, narrow plantations of pine, and its ravines and gullies create a highly varied internal landscape, affording adventure, education, solitude, and natural beauty. With metropolitan Chicago to the north and flat cornfields to the south, Thorn Creek Woods is a curious anomaly, the last privately-owned woods of its size in northeastern Illinois.[63]

As with many environmental controversies, the dispute over Thorn Creek Woods grew out of the fact that the site's varied physical terrain was randomly criss-crossed by county, municipal, and private boundaries. The town of Park Forest to the north had acquired two parcels in the woods, and the Cook County Forest Preserve District had purchased another section. But Park Forest South and its portion of the woods were situated in a corner of rural Will County, which had little interest in preserving the woods. In addition, the state of Illinois had proposed the construction of a new highway through the woods, along with the development of a nearby state university campus. Moreover, the developer's property within the woods was adjoined on three sides by other owners. As developer Lewis Manilow saw it, the major cost

of preserving the woods would fall on him while the benefits would be an undeserved windfall to neighboring property owners.

Before 1970, there would have been little hope for Thorn Creek Woods, largely because of the discontinuity between the site's physical geography and its political/legal geography. Despite avid lobbying by the local Thorn Creek Preservation Association, no entity had a sufficient interest in and the means of keeping the woods intact. If it were not for major changes already in the air, Park Forest South would have proceeded with its plan, probably winning a design award for its mix of uses and housing styles in their wooded setting. But on January 1, 1970, President Richard Nixon signed the National Environmental Policy Act (NEPA). That brief statute, never since amended, declared a "continuing policy of the federal government, in cooperation with the state and local governments . . . to foster and promote the general welfare, to create or maintain conditions under which man and nature can exist in productive harmony, and fulfill the social, economic, and other requirements of present and future generations of Americans."[64] In addition, the act requires an "environmental impact statement" (EIS) to be prepared for any proposed "major federal actions significantly affecting the quality of the human environment."[65]

With respect to Thorn Creek Woods, the first issue was the proposed highway. Section 4(f) of the Federal Aid Highway Act of 1966 discouraged building new highways through public parks and wildlife areas. Of course, Thorn Creek Woods was not yet a public park, and—in a catch-22—the state declared that it could not acquire the land because it was planned for a highway corridor. Remarkably, all local interests, including the PFS developer, jointly invoked Section 4(f) to persuade

The "Jigsaw" Plan for Thorn Creek Woods

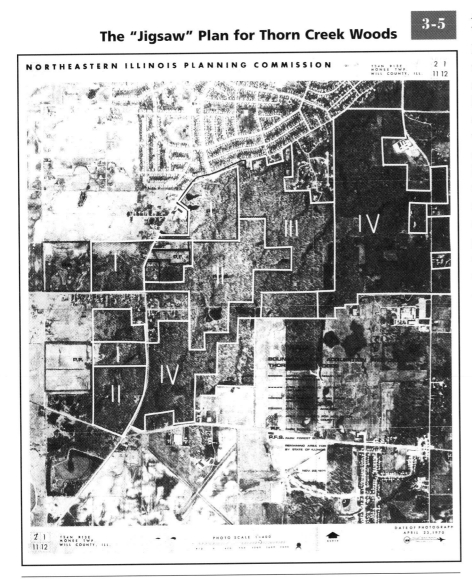

The plan came together when the multiple jurisdictions cooperated to designate areas to be acquired.

Source: Northeastern Illinois Planning Commission.

Ad Hoc Committee on Thorn Creek Woods, convened by the Northeastern Illinois Planning Commission, brought together all relevant stakeholders to formulate a "jigsaw plan" under which various entities pledged to acquire a piece of the woods and thereafter cooperate with one another in the management of the woods as a whole. The next breakthrough came from HUD, which, under the New Communities Act, could add an extra 20 percent to the already available 50 percent federal grants for state and local government open-space acquisition. HUD's offer sparked interest from the various governments such that the "jigsaw" approach finally succeeded in motivating the state of Illinois, Will County, the village of Park Forest South, and the new Governors State University to commit to acquiring parts of the woods. As the acquisition of the woods moved ahead, the development company quickly made a virtue out of necessity, as evidenced by excerpts from Park Forest South advertising brochures:

> At the edge of Thorn Creek Woods, one of the last natural forests in Illinois—a new town is being born, a town in which nature's blessings may be found in abundance. And this beautiful setting—grassy meadows, hills, ravines, creeks, lakes—so evident today—will remain forever.

Today, Thorn Creek Woods provides environmental education, recreation, and a natural oasis amid the continuing southward thrust of Chicago's metropolitan development.[67]

The Wachusett Watershed Protection Plan. The rural and urban landscapes of the United States have evolved in tandem with the development and management of water resources. From New England's 19th century mill dams and canals to the vast irrigation and water transfer projects of the West and from New York City's

the state highway department to consider and ultimately adopt a route that entirely avoided the woods.

Then, in 1970, Congress amended the 1968 New Communities Act to require new communities, Park Forest South potentially among them, to help "preserve or enhance desirable aspects of the natural and urban environment." While vague, the language was helpful to environmental advocates of Thorn Creek Woods. Ultimately, the backers turned to the new National Environmental Policy Act (NEPA) to gain time for further review by all parties. After prodding by HUD and threats of litigation from the Thorn Creek Preservation Association (TCPA), the developer agreed "to use its best efforts to establish a comprehensive Thorn Creek Woods program in cooperation with other owners and governmental agencies . . . ."[66]

It was now up to the TCPA to produce an acquisition plan by January 1972, at which time the developer reserved the right to proceed with his plan. The

Croton River Dam and aqueduct built in the 1840s to its mammoth "third water tunnel," the use of land has been inextricably linked to the capture, transfer, treatment, and distribution of water. Today, a major federal initiative under the Safe Drinking Water Act of 1973, as amended, has led to unexpected efforts among certain cities, notably Boston and New York, to protect their water supplies through elaborate watershed management programs.

The delivery of public water in the United States is not predominantly a national or state responsibility but rather has been largely the province of regional, municipal, and private water agencies. Water suppliers range in size from tiny municipal utility districts to immense regional systems serving millions of people. Today, the American system of public water supply is in transition. The politics of scarcity is giving way to the politics of sustainability. The myth of unlimited sources of new supply is yielding to the reality that existing supplies must be managed, protected, and wisely allocated. Increasing, too, is the recognition that water supply management is not an isolated, single-purpose enterprise but rather is part of the larger context of multiple-purpose, sustainable water resource and land management programs.

Fortuitously, the protection of surface and groundwater supplies yields benefits in terms of maintaining the integrity of large tracts of watershed and aquifer recharge lands. Public ownership of water supply drainage areas also helps protect the quantity and quality of runoff to reservoirs (or recharge to groundwater) while providing open space for natural habitat, recreation, and separation of urban communities. On the other hand, many rural watersheds that drain into public reservoirs remain substantially in private ownership and thus vulnerable to contaminants from agriculture and poorly treated wastewater.

Recent changes in federal law are motivating water suppliers to protect their source water against contamination by, for example, expanding public ownership and control of land uses within reservoir catchment areas. Pursuant to the 1986 amendments to the Safe Drinking Water Act,[68] the U.S. Environmental Protection Agency (EPA) issued a Surface Water Treatment Rule (SWTR) that requires most drinking water to be filtered before it is distributed to consumers unless a water supplier can satisfy EPA criteria relating to giardia and virus inactivation, the absence of waterborne-disease outbreaks, disinfection, monitoring, and watershed management, including land acquisition.

Both the metropolitan Boston and New York City water systems are seeking to prove that watershed management can forestall the need to build high-cost filtration plants. In Boston's case, the pristine Quabbin Reservoir, surrounded by state-owned land, easily secured a filtration waiver from the EPA. But the Wachusett Reservoir watershed, which lies at the cusp of the expanding Worcester metropolitan area, is two-thirds in private ownership. Given that Quabbin water passes through Wachusett before delivery to user communities in eastern Massachusetts, degradation of the Wachusett Reservoir will endanger the quality of the entire metropolitan Boston water supply.

In 1990, in response to the EPA's Surface Water Treatment Rule, the Massachusetts Department of Environmental Protection (DEP) issued the Watershed Resource Protection Plan Policy. The policy led to the development of the Wachusett Reservoir Watershed Protection Plan (WPP), which is a blueprint for a comprehensive, long-range land use and water quality program for the Wachusett watershed. Among the major threats addressed in the WPP are on-site septic systems, stormwater runoff, gasoline and petroleum storage, various types

of uncontrolled releases, and future developable areas.[69] Overall, the WPP involves land use regulation in sensitive areas, land acquisition, remediation of failing septic systems, construction of sewage collection and treatment facilities, monitoring, and remediation of hazardous materials from leaking storage tanks or transportation accidents.

Wastewater is one of the most important concerns in the Wachusett watershed. Of the 8,350 acres of watershed land currently in residential, commercial, and industrial use, only about 1,792 acres are served by conventional sewer systems; the other 6,558 acres are served by on-site septic systems. Thus, strict rules adopted in 1991 for the inspection and remediation of septic systems throughout Massachusetts are incorporated into the WPP.[70] In addition, new sewer systems are scheduled to be constructed in the towns of West Boylston and Holden with costs to be shared by the state, the Massachusetts Water Resources Authority (MWRA), and the two towns.

Further, the Massachusetts legislature enacted the Watershed Protection Act in 1992 to reduce nonpoint source pollution entering Massachusetts Water Resources Authority reservoirs from farms, failing septic systems, and urban runoff.[71] The law prohibits most development within 200 feet of a "bank of a tributary or surface waters and within 400 feet of the bank of a reservoir."[72]

The Wachusett Watershed Protection Plan calls for the commitment of $20 million to purchase about 10,500 acres of land over the next decade, thereby increasing public ownership from 14 to 25 percent of the watershed; another 25 percent is to be protected by other entities. The 1992 Watershed Protection Act also created a $135 million fund to purchase the development rights to environmentally sensitive property within MWRA system watersheds. The combination of public land acquisition and public compensation for landholders whose development rights are limited by the watershed plan will ensure the future quality of Boston's water supply.

San Diego's Multiple Species Conservation Program.[73] With a population increase of over one-third since 1980, San Diego is now the sixth-largest city in the United States. Adjoining areas in San Diego County are growing at a similarly rapid rate. One result of the region's explosive growth is that urbanization is severely threatening the biological viability of San Diego County's unique ecosystem. The county contains over 200 plant and animal species identified for protection under the federal or state endangered species programs. More than half of the species occur in a 900-square-mile region in southwest San Diego County that accounts for about 20 percent of the county's total area.[74] It was these circumstances that led to the creation of the Multiple Species Conservation Program (MSCP), an ambitious and complex initiative to protect entire landscapes while allowing continued development. Federal and state policy makers are closely watching the program to determine if it might provide a long-sought model for conservation planning elsewhere in the nation.[75]

Specifically, the MSCP was a response to the rising number of individual conservation planning efforts that had been initiated throughout the county under the Habitat Conservation Plan provisions of the Endangered Species Act. Not only were such efforts costly to both public and private participants, but the resultant agreements were also vulnerable to discoveries of additional endangered species on lands that the plans had committed to development.

As the cornerstone of federal efforts to protect endangered or threatened flora

and fauna, the Endangered Species Act (ESA) of 1973[76] permits the development of habitat conservation plans. The intent of Congress in adopting the ESA was "to provide a means whereby the ecosystems upon which endangered species and threatened species depend may be conserved . . . ."[77] In fact, the ESA ushered in a new era of ecosystem management in the United States that extends well beyond merely wildlife management and traditional public land management.[78] For the first time, individual species, listed as endangered or threatened, were granted various protections from potentially harmful activities. Most stringent among the ESA's various provisions is the rule that no person shall "*take* any such species within the United States or the territorial sea . . . ."[79] Prohibited activities include both direct actions (e.g., shooting a bald eagle) and indirect actions with no intent to cause harm (e.g., timber sale or construction of a hydropower project or housing development). Land development that harms listed species by altering or destroying habitat potentially constitutes a "take" in violation of the ESA.[80]

In response to landowners' widespread opposition to the ESA's "take" rule, Congress amended the act in 1982 to authorize limited "takes" of designated habitat (and listed species) pursuant to a "habitat conservation plan" (HCP) for a specific area. An HCP requires a formal planning process that involves all interested parties, including landowners, developers, local governments, state and federal wildlife agencies, and private environmental organizations. Overseen by the U.S. Fish and Wildlife Service (FWS), the process is intended to achieve an agreement among all parties that specifies the impacts that will result from proposed land use changes; steps to be taken to minimize and mitigate such impacts and funding to implement those steps; and alternatives to the "take" and why they were not adopted.[81]

Increasingly, private landowners turned to the HCP process as a way to conduct economic activities on their lands while still complying with the law. The private sector "is drawn to the conservation planning process and kept at the table by the promise of assurances and certainty—guarantees of streamlined regulations . . . and a clear picture of future obligations."[82] By January 1999, the FWS approved 236 HCPs, with about 200 additional plans under development.

Despite the conflict-resolution purpose of HCPs, many plans have generated significant controversy, with opposition voiced by both land development interests and environmentalists. Only recently has the HCP process come to be viewed as a method for working out a compromise that allows developers a measure of predictability and fairness while protecting biodiversity.[83] Still, some conservationists and scientists believe that the plans condone the destruction of important habitat without adequate consideration of the recovery needs of the affected species.[84] One central concern among conservationists is the "no surprises" policy, which provides landowners with an opportunity to "lock in" their ESA obligations for periods of up to 100 years.[85] The policy is intended to encourage landowner participation in the planning process by giving assurances that, once land management agreements are in place, such agreements cannot be renegotiated at a cost to the landowner if new species listings are issued or the status of a species changes.

Given the intense controversy surrounding HCPs, a revised approach was needed to reconcile preservation goals with the demands of urban development. Initially, most HCPs focused on the protection of a single species, such as the mission blue butterfly in the San Francisco Bay Area's

San Bruno Mountains, the Coachella Valley fringe-toed lizard in the Coachella Valley Desert in California, and the piping plover on Atlantic Coast beaches. But, over time, habitat conservation planning has gradually evolved from its earlier emphasis on single-species management to comprehensive planning efforts aimed at protecting a variety of species dependent on or associated with a well-defined natural community. Indeed, the Natural Communities Conservation Planning Program initiated by the state of California in 1991 recognized that "because many of the natural communities in California are already highly endangered, developing conservation plans for one species at a time, without

attention to the larger landscape or ecological processes, only ensures that other species will be listed and need conservation planning relatively soon. Given the high cost of participating in conservation plans, the species-by-species or last-ditch effort approach provides little incentive for most private landowners to cooperate."[86]

San Diego's MSCP is an early and innovative example of planning aimed at protecting habitats that are home to several wildlife species, many of them threatened or endangered, while allowing compatible development. Initial efforts to design and implement the MSCP plan began in 1997 when U.S. Secretary of the Interior Bruce Babbitt

assigned responsibility for protecting the threatened California gnatcatcher to the state of California. With that grant of authority, the state defined the San Diego MSCP study area to include the city of San Diego, portions of the unincorporated county of San Diego, ten additional city jurisdictions, and several independent special districts; the area accounts for 315,940 acres of natural habitat, about two-thirds of which is privately owned. The plan identifies 16 core biological resource areas and associated habitat linkages for a total of about 202,700 acres of habitat. To reach a preservation target of 171,920 acres, the public sector will provide about two-thirds of the acreage and private developers one-

The Jurisdictions Taking Part in Multiple Species Habitat Conservation Planning for San Diego County 3-6

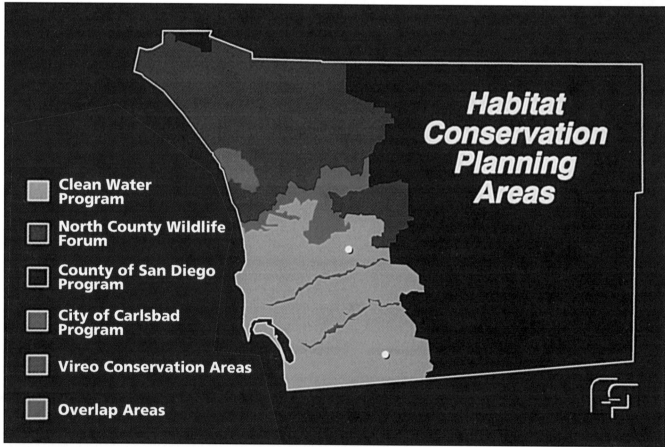

Habitat Conservation Planning Areas

- Clean Water Program
- North County Wildlife Forum
- County of San Diego Program
- City of Carlsbad Program
- Vireo Conservation Areas
- Overlap Areas

Planning for multiple species habitat protection resulted from a collaboration among municipal, county, water, and conservation organizations. The plan identified areas to be conserved or restored and areas that could be developed, saving millions of dollars compared with planning costs for individual projects.

third. The federal and state governments will commit 36,510 acres to permanent habitat conservation and management, including 24,510 acres managed by the Bureau of Land Management, three existing National Wildlife Refuges, and several state parks and reserves. The MSCP predicts that 85 species will be adequately "covered" by the MSCP.[87]

By identifying priority areas for conservation and other areas for future development, the MSCP will streamline existing permit procedures for development projects that affect habitat. The program establishes a framework or overlay within which local jurisdictions (including utilities and special-purpose agencies as well as governments) administer their own subarea plans and implementing agreements as approved by state and federal wildlife agencies.[88] Subarea plans embody criteria (e.g., conservation targets, mitigation standards, and/or development encroachment limits) to ensure that habitat preservation proceeds in step with development. Subarea plans also include various mechanisms to avoid or minimize project impacts on the preserve. Together with a specific implementing agreement,[89] subarea plans serve as the basis for federal and state "take authorizations" that allow impacts on covered species incidental to land development. Local jurisdictions will implement the MSCP through their approved subarea plans and amend their overall land use plans, development regulations, and codes and guidelines as needed to ensure that development projects are consistent with subarea plans and that conservation targets are met.

Based on a 30-year benefit assessment program, the total cost of the MSCP to local jurisdictions, residents, and businesses is estimated to range from $339 to $411 million (1996 dollars). The cost covers land acquisition and costs for preserve management, biological

monitoring, and program administration. Local jurisdictions and federal and state funding programs (e.g., the federal Land and Water Conservation Fund, National Fish and Wildlife Challenge Grants) will share program costs.

The MSCP has met with mixed reaction since its adoption. Led by the Southwest Center for Biological Diversity, 14 conservation groups filed suit in December 1998 to block implementation of the plan. The groups claimed that the MSCP fails to protect wetlands species.[90] On the other hand, the plan has its supporters. A Washington, D.C., national conference on HCPs in 1997 hailed the San Diego MSCP as the first opportunity for significant species recovery.[91] The MSCP process has also earned commendations for its noteworthy stakeholder involvement. Several regional and national conservation groups, such as the Endangered Habitats League and the San Diego Chapter of the Sierra Club, participated with development interests and government agency staff in developing the program. By employing a partnership approach, the MSCP process benefited from the leadership asserted by the city of San Diego and other local government agencies.[92]

The evolution to multiple-species habitat planning is relatively recent, and current attempts are still unproven. Perhaps as a result of the multiyear downturn in southern California's real estate market, only four of the 11 required subarea plans have been completed as of this writing. No "take authorizations" have yet been issued, and the MSCP implementation schedule is unclear due to the pending environmental lawsuit. Clearly, however, the MSCP process provides one means for serving the goals of sustainable development.

The Hackensack (New Jersey) Meadowlands Special Area Management Plan.

The Hackensack Meadowlands lies across the Hudson River from Man-

hattan Island and is a 20,000-acre expanse of much-degraded brackish wetlands and low-lying drier ground within sight of the World Trade Center. Over three centuries, forests were cleared and wetlands drained to provide croplands and control mosquitoes. The creation of the Oradell Reservoir in 1922, upstream on the Hackensack River, impeded fresh water flow and allowed the introduction of salt water, creating a brackish, estuarine wetlands system. Vegetation is dominated by nearly monotypic stands of the common reed *Phragmites australis*. Today, the Meadowlands claims more than 8,000 acres of wetlands and 12,000 acres of former wetlands.

By the late 1960s, the Meadowlands's landscape had undergone significant alteration. Transportation arteries of all types criss-crossed the area without regard to its natural attributes. The region's low topography invited the dumping of industrial and household waste from surrounding communities, including New York City. Scores of landfills covered an estimated 1,600 acres of wetlands. And then there were the over 200 known or suspected hazardous waste sites, including three Superfund sites as well as several combined-sewer overflows, all of which continue to cause the cumulative degradation of the area's environment.[93] Meanwhile, development pressures on the remaining undeveloped wetlands and open waters were mounting, driven by the growth of the New York metropolitan area's population and economy. At the same time, conservation interests were pressing for the protection of the Meadowlands's natural resources. Land values exceeded $3 million per acre.[94]

In 1968, the New Jersey legislature[95] created the Hackensack Meadowlands Development Commission (HMDC). The newly created state agency was accorded jurisdiction over 19,730 acres, an area larger than Manhattan lying within 14 municipalities in

Jurisdictions in the Hackensack Meadowlands

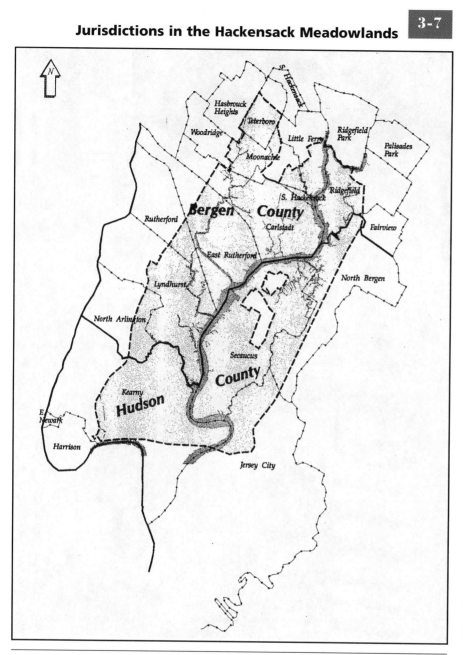

The commission exercises its powers in parts or all of 14 municipalities and two counties in northern New Jersey.

In addition, the commission has undertaken a variety of efforts to expand public outdoor recreation opportunities and to manage environmental resources. In 1997, for example, the HMDC revised its open-space plan to ensure the protection of more than 8,400 acres, nearly 80 percent of the undeveloped acreage remaining in the Meadowlands District. The plan calls for greenways, landfill conversions to parks, footpaths and cycle trails, ball fields, and environmental education facilities. Many of the district's most important wetlands are to be restored and preserved.

Landfill remediation is another component of the HMDC's environmental protection program. In 1997, the HMDC collected nearly 2 billion cubic feet of methane gas from landfills and provided energy to thousands of homes. At the same time, the HMDC is working to control the effects of excessive amounts of leachate from landfills (e.g., polluted groundwater and water quality impacts on the Hackensack River). The commission has also started to clean up nearly 2,000 acres of wetlands scarred by wastes and has permanently ended the massive dumping of residential solid waste in the district.[98]

During the mid-1980s, however, a simmering dispute between development and conservation interests increasingly hampered further development. The dispute resulted in part from the arcane nature of federal laws governing wetlands protection and the fact that most of the land available for future development in the Meadowlands was classified as wetlands. The laws, which are embedded in several federal statutes primarily concerned with other matters such as water pollution, agricultural production, fish and wildlife habitat, and selected federal benefit programs, focus principally on wetlands protection and thereby prevent the development of public and private projects beneficial to the public interest.[99] Furthermore, the piece-

Bergen and Hudson counties. The HMDC focused its efforts on three mandates: economic development of the 32-square-mile Meadowlands, preservation and enhancement of the area's delicate balance of nature, and provision and management of areawide solid waste disposal facilities.

The commission rather than the 14 affected jurisdictions administers land use planning and development controls for the Meadowlands District. The HMDC regulates land development in and around wetlands through a master plan and accompanying zoning regulations (originally adopted in 1972) as well as through subdivision reviews and building permits.[96] The HMDC continues to review applications for large-scale development projects and, by 1997, completed three major redevelopment initiatives.[97]

meal legal structure has produced a confusing array of definitions, prohibitions, and policies applicable to activities in or concerning wetlands and, even today, continues to cause jurisdictional and enforcement problems for the regulatory agencies charged with oversight of the nation's wetlands.[100]

The primary statute that regulates activities in wetlands of the United States is Section 404 of the Clean Water Act.[101] Ironically, the statute never mentions "wetlands" as such. Instead, it charges the U.S. Army Corps of Engineers (Corps) with administering a permit program for the discharge of dredged or fill material into "waters of the United States" and delegates power to the EPA to establish environmental guidelines—the so-called 404(b)(1) Guidelines[102]—to be followed by the Corps. The guidelines and the Corps's own regulations (pursuant to court order) clarify that wetlands are to be regulated as "waters of the United States." The joint administration of the Section 404 program by the Corps and the EPA—a bureaucratic "Odd Couple"—has been fraught with controversy and frustration. Matters of contention include definitions of wetlands, how to balance the values of existing versus constructed wetlands, and in what ways wetlands regulation can limit impacts on or provide compensation for property owners.

In recent years, landowners and developers frustrated with the process of obtaining individual permits placed another question on the table: How can we provide regulatory certainty for development projects while preserving the ecological integrity of the ecosystem as a whole? Two federal processes have emerged as at least partial answers: advance identification of wetlands (AVID) and special area management plans (SAMP). AVIDs are designed to shorten the permit process and increase the predictability of the Section 404 regulatory program. SAMPs are com-

prehensive plans that guide future land use in sensitive coastal areas.

In 1988, to overcome an approaching stalemate between development and environmental interests, the HMDC entered into a Memorandum of Understanding (MOU) with the EPA, the Corps of Engineers, the New Jersey Department of Environmental Protection, and the National Oceanic and Atmospheric Administration (NOAA) to develop and implement a special area management plan. The MOU defined the intended outcome:

> The SAMP process is a comprehensive plan providing for natural resource protection and reasonable economic growth containing a comprehensive statement of policies and criteria to guide uses of lands and water and mechanisms for implementation in specific geographic areas. The SAMP will result in a definitive regulatory product.[103]

The parties to the SAMP developed the plan in the following sequence: definition of the district's growth needs; assessment of existing wetlands functions and preparation of a map that compared the relative functions of the wetlands; development of alternative land use configurations that would meet the district's projected growth needs, along with an analysis of the alternatives' impacts; selection of the preferred alternative; development of mechanisms to mitigate unavoidable impacts; and development of products and processes by which the SAMP is to be implemented, including "advance identification" of wetlands eligible for development.[104]

As part of the SAMP process, the HMDC proposed an Environmental Improvement Program (EIP) to remedy existing environmental degradation and mitigate potential adverse impacts aris-

ing from future development.[105] The EIP would provide a centrally managed approach to environmental remediation and natural resource protection projects carried out within the district, including solid waste management and landfill closures, water resources protection and monitoring, flood control and stormwater management, and reclamation of contaminated land. Costs over 20 years are projected at about $900 million. Part of the funding will come from landfill closure fees and state and federal programs; about 35 to 40 percent of the funding is expected to come from fees generated by development.[106]

The Draft SAMP Preferred Alternative calls for the following: a land use plan allocating 2,200 acres of land for development, of which 842 acres will be wetlands; transportation improvement projects; a compensatory wetlands mitigation program involving the enhancement of over 3,400 acres of existing wetlands; the Environmental Improvement Program; state and federal regulatory reform; an out-of-district program; a program of transferable development rights that will provide a mechanism for compensating property owners whose land is not proposed for development; and a monitoring and review process.

The preferred alternative was opened to public comment in August 1995. Many comments were highly critical of the SAMP, especially the extent of proposed development (14,000 residential units, 18.5 million square feet of office space, 15.3 million square feet of secondary office space and warehousing, and 2.5 million square feet of commercial space). Several interest groups even questioned whether the extent of the specified development was consistent with current market trends and forecasts. Another closely related concern focuses on the proposed filling of up to 842 acres of wetlands to accommodate projected development. Environmentalists argued that the

Hackensack River estuary cannot withstand any more fill activity. Some environmentalists went further, flatly rejecting the SAMP's essential principle: balancing new development against restoration/preservation of the district's remaining wetlands. Ironically, the restoration of wetlands under the SAMP strategy depends on fiscal revenue derived from the impact fees and assessments levied on new Meadowlands development. According to NOAA, without the projected $200 million in EIP funding derived from new wetlands fill, "significant, cumulative degradation of the aquatic ecosystem greater than the impacts likely to result from the new development would occur."

Since the 1995 public comments, disputes between developers and environmentalists have continued to fester. In an attempt to resolve the heightening tensions, federal agencies tried to work out their own differences and provide a unified front. On April 22, 1999, the federal and state agencies cooperating in the Hackensack Meadowlands SAMP announced in the *Federal Register* their intent to complete the SAMP process by September 15, 1999. That date came and went without resolution of outstanding issues. And so after 11 years, the Hackensack Meadowlands Special Area Management Plan continues to evolve. Without question, though, the stakes are huge: billions of dollars in development balanced against restoration of thousands of acres of wetlands at the doorstep of New York City. In light of the costs and competing demands, a planning process measured in decades rather than years may be unavoidable.

The Changing Landscape: A Closer Look

Today's human landscape is not outwardly much different from what it was three decades ago when Hardin, McHarg, and Whyte offered new ways of thinking about and interacting with the physical

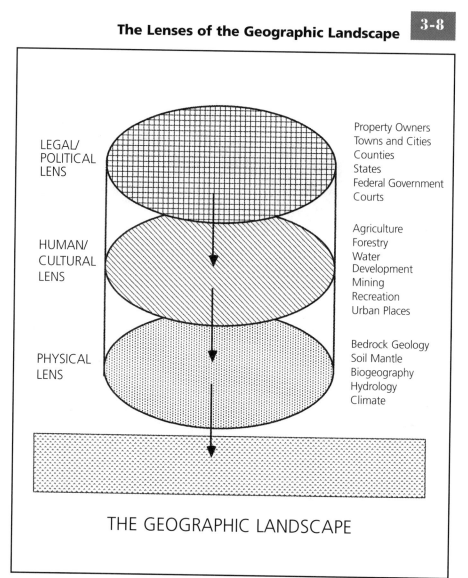

LEGAL/
POLITICAL
LENS

Property Owners
Towns and Cities
Counties
States
Federal Government
Courts

HUMAN/
CULTURAL
LENS

Agriculture
Forestry
Water
Development
Mining
Recreation
Urban Places

PHYSICAL
LENS

Bedrock Geology
Soil Mantle
Biogeography
Hydrology
Climate

THE GEOGRAPHIC LANDSCAPE

environment. Suburban and exurban development has continued to push farther out from the older core cities. The Boston metropolitan region extends west of Interstate 495, north into New Hampshire and Maine, and south to Cape Cod and the Providence area. "Chicagoland" spreads well into northwestern Indiana and southeastern Wisconsin and westward halfway to the Mississippi River. Atlanta is pushing out in all directions. Denver, after encroaching into the foothills of the Rocky Mountains, is filling in gaps north and south along the Front Range and spilling into the high plains around the new airport and into the semiarid reaches of Douglas County,

which is one of the nation's fastest-growing counties. The booming Pacific Northwest metropolitan areas of Portland and Seattle are reaching toward each other and ever farther into their mountain hinterlands. Despite chronic water problems, the Southwest desert continues to be converted to golf courses, condominiums, and casinos. Southern California just grows, as does its traffic.

However synoptic and gloomy this overview, it misses the finer grain of what is happening to the American metropolitan landscape. A higher-powered level of resolution reveals a much more detailed picture that

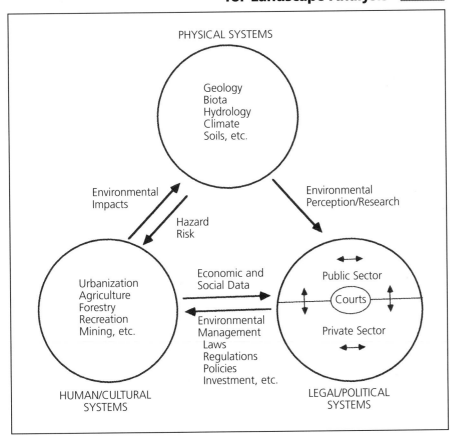

dictions that collectively determines the use of land. The broad classes of data perceived by each "lens" are composites of more specific variables listed in figure 3-10. While a checklist for each variable is unnecessary, the inventory in the box suggests the range of characteristics that might be included in a contemporary landscape inventory.

It should be apparent that the classes of data perceived by each "lens" are interactive. That is, the physical landscape is modified by human activities, which themselves are affected by the physical character of an area or region. As decision makers perceive changes in the physical and human-built systems, they advance new sets of policies, laws, rules, or decisions that may in turn change the way human activities interact with the natural environment. Figure 3-9 depicts the interactive version of the "three-lens model."

Over the past 50 years, the concerns and styles of real estate development have undergone a sea change marked by growing attention to the long-term effects of development on the environment. Developers, builders, lenders—and consumers—are more aware than ever before of the importance of sustainable forms of development. One particularly important influence on the way we reshape our landscape is the increasingly pervasive role of government programs—i.e., a major alteration of the "legal lens." Theoretically, planning and regulation of private land are state and local functions. Indeed, both state and local governments are moving toward sustainable development by stepping up their interest in saving open space and protecting natural resources. At the same time, though, the federal environmental programs of the past three decades have both directly and indirectly influenced the use of land.[108] Among the many federal laws adopted during the hectic period 1968–1980 that today influence land development or redevel-

includes not only the dreary loss of farmland, field, and forest but also some notable environmental successes—for example, the Appalachian Trail and its analogues, the I & M Canal, the Midewin National Tallgrass Prairie in Illinois, the Indiana Dunes National Lakeshore, and a host of other nontraditional national, state, and local parks. Added to the well-publicized successes are the myriad local park improvements, rail trails, greenways, nature centers, museums, river and coastal cleanups, and other "thousand points of green." In the words of Tony Hiss, small and large "sacred places"[107] range from the sublime to the minuscule, from the Cape Cod National Seashore to the cleaned-up neighborhood vacant lot.

The landscape is defined not only by the evidence of human activities and the

institutions that conduct or influence those activities, but, as McHarg taught, also by nature. The physical landscape is the stage on which the human drama is played out, and that landscape affects the outcome of the drama.

The landscape is best understood in terms of three "lenses" of spatial data, an amplification and extension of McHarg's data overlays that inventory and evaluate natural conditions. As described in chapter 1, McHarg's inventory lays the groundwork for understanding and conserving natural functions in areas subject to development. Figure 3-8 illustrates that the three major lenses or sets of spatial data are physical—patterns of the landscape as "nature made it"; human/cultural—patterns of human land use and settlement; and legal/political—the mosaic of legal interests and government juris-

THE PHYSICAL LENS

Bedrock Geology
  Sedimentary
  Granitic
  Limestone/karst
  Basalt
  Metamorphic
  Other
Surficial Landforms
  Topography (uplands and lowlands)
  Soils
  Glaciation
  Floodplains
  Weathering (wind, ice, water)
  Vulcanism (volcanoes)
Hydrology
  Hydrologic cycle
    Precipitation
    Surface and groundwater flows
    Evapotranspiration
    Watersheds (river and drainage basins)
    Floodplains (coastal, riverine, other)
    Groundwater aquifers
    Ice and snow
    Surface waters (fresh, salt, brackish)
    Wetlands (fresh, salt, estuarine, and so forth)
    Water quality
Oceanography
  Bathymetry
  Tides
  Currents
  Storms
Climate
  Precipitation (aridity/humidity)
  Growing season
  Air quality
  Extreme events (hurricanes, northeasters, tornadoes, blizzards, El Niño, and so forth)
Vegetation
  Dependence on climate, hydrology, altitude, latitude, and so forth
  Biodiversity
  Ecosystems/bioregions (forest, grassland, desert, alpine, wetlands, and so forth)

THE HUMAN/CULTURAL LENS

Nonurban
  Agriculture
    Irrigated/nonirrigated
    Organic/inorganic
    Cropland
    Livestock
    Orchard
    Nursery/horticulture
    Aquaculture
    Farmsteads
  Forestry
    Managed/nonmanaged
    Clearcut/selective cut
    Monoculture/species diversity
  Wetlands
    Dredged, filled, drained, polluted, farmed, developed
    Protected
    Restored/created
  Grassland
    Fenced
    Grazed
  Recreation
    Ski slopes
    Golf courses
    Water-based (marinas, boatyards, artificial lakes, and so forth)
    Trails, greenways, bikeways, and so forth
  Mining
    Strip mines and open pits
    Processing and transport facilities
    Reclamation
Urban
  "Megalopolis" (Boston-Washington, Great Lakes, West Coast, and so forth)
  Metropolitan Statistical Areas (MSAs)
  Cities and suburbs
  Neighborhoods
  Developments (malls, office and industrial parks, subdivisions)
  Parcels
  Linkages
    Transportation (highways, rail, air, waterways)
    Energy (dams, power stations, pipelines, transmission lines, and so forth)
    Water (reservoirs, aqueducts, pipes, treatment facilities, and so forth)
    Information (telephone, satellite, Internet, television, cable, and so forth)

THE LEGAL/POLITICAL LENS

Government (public sector)
  Federal (highways, tax policies, parks, wetlands, flood insurance, and so forth)
  State (highways, tax policies, parks, wetlands, economic development, and so forth)
  County
  Regional/special district (depending on assigned function)
  Municipal (planning, zoning, subdivision regulations, and so forth)
  Judicial (federal and state court decisions)
Nongovernment (private sector)
  Corporations
    Business
    Nonprofit (environmental, community, religious, educational, and so forth)
  Households and individuals

opment are the following (some of which were already noted) (later amendments not listed): the National Flood Insurance Act (1968), National Environmental Policy Act (1969), Clean Air Act (1970), Clean Water Act (1972), Coastal Zone Management Act (1972), Endangered Species Act (1973), Safe Drinking Water Act (1974), Resource Conservation and Recovery Act (1976), and "Superfund" Act (1980).

In addition to increasingly direct government involvement in maintaining and restoring the nation's resources, today's "legal lens" recognizes a much stronger role for nongovernmental organizations on all sides of land development proposals—environmentalists, NIMBY interests, taxpayer organizations, chambers of commerce, civil rights organizations, and ad hoc advocacy groups convened to save this or oppose that. New doctrines of "legal standing" and "class actions" have facilitated direct legal intervention by many types of interest groups. In addition, the media widely air competing viewpoints. Thus, the process of shaping today's "last landscape" engages a broader range of participants and diversity of voices than in the 1960s.

Finally, the realm of science is more influential now than in the 1960s in terms of public and private environmental management. In the tradition of Rachel Carson and Barry Commoner, present-day Jeremiahs warn of threats such as biodiversity decline, global warming, a rise in sea level, water contamination and scarcity, soil erosion, natural hazards, and aesthetic blight. Scientific research into these and other problems, as communicated by the scholarly and popular media and by environmental and professional organizations (such as the Urban Land Institute), helps inform decisions by legislatures, administrative agencies, courts, lenders, developers, and owners. For example, the trend toward "ecosystem management" is replacing earlier emphasis on "multiple-use/sustained yield" as a framework for many types of government resource management programs.[109]

Public laws and programs, nongovernmental organizations, and science— all have changed the way in which the human landscape is shaped in the United States. The unfolding of urban development over the last three decades has gradually—albeit imperceptibly in many places—begun to pay more than lip service to the natural environment. Under the National Environmental Policy Act (NEPA), environmental impacts must be studied and avoided where possible when federal funds or permits are involved. Counterpart state environmental policy acts require comparable reviews for actions involving state funds or permits. And several local governments require an impact assessment as part of their subdivision or site plan approval process. Many other federal laws and their state counterparts demand closer scrutiny of the impacts of land development on the biophysical landscape and vice versa.[110]

Conclusion

Taking a historical perspective, this chapter has surveyed the relationship between ecology and land development in the United States. The central challenge before planners and developers for the next half-century is how to accommodate another 120 million people and develop 75 million dwellings and associated land uses while minimizing further degradation of the nation's natural resources. Earlier forms and functions of preserved open spaces within American cities have yielded a diverse legacy of commons, large and small parks, civic plazas, greenways, trails, conservation areas, and informal green spaces—all of which embellish our metropolitan regions. Ecological concerns were intrinsic to the early colonial commons, irrelevant to the designed landscapes and civic plazas of the 19th and early 20th centuries, and now enshrined in the post–*Silent Spring* and *Sand County Almanac* era. From the humble "green patch across the street" to the national seashores and lakeshores, from gritty canal corridors and rail trails lined by native habitat to wetlands in the Hackensack Meadowlands, open spaces of all sizes and types are today the target of protection in the name of sustainable development.

1 National Association of Home Builders, "NAHB's Statement of Policy on Smart Growth: Where We Live, Work, and Play," adopted March 15, 1999.

2 Bureau of the Census, *Current Population Reports*, P25-1095 and P25-1104.

3 Bureau of the Census, *U.S. Statistical Abstract 1995-1996*, Table 65.

4 George B. Brewster, *The Ecology of Development: Integrating the Built and Natural Environments*. Working Paper 649 (Washington, DC: Urban Land Institute, 1997), p. 9.

5 Openlands Project, "Under Pressure: Land Consumption in the Chicago Region: 1998–2028" (Chicago: Openlands Project, 1999), p. 3.

6 National Association of Home Builders, "NAHB's Statement of Policy on Smart Growth."

7 Quoted in Steen Eiler Rasmussen, *London: The Unique City* (Cambridge: MIT Press, 1934/1967), p. 68.

8 Rutherford H. Platt, Rowan A. Rowntree, and Pamela C. Muick, eds., *The Ecological City: Preserving and Restoring Urban Biodiversity* (Amherst, MA: The University of Massachusetts Press, 1994), Ch. 1.

9 John Stilgoe, "Town Common and Village Green in New England: 1620 to 1981" in Ronald Lee Fleming and Lauri A. Halderman, *On Common Ground: Caring for Shared Land from Town Common to Urban Park* (Cambridge: The Harvard Common Press, 1982), p. 12.

10 Ibid.

11 John W. Reps, *The Making of Urban America: A History of City Planning in the United States* (Princeton: Princeton University Press, 1965), p. 128.

12 Ibid., pp. 160-161.

13 Ibid.

14 Walter Muir Whitehill, *Boston: A Topographic History*, 2nd Edition (Cambridge: Harvard University Press, 1974), p. 156.

15 Kenneth T. Jackson, *Crabgrass Frontier: The Suburbanization of the United States* (New York: Oxford University Press, 1986).

16 Rutherford H. Platt, *Land Use and Society: Geography, Law, and Public Policy* (Washington, DC: Island Press, 1994), p. 191.

17 Frederick Law Olmsted, "Boston: Parks and Parkways—A Green Ribbon," in S.B. Sutton, ed. *Civilizing American Cities: A Selection of Frederick Law Olmsted's Writing on City Landscape* (Cambridge: MIT Press, 1979), p. 255.

18 Lewis Mumford, *Sticks and Stones: A Study of American Architecture and Civilization* (New York: Dover, 1955), p. 147.

19 Ebenezer Howard, *Garden Cities of Tomorrow* (Cambridge: MIT Press, 1899/1965).

20 Rutherford H. Platt, "From Commons to Commons: Evolving Concepts of Open Space in North American Cities," in Platt, Rowntree, and Muick, eds., *The Ecological City*, Ch. 1.

21 Peter Hall, *Urban and Regional Planning* (London: George Allen & Unwin, 1982), Chs. 3 and 4.

22 Lewis Mumford, "Introduction" to republication of Benton MacKaye, *The New Exploration: A Philosophy of Regional Planning* (Urbana: University of Illinois Press, 1928/1962), p. vii.

23 Mumford's 1938 text *The Culture of Cities* was, in Peter Hall's phrase, "almost the Bible of the regional planning movement." Peter Hall, *Urban and Regional Planning*, note 22, p. 66.

24 Lewis Mumford, "The Natural History of Urbanization," in William L. Thomas, Jr., et al., eds. *Man's Role in Changing the Face of the Earth* (Chicago: University of Chicago Press, 1956), p. 386.

25 Ibid., p. 397.

26 Aldo Leopold, "A Land Ethic," in *A Sand County Almanac* (New York: Oxford University Press, 1949/1966), p. 240.

27 J. Ronald Engel, *Sacred Sands: The Struggle for Community in the Indiana Dunes* (Middletown, CT: Wesleyan University Press, 1983).

28 Ibid., p. 12.

29 Rutherford H. Platt, *The Open Space Decision Process: Spatial Allocation of Costs and Benefits*. Research Paper No. 142 (Chicago: University of Chicago Department of Geography, 1972).

30 Editors of *Fortune, The Exploding Metropolis* (Garden City, NY: Doubleday Anchor Books, 1958).

31 Edward Higbee, *The Squeeze: Cities without Space* (New York: William Morrow, 1960).

32 New York Regional Plan Association, *The Race for Open Space* (New York: RPA, 1960).

33 Jean Gottmann, *Megalopolis: The Urbanized Northeastern Seaboard of the United States* (Cambridge: MIT Press, 1961).

34 Jane Jacobs, *The Death and Life of Great American Cities* (New York: Vintage Books, 1961).

35 James A. Kushner, *Subdivision Law and Growth Management* (Deerfield, IL: Clark, Boardman, Callaghan, 1992), sec. 6.02[1].

36 Ibid., sec. 6.04; Alexandra D. Dawson, *Land-Use Planning and the Law* (New York: Garland STPM Press, 1982), p. 50.

37 Kushner, note 35, sec. 6.04[2].

38 114 S.Ct. 2309 (1994).

39 Platt, *Land Use and Society*, p. 128.

40 Lloyd W. Bookout, Jr., et al., *Residential Development Handbook*, Second Edition (Washington, DC: Urban Land Institute, 1990), pp. 144-145.

41 Douglas Porter, *Managing Growth in America's Communities* (Washington, DC: Island Press, 1997), p. 61.

42 Garrett Hardin, "The Tragedy of the Commons," *Science* 162: 1243-1248 (December 13, 1968).

43 Ian L. McHarg, *Design with Nature* (New York: Natural History Press, 1969).

44 William H. Whyte, *The Last Landscape* (Garden City, NY: Doubleday, 1968).

45 Roderick Frazier Nash, *American Environmentalism*, 2nd ed. (New York: McGraw-Hill, 1990); Platt, *Land Use and Society*, p. 400.

46 American Farmland Trust, "Fact Sheets of State and Local Purchase of Agricultural Conservation Easement Programs" (Washington, DC: American Farmland Trust, 1999).

47 Phyllis Myers, *Livability at the Ballot Box: State and Local Referenda on Parks, Conservation, and Smarter Growth, Election Day 1998*. Prepared for the Brookings Institution Center on Urban and Metropolitan Policy, January 1999.

48 Charles E. Little, *Greenways for America* (Baltimore: Johns Hopkins University Press, 1990).

49 William Cronon, *Nature's Metropolis: Chicago and the Great West* (New York: W.W. Norton, 1991).

50 Canal Corridor Association, *Prairie Passage: The Illinois and Michigan Canal Corridor* (Urbana: University of Illinois Press and the Canal Corridor Association, 1998). This handsome volume of photographs and interpretive text further communicates the significance of the original canal and its heritage corridor reincarnation. (Photographs by Edward Ranney. Text by Tony Hiss, Emily J. Harris, and William Least Heat-Moon).

51 For more information on the revival of urban rivers, see David Salvesen, "Urban River Revival," *Urban Land,* June 1997, pp. 31-34.

52 At the Federal Army Arsenal at Joliet, Illinois, 19,000 acres recently were transferred to the U.S. Forest Service to become the Midewin National Tallgrass Prairie.

53 Remarks by Carol M. Browner, administrator of the U. S. Environmental Protection Agency, to the Urban Land Institute Conference on Incentives for Smart Growth, Chicago, Illinois, April 19, 1999.

54 Rutherford H. Platt, *Disasters and Democracy: The Politics of Extreme Natural Events* (Washington, DC: Island Press, 1999), Chs. 4 and 5.

55 Platt, "From Commons to Commons", p. 37.

56 The U.S. Department of Agriculture's five-year report on the nation's inventory of natural resource lands, published in 1999, showed that metropolitan areas are losing their trees as development pushes out into the countryside. About 13 percent of the Washington metropolitan area, for example, was covered by trees in 1997, compared with 37 percent in 1973. William K. Stevens, "Sprawl Quickens Its Attack on Forests," *New York Times,* December 7, 1999, p. D6.

57 Michael Hough, "Design with City Nature: An Overview of Some Issues" in Platt, Rowntree, and Muick, eds., *The Ecological City,* p. 41.

58 Richard Mabey, *Unofficial Countryside* (New York: Collins, 1973).

59 David Nicholson-Lord, *The Greening of the Cities* (London: Routledge & Kegan Paul, 1987), p. 82.

60 Platt, "From Commons to Commons", pp. 36-38.

61 Platt, *Land Use and Society,* Ch. 12.

62 Burt Schorr, "New Federal Programs May Strengthen Effort to Guard Environment," *Wall Street Journal,* October 27, 1970, p. l.

63 Rutherford H. Platt, "Thorn Creek Woods: The Place and the Controversy." Unpublished manuscript, November 1974.

64 PL 91-190, sec. 101(a).

65 PL 91-190, sec. 102(C).

66 Exhibit G of Project Agreement between Park Forest South Developers, Inc., and the U.S. Department of Housing and Urban Development, March 17, 1971, p. 16.

67 Unfortunately, Park Forest South became a casualty of a real estate downturn in the mid-1970s and the development firm defaulted on its HUD-backed loans.

68 PL 99-339; 42 U.S.C. sec. 300g et seq.

69 Metropolitan District Commission/Massachusetts Water Resources Authority, *Wachusett Reservoir Watershed Protection Plan,* 1991, Table 3-4.

70 310 *Code of Massachusetts Regulations,* sec. 15.001 et seq.

71 *Mass. General Laws Annotated,* Ch. 92, sec. 107A. The act is discussed in David P. Hutchinson, "A Setback for the Rivers of Massachusetts? An Application of Regulatory Takings Doctrine to the Watershed Protection Act and the Massachusetts River Protection Act," *Boston University Law Review,* 73:237-270, 1993.

72 Ibid. Potential pollutant sources must be 200 to 400 feet from tributaries, floodplains, wetlands, and areas overlying major aquifers that affect reservoirs. The Watershed Protection Act applies only to the MWRA system and does not directly affect other public water supply systems in the state. The Massachusetts River Act (Laws of 1996, Ch. 258) restricts building and other land uses to a distance of 200 feet from any river in the state (or 25 feet in certain urban areas).

73 This section and the following one on the Hackensack Meadowlands were researched and coauthored by Jessica Spelke Jansujwicz, Department of Geosciences, University of Massachusetts at Amherst.

74 San Diego County, *Multiple Species Conservation Program, MSCP Plan,* Volume I, August 1996.

75 William K. Stevens, "Disputed Conservation Plan Could Be Model for Nation," *New York Times,* February 16, 1997, p. 18.

76 16 USCA, secs. 1631-1643, as amended.

77 ESA, sec. 2b, emphasis added.

78 Reed F. Noss, Michael A. O'Connell, and Dennis D. Murphy, *The Science of Conservation Planning: Habitat Conservation Under the Endangered Species Act* (Washington, DC: Island Press, 1991), p. 25.

79 ESA, sec. 9(1)(B), emphasis added.

80 Timothy Beatley, "Reconciling Urban Growth and Endangered Species: The Coachella Valley Habitat Conservation Plan" in Platt, Rowntree, and Muick, eds., *The Ecological City,* p. 231.

81 ESA, sec. 10(a).

82 Michael J. Bean, S.J. Fitzgerald, and Michael A. O'Connell, *Resolving Conflicts Under the Endangered Species Act: The Habitat Conservation Planning Experience* (Washington, DC: World Wildlife Fund, 1991).

83 Information supplied to the author in 1999 by Lindell L. Marsh, a southern California attorney involved in the San Bruno Mountain HCP process and later HCP efforts.

84 John Kostyack, "Reshaping Habitat Conservation Plans" (Introduction to a series of articles on habitat conservation plans), *Environmental Law,* Northwestern School of Law of Lewis and Clark College, Fall 1997, 27(3): 755-765.

85 John Kostyack, "Surprise!" *The Environmental Forum: the Policy Journal of the Environmental Law Institute,* March–April 1998, 15(2): 19-28.

86 California Native Plant Society, *Manual on the HCP-NCCP Process,* June 1998, Public Release 1.0., p. 27.

87 "Covered" species include species listed as endangered or threatened as well as currently unlisted species. If an unlisted "covered" species is subsequently listed, it will automatically fall within the "take" provisions of the HCP.

88 The MSCP area encompasses 11 planning subareas in various stages of plan development. Approved subarea plans to date include the Poway Subarea Plan and the City of San Diego Subarea Plan. For more information and an NCCP update, visit http://ceres.ca.gov/CRA/NCCP/updates.htm.

89 An implementing agreement is a binding contract signed by the local jurisdiction (or other take authorization holder) and the wildlife agencies, which identifies the roles and responsibilities of the parties to implement the MSCP and subarea plan. The agreement also specifies assurances and remedies if parties fail to perform their obligations.

90 National Wildlife Federation, *HCP Update,* January 26, 1999.

91 Discussion during break-out session: "HCPs and the Recovery Goal" by Jacqui Bonomo, National Conference on Habitat Conservation Plans, Washington, DC, May 17–18, 1997. Summary of conference is found at National Wildlife Federation Web page, www.nwf.org.

92 John Kostyack, "Habitat Conservation Planning: Time to Give Conservationists and Other Concerned Citizens a Seat at the Table," *Endangered Species UPDATE,* University of Michigan School of Natural Resources and Environment, July/August 1997, 14(7&8): 51-55.

93 Mary Ann Thiesing and Robert W. Hargrove, *The Hackensack Meadowlands Special Area Management Plan (SAMP): Using a Watershed Approach to Achieve Integrated Environmental Protection* (New York: U.S. Environmental Protection Agency, Region II, 1996).

94 Sandra Crane, Jan Goldman-Carter, Heidi Sherk, and Michael Senatore, *Wetlands Conservation: Tools for State and Local Action: A Guide to Federal, State, and Local Regulatory Programs for Managing Wetlands Resources* (Washington, DC: World Wildlife Fund, 1995).

95 Hackensack Meadowlands Reclamation and Development Act, Ch. 404, Laws of 1968, c. 13:17-1.

96 Rutherford H. Platt, *Coastal Wetland Management: Strengthening EPA's Role* (Amherst: Land and Water Policy Center, University of Massachusetts, 1987).

97 Ibid.

98 Hackensack Meadowlands Development Commission, *1997 Annual Report.*

99 Anthony Scardino, Jr., executive director, Hackensack Meadowlands District Commission, Public Hearing testimony, August 29, 1995.

100 Margaret N. Strand, *Wetlands Deskbook.* Environmental Law Institute, 1997.

101 33 USCA, sec. 1344.

102 40 CFR Part 230.

103 Memorandum of Understanding for the Special Area Management Plan Process for the Hackensack Meadowlands District, August 26, 1988.

104 Theising and Hargrove, *The Hackensack Meadowlands Special Area Management Plan.*

105 Crane et al., *Wetlands Conservation.*

106 Ibid.

107 Tony Hiss, Introduction to *Prairie Passage,* note 41.

108 Platt, *Land Use and Society,* Ch. 12.

109 Hanna J. Cortner and Margaret A. Moote, *The Politics of Ecosystem Management* (Washington, DC: Island Press, 1999).

110 E.g., Raymond J. Burby, ed., *Cooperating with Nature: Confronting Natural Hazards with Land-Use Planning for Sustainable Communities* (Washington, DC: Joseph Henry Press, 1998).

THE CONNECTION BETWEEN SUSTAINABILITY AND ECONOMIC DEVELOPMENT

Christopher Leinberger

For the first time in over a century, a connection between sustainability and economic development has evolved, and it is a response to the emergence of the knowledge economy. In the former industrial economy, which was dominant from the mid-19th century until the 1970s, that connection did not exist. In fact, unsustainable economic development practices were responsible for economic expansion. Smokestacks came to symbolize progress and job growth. We sacrificed quality of life and environmental protection to earn a living. The industrial-era tradition of total separation of land uses is reflected in today's sprawl, which is the most visible reminder of our outdated thinking. Today, we are having a difficult time accepting the notion that the connection between economic growth and sustainability is not only beneficial but also essential for both the environment and the bottom line.

The knowledge economy encourages recognition of the long-term value of development and distinctive developed places associated with sustainable natural surroundings. Workers in the knowledge economy value high-quality living and working environments; they are increasingly attracted to thriving urban neighborhoods and to business locations in revitalized employment centers. They and their families enjoy the benefits of conserved natural spaces. They pay greater attention to the cost effects of development—on natural resources, on public services such as transportation and utilities, and on social and economic interactions. To respond to these interests, we must cultivate economic paradigms that support sustainable forms of development, including approaches to financing private development that recognize the long-term value of development and public fiscal policies that reflect the cost differentials of delivering services to conventional versus sustainable development.

The Legacy of the Industrial Economy

To understand what changed when the method by which we earn our livings shifted from an industrial to a knowledge base, we need to consider the five ways that value is added in any economy—agricultural, industrial, or knowledge:

- the conversion of raw material, such as oil, iron, wheat, and so forth, to produce tangible goods;

- reliance on skilled and unskilled labor to manipulate raw materials;

- research and development to create and refine technologies that result in new products, either tangible or intangible;

- marketing and distribution to understand, create, enhance, or respond to consumer demand and to transport the product to the end user; and

- the management and financing of the enterprise.

In the industrial economy, raw material extraction and labor to manipulate that raw material added 60 to 80 percent of value to the final product. The production of steel, the prototypical industrial product, required a huge investment in mines, the shipping of raw materials, and labor-intensive production processes, all of which accounted for about 70 percent of the cost structure of manufactured steel. Factories in the industrial era had no choice but to locate close to the source of raw material, particularly if the material was difficult to transport. The result was an explosion in economic and population growth in the resource-rich Midwest, particularly in cities with water transportation such as Detroit, Chicago, Pittsburgh, Cleveland, and Milwaukee. Water transportation allowed for inexpensive inbound shipment of raw materials and outbound shipment of finished products. While labor was demeaned and undervalued during the early years of the industrial era, the middle years of the 20th century saw the rise of labor unions, forcing management to recognize the value of labor's input. The power of unions allowed the real wages of skilled and unskilled workers to rise to middle-class levels for the first time in history.

The industrial era peaked just after World War II, when 45 percent of all jobs were in the manufacturing sector. Today, industrial jobs account for 16 percent of all jobs but, by 2010, they will likely represent 10 percent, according to forecasters. Despite the projected drop, industrial production as a percent of GDP hovers around 25 percent, as it has for decades; the reason is increased productivity.

The rapid decline in a basic sector of the economy is not without precedent. Before the industrial era, agriculture drove the economy. During the early 19th century, over 75 percent of the workforce was employed on farms. Today, the agricultural sector of the economy, which is one of the nation's most productive and most successful export sectors, employs less than 3 percent of the total workforce.

The industrial economy began at a time when resources and land were considered inexhaustible. The continent was so large and raw materials so plentiful, especially in view of the 19th century's small population base, that few Americans felt the need to conserve. The belief that the continent offered unlimited land and resources had its basis in the largest and least contentious transfer of land ever witnessed in history: the conquest of the Western Hemisphere by Europeans. Never has so much land been transferred from one group of peoples to another group with such relative ease.

By some estimates, approximately 40 million Native Americans populated North and northern South America in 1492. Large population centers of Native Americans dotted what is now the eastern United States, the Mississippi River Valley, the Southwest, central Mexico, and Peru. The early-19th century journals of the Lewis and Clark expedition describe the expedition's winter camp at the mouth of the Columbia River in Oregon as having what we would consider today's suburban densities. And in the Mississippi Valley, the Pueblo Indians of the Southwest, the Aztec civilization of central Mexico, and the Incas of Peru achieved significant urban-density concentrations. It was not until the mid-19th century that the population of European settlers reached the 15th-century level of the native populations.

After the arrival of the Europeans, however, over 90 percent of the native population was wiped out, primarily due to European diseases such as smallpox, measles, and tuberculosis. In fact, the European advantage in weaponry was of only secondary importance. Smallpox, probably brought by early French trappers even before significant European exploration took place, eliminated the Mississippi Valley culture. As for

the Aztec nation, which was a militant civilization of about 20 million, an invading force of 600 under Hernán Cortes was responsible for a smallpox epidemic that, in a little less than a year, killed over half the population, including the emperor. The surviving Aztec defenders were disheartened that the deadly disease affected only them, not their Spanish conquerors. Within 100 years of conquest, the native population of Mexico had dropped to less than 2 million.

With less than 10 percent of the Native American population left to defend its land, the European invaders found the land takeover relatively easy. In fact, the land-starved European lower classes, which made up most of the immigrant population, claimed a gift of land and resources beyond any previous historical precedent. One can only speculate about the different scenario that would have played out if European germs were the equal of Native American germs, pitting the small groups of travel-weakened European invaders against 40 million well-entrenched defenders. The fight put up by the small remnant of native Americans inspired the heroic myths of the frontier while the inevitable outcome fueled the American sense of "manifest destiny."

In thrall to manifest destiny, early European settlers and their descendants assumed that the continent's natural resources and land were unlimited and free—or at least cheap. There was always another rich valley over the next hill. For example, the transformation of the upper Midwest during the late 19th century resulted in the destruction of one of the world's largest forests, the corporate-financed near-extinction of the buffalo, and the transformation of the prairie into the farmland we know today. Manifest destiny mentality was responsible for denuding what was a once an environmentally rich continent.

Writing in the January 1929 issue of *Harper's Magazine*, Malcolm Cowley, one of America's great essayists of the early 20th century, wrote about growing up in central Pennsylvania around 1915:

> There were no longer any deer in my country. The white pines, which once covered it, were reduced to a few weevily saplings. The trout had been poisoned by sawmills or sulphur from the mines. The young men were dispersing, the farms neglected, and soon my country would be a fire-blackened wilderness with a few old houses crumbling in the midst of overgrown fields.

Cowley spoke of old men remembering "when panthers skunk after white-tailed deer, when every creek was full of shadowy trout." Meanwhile, "the young men [of 1915] tramped off to Pittsburgh to look for work in the mills" and further denigrated the environment. But, with limited alternatives for economic growth, wealth creation, or the provision of family necessities, few voices questioned the tradeoff between economic necessity and environmental destruction.

With the advent of the knowledge economy in the 1970s, the economic rules began to change. Automation reduced labor inputs as the dirtiest and most dangerous jobs moved abroad to take advantage of lower labor costs and less stringent regulatory regimes (actions that are not without sustainability impacts). Tangible products became smaller and lighter, minimizing raw material inputs. Intangible products, such as professional services and software, now dominate the marketplace and account for the fastest-growing sectors of the economy. The R&D required to create smarter, tangible products is the only input into intangible products and therefore is of paramount importance. Understanding

the consumer and even stimulating consumer desire in an increasingly wealthy society means the difference between product/service success and failure. Developing "smart" distribution systems to move products to consumers when and where they want them, in a "just-in-time" manner, has become a major component of corporate strategy. Finally, two areas of pursuit—managing the complex process of product/service R&D, marketing, and distribution and providing finances through a highly sophisticated worldwide network of investors and bankers—now account for the economy's most highly compensated activities.

Today, the value added by R&D, marketing, and distribution and by management and finance dwarfs the value of raw material and labor. The laptop computer used to create this text retailed for about $2,000. The actual cost of producing that computer—the plastic, metal, and battery—totaled less than $200, FOB. The rest of the cost paid for amortizing R&D, enticing the consumer through advertising, providing customer support through call centers, and financing and managing the enterprise.

So how has the agricultural- and industrial-era mentality influenced how we use the land and build the places where we live, work, and play?

Emerging Metropolitan Development Patterns

The few following factors define how the real estate industry and government have shaped development of the nation's metropolitan areas:

- through the location of executive housing concentrations, which tend to be in one general part of the metropolitan area, although a few of the largest metropolitan areas have two or three concentrations;

- through the location of local minority group concentrations, which tend to be in opposite directions from the executive housing concentration(s); and

- through the freeway system.

In other words, employment locations tend to be driven by proximity to executive housing (the bosses make employment location decisions) and by access to the regional freeway network. Where employment goes, metropolitan development follows. These factors have combined to push the metropolitan fringe farther and farther out, suburbanizing the rural countryside at an ever-increasing pace.

The last 50 years have witnessed a geometric expansion in the land area occupied by metropolitan development. Stated more precisely, the land area subject to development grew at least seven times as fast as the population during the second half of the 20th century, with 80 percent of the nation's population increase of 120 million settling in metropolitan areas. During the early to mid-1990s, in particular, the bounds of our metropolitan areas pushed outward even more rapidly than in previous decades. The edge cities of one decade become the inner suburbs of the next decade as new edge cities are built farther out. Commercial developments have exploded at the metropolitan fringe, such as toward the Alliance Airport area of Dallas/Fort Worth, toward north Scottsdale in Phoenix, and into Cobb and Gwinnett counties 40 miles north of downtown Atlanta.

In their choices of where to live and work, the executive decision makers in the knowledge economy are driving continued suburbanization. Highly educated and trained engineers, marketing specialists, finance professionals, scientists, investors, and managers constitute the most important input into the knowledge economy—not raw materials or the skilled labor needed to manipulate raw materials. Knowledge workers are well-traveled and sophisticated and exercise great discretion. They have choices. Given their power to choose, they tend to live in high-quality-of-life places that offer unique environmental features. They select office and plant locations close to their homes that may even be their homes. They can locate their workplaces near their generally high-end housing because the knowledge economy is nearly pollution-free, except for the air, water, and noise pollution caused by lower-level workers' daily commute.

These factors have led to the emergence of the "favored quarter," where most new and relocating jobs settle and 70 to 80 percent of infrastructure dollars are spent. But the success of the new knowledge economy has not been paralleled by success in building workable metropolitan areas. Americans still operate with the pioneer belief in unlimited resources and land availability. After all, an airplane trip across the country reveals an abundance of seemingly unused land; indeed, we use only 5 percent of our land to house 80 percent of the population. And the current industrial-era interpretation of the American dream gives anyone the right to a large lot, privacy, and easy access to work by automobile. The vision of how we should be able to live is so strong that it is embedded in our zoning codes, financing mechanisms, and real estate strategies. As long as lower-level workers are closed out of the favored quarter, our metropolitan areas will continue to be plagued by long commutes, traffic congestion, loss of valued natural features, and air pollution. With all of us trying to live the same dream, the age-old phenomenon of the "tragedy of the commons" sets in.

The tragedy of the commons refers to the pre–17th century British countryside practice of making common pastureland available for the sheep farmers in a particular area. Anyone was free to graze sheep on the commonly owned pasture. However, because no one owned the land, no one took responsibility for preserving it in the face of mounting pressures for pasturage. If one farmer did not exploit the use of the pasture, the next one would; so why not strip the pasture of grass? Today, the tragedy of the commons is leading to the environmental degradation of American metropolitan areas as the scourge of air, water, and noise pollution and traffic congestion compromise our quality of life. With the indirect costs of suburban sprawl passed off to society as a whole, there is no incentive for any individual to conserve.

The other side of the tragedy of the commons is the monoculture we are creating by following the industrial-era version of the American dream. With few exceptions, American metropolitan areas have adopted a "one-size-fits-all" approach to real estate development. If you want an executive home, you can choose a single-family house or a single-family house. If you want to shop near your single-family house, you can go to a strip retail center or a strip retail center. For a nation that prides itself on offering the widest array of consumer options, we offer little choice in our living environments. As Tom Wolfe said in *A Man in Full*, when commenting on the infamous American commercial strip, "the only way you could tell you were leaving one community and entering another was when the franchises started repeating."

Conventional Formulas for the Built Environment. Our monoculture can now be boiled down to a few standard product types that the real estate industry, Wall Street, and institutional investors can easily finance, build, and sell. Perhaps the most common examples of "slam-dunk" products are:

- grocery store– and drugstore-anchored neighborhood centers of between 80,000 and 150,000 square feet, with surface parking, and designed to draw from the "neighborhood" within a two- to four-mile radius;

- two- and three-story rental apartment buildings of 100 to 500 units with surface parking, though more attached garages are expected;

- move-up detached housing on one-third-acre lots with houses between 1,800 and 3,000 square feet;

- two- and three-story office buildings between 50,000 and 100,000 square feet, with surface parking limited to outer-suburban areas;

- one-story 100,000-plus-square-foot warehouses with a minimum of a 22-foot clear-span height and laser-leveled floors to accommodate automatic storage and retrieval systems; and

- power centers comprising several big-box, category-killer retailers such as Circuit City and Home Depot, totaling between 200,000 and 400,000 square feet, with surface parking and drawing from a three- to five-mile radius.

Figure 4-1 presents 19 standard products the real estate industry is accustomed to producing with ready acceptance by investors.

Even though supply and demand pressures ensure that the product formulas in figure 4-1 are not perfectly static, the formulas are nonetheless extremely limiting. The major land use implication of standardization is an acceleration of the trend toward a homogeneous built landscape. With the possible exception of superficial architectural details, an apartment building in Atlanta looks like one in Los Angeles; a housing sub-

Income Products
Office
  Build-to-suit
  Speculative suburban low-rise
Industrial
  Build-to-suit
  Speculative warehouse
  (greater than 28-foot clear span)
  Research and development/flex
Retail
  Neighborhood (between 80,000 and 120,000 square feet)
  Power (between 120,000 and 400,000 square feet)
  Urban entertainment
Hotel
  Limited service
  Full-service business
Apartment
  Low-density suburban (over 150 units at 15 to 20 units per acre)
  High-density suburban (over 200 units at greater than 20 units per acre)
Miscellaneous
  Self-storage
  Assisted living

For-Sale Products
Residential
  Entry-level attached
  Entry-level detached
  Move-up/-down attached
  Move-up/-down detached
  Executive detached

Source: Robert Charles Lesser & Co.

division in Kansas City looks like one in Orlando. And the commercial strip is ubiquitous and probably the most significant American contribution to 20th century architecture. Standardization has led to biting commentaries over the past 30 years. In *The Geography of Nowhere,* James Kunstler refers to the American built landscape as a "hostile cartoon environment."

How are Americans reacting to the formula-driven environment that has been created across the country? "Visual preference surveys" by Anton Nelessen, a Princeton-based planner, yield a nearly universal conclusion: Conventional,

formula-codified development is considered "an evil unleashed on the community." In what may appear to be a blinding flash of the obvious, Nelessen has consistently shown that Americans overwhelmingly and consistently prefer a pedestrian-oriented retail village versus eight lanes of traffic separating the local Wal-Mart from the McDonald's.

If such findings reflect antipathy toward current real estate industry development patterns, how can we explain the obvious acceptance of such patterns? Critics of conventional developments, such as Peter Calthorpe, one of the leaders of the new urbanism movement, would

say that acceptance reflects the dearth of alternatives to today's cookie-cutter products. That observation is borne out by the protective behavior evidenced by the residents and patrons of many neighborhoods and commercial areas built before World War II. Examples include Country Club Plaza in Kansas City, the German Village neighborhood in Columbus, Ohio, and the upper east and west sides of Manhattan, places that violate the formulas of today's codified products. Elected officials or developers who attempt to change the character of these and other highly treasured places do so at huge risk.

However, a major reason for the success and consumer acceptance of the limited number of standardized products is that Americans have obviously traded off character for efficiency. In retailing, for instance, strip commercial development allows the average consumer to spend far less on food than consumers in the rest of the industrialized world. Wal-Mart is cheaper and offers a wider selection than the old five-and-dime store. And homes in the United States are far larger for the same or less cost than dwellings in other nations. Clearly, the standardization of our real estate has led to significant cost efficiencies, yet it has occurred at an environmental and societal cost that has been pushed off to society as a whole.

In the head-long rush to implement the industrial-era vision of the American dream, we were initially successful in having it all: privacy, automobile-based convenience, and environmental quality. But we pursued that dream before its unforeseen environmental consequences became evident. The real estate industry now provides only a few low-density standard options. And that is where the tragedy of the commons sets in. We end up loving to death the very environmental features that propelled us farther and farther to the fringes of our metropolitan areas.

Atlanta: The Epitome of Nonsustainability. Nowhere is the tragedy of the commons more evident than in 1990s Atlanta. Blessed with a Sunbelt location and unlimited land with few topographic barriers, Atlanta entered the 1990s as America's premier corporate location, according to every leading business magazine. Southern charm and Northern-financed economic growth combined to make Atlanta the fastest-growing metropolitan economy of the decade. In addition, the metropolis experienced the fastest rate of human settlement in history with respect to physical expansion. The Atlanta area started off the decade with a north/south commuter shed of 65 miles; it ended the decade with a 110-mile commuter shed. That growth has resulted in massive traffic congestion and some of the poorest air quality in the country—along with two unforeseen consequences. First, the federal government, recognizing that metropolitan Atlanta was in violation of EPA clean air standards, cut off all federal highway funds for the region. Second, Atlanta has dropped off the charts as a business location. In fact, Hewlett-Packard recently declined to move additional jobs to the region and may even start moving jobs out as a result of the declining quality of life.

Largely because Atlanta enjoys a history of extremely progressive business leadership, particularly in the real estate community, the leaders of the Atlanta metropolitan area and the state reacted rapidly to a deteriorating situation. John Williams, president of the chamber of commerce during the late 1990s and CEO of Post Properties, set the pace for a new direction when he shifted the strategy of his $2 billion REIT (real estate investment trust) from suburban apartment development to mixed-use urban complexes. In addition, Williams, along with others, recognized the cost of conventional development and even went so far as to oppose the construction of the proposed outer freeway loop, singling out the Atlanta chamber as the only chamber in the nation to disapprove of a freeway project. Moreover, the chamber and other business groups joined forces with the environmental community in a one-of-a-kind coalition to obtain the passage of legislation creating the unprecedented Georgia Regional Transportation Authority (GRETA). GRETA, authorized by the legislature in early 1999, was granted broad power to control sprawl in the 20-county metropolitan area, including the authority to veto the actions of the heretofore all-powerful Georgia Department of Transportation.

Atlanta has come to realize that conventional development promotes an ideal that is self-defeating; the image of privacy, open space, and freedom of movement is illusory. As more people try to achieve the ideal, the more the ideal is unachievable for all. The ultimate irony is that the sale of every additional house often erodes the value of the conventional housing project or master-planned community. The evidence is most pronounced among homeowners' associations that fight the next phase of construction in their own communities. As many homebuilders have come to realize, the sale of every house means opposition to further development.

The Fiscal "Bottom Line" of Conventional Development

During the 1980s, local governments took advantage of a new methodology for measuring the fiscal impact of new economic and real estate development. Fiscal impact analysis helped government officials determine the costs and benefits of a new industrial location or other forms of real estate development. Since the advent of fiscal impact analysis, several accepted conclusions have emerged, including the following:

- Providing tax breaks for corporate relocations, particularly relocations that employ unskilled or semiskilled labor, is a give-away that most times is never paid back over the short or mid-term and possibly never.

- Residential development, particularly entry-level and move-up projects aimed at the family market, pays about 70 percent of the costs of the services provided by local government; the shortfall is attributable to the cost of public education.

- Assuming no subsidies, office and industrial development tends to pay its own way through the various taxes imposed on it.

- Retail development almost always pays for itself if local governments participate in the distribution of sales tax revenues.

Recent work conducted by Myron Orfield has shown that the metropolitan development patterns discussed above have evolved in part due to the great disparity in where infrastructure dollars are spent. Based on the results of surveys in many of the nation's major metropolitan areas, Orfield has determined that the largest share of new infrastructure spending is concentrated in the favored quarter. Given that most of the taxes levied to pay for new roads and sewer and water line extensions are collected from throughout a region, middle- and lower-income households frequently subsidize the areas where well-to-do executive households tend to locate. This imbalance obviously needs to be addressed. The favored quarter is probably not interested in additional highway lanes and the associated sprawl while the three-quarters of the metropolitan area that lies outside the favored quarter—and typically embraces a region's older areas—would appreciate the infrastructure improvements.

Components of Sustainable Economic Development

In the long run, conventional development is unsustainable in many respects, from fiscal subsidies to environmental damage. Ultimately, though, it hurts business, especially given that business decisions are increasingly driven by quality-of-life considerations. And more than ever, high quality of life means environmental sustainability. Eventually, communities will arrive at the conclusion that investing in education, parks, and pedestrian-oriented places is a far better economic development decision than subsidizing sprawl and the relocation of companies. No one provides subsidies to attract new companies to Seattle, Portland, Austin, or the Silicon Valley.

So what is the new model that will allow for sustainable development? The new model must contain a variety of elements that are environmentally sustainable, financially sustainable at the project level, and fiscally sustainable for local governments. The model must also appeal to a rapidly changing market and provide business with a place that draws knowledge workers and in turn attracts corporate investment. What results from a sustainable development model is an upward spiral of self-reinforcing elements that are both synergistic and self-sustaining.

We can see elements of the model in changes occurring today in the marketplace. During the late 1990s, as the nation's economic recovery continued to set records and the expectation of further sprawl fueled community and political opposition, something unexpected may have begun. Based on anecdotal evidence, the late 1990s may have signaled the beginning of the end of sprawl. Of course, expansion at the metropolitan fringe will continue and suburban subdivisions will rise on former farmland. Huge build-to-suit offices and plants will still be sited on greenfield parcels 40 to 60 miles from central-city downtowns.

It appears, nonetheless, that a small but significant shift is occurring in the location of selected types of new development, namely, more infill and downtown sites. Atlanta may not expand into Tennessee as most observers have predicted, and the New York metropolitan area may not make Philadelphia a suburb, but something different from the past half-century is happening and may portend a structural shift in how we build metropolitan areas and how Americans want to live. And while a change in public policy might accelerate the end of sprawl, what is at work seems to be a market shift that no amount of government intervention can fundamentally alter. This trend offers hope that sustainable forms of development are starting to take hold.

For real estate firms, sustainable development starts with identifying and taking environmental *and* financial responsibility for the development product. The ideal development combines responsible environmental conservation with the least long-term (ten-year-plus time horizon) cost. Each of these elements is explored below in greater depth.

The Economics of Environmental Sustainability. In much of today's development, environmental damage stems from the basic components of infrastructure needed by a household or business, including transportation, energy (electricity, heating oil, and natural gas), water, and sewer service/ refuse removal. By far, the most important infrastructure need is transportation. Responsible for over 20 percent of the typical family budget, transportation is also the major contributor to environmental degradation. More than 90 percent of all household trips and business shipments (number of shipments, not shipments by weight) take place by automobile or truck, generating the largest share of airborne, runoff-related, and noise pollution.

By working at home or relying on transit, walking, and/or cycling, at least one household member can contribute to important energy savings and a decline in pollution. Reduced reliance on the automobile gives the metropolitan area a more urban character and further enhances the market appeal of its neighborhoods. Environmental sustainability is a logical byproduct of the market's growing acceptance of and preference for urban lifestyles, as discussed below.

Business transportation also must face up to long-term needs for reducing the environmental degradation that will result from the nation's gradual shift from a tangible product economy to a more intangible product–based economy. Obviously, tangible products, from soap to shoes to turbines, will continue to be a part of the economy. But, as services and high knowledge–based products account for a larger share of GDP, the shift in value added to R&D, marketing and distribution, and management and finance will account for a relative reduction in the percent of business transport of tangible products.

For many basic services, pricing mechanisms mask real costs as well as the full range of environmental effects. For example, 80 percent of the country's light bulbs waste half the electricity they use. Upgrading bulbs and fixtures has a three-year payback, but the short-term bias in our capital allocation system and a business and consumer energy management system that hides energy costs from the ultimate bill payer works against the longer view and forecloses opportunities for conserving energy. In particular, property managers and building owners typically pay for fixtures and bulbs out of their capital and operating budgets and thus often pass energy operating costs on to unknowing tenants through common area maintenance charges.

A similar issue arises with water supply. In the near future, a water shortage will likely occur in various parts of the country, particularly west of the 100th meridian. The shortage will result from the illogical pricing system now in place and, consequently, the inefficient means by which we use water. Water delivery is incredibly capital-intensive and usually handled by government agencies or government-regulated private companies. In either case, the amortized cost of capital is inadequately valued; pricing is set in accordance with variable operating costs, which tend to be low relative to capital costs.

The solution is obvious; at a minimum, utilities must charge for water based on the total unit cost of delivery, including operating and capital costs. Pricing based on actual costs will particularly affect development at the low-density fringe but, in any event, should be introduced over a number of years so that households and businesses can more easily adjust to it. At the same time, pricing based on actual cost would encourage the introduction of a series of sustainable practices that are well known but not technologically sophisticated. The most significant practice relates to the biological treatment of sewage, which permits the reuse of water time and time again. As described in detail in chapter 6, decentralized marsh-based wastewater treatment systems are well understood, less costly to install than centralized sewage treatment systems, and relatively inexpensive to maintain. In addition, they provide an odor-free natural amenity for a community. The reason for their current lack of acceptance is merely bureaucratic resistance to a better-known technology. For example, efforts in the Southwest a few years ago to convince a municipal water and sewer district to allow a marsh treatment process for a master-planned communi-

ty spurred the following response from the water district: "You do not buy water from us, you rent it . . . and you can only use it once then you must send it to our new sewage treatment plant."

Pricing that recognizes environmental risks is particularly important for reducing and recycling solid waste. Indeed, waste reduction/recycling is entirely feasible if the will exists to raise prices to their full cost. Besides, properly sealed dumps can be considered temporary storage locations for products not worth salvaging today. Undoubtedly, the economic value of the things we "throw away" will change; for example, plastics will eventually be worth relatively more in the future. As a result, landfills will be "mined" some day for the treasures they contain.

Financial Sustainability at the Project Level. Modifying the method of evaluating capital investment decisions is probably the most important "soft" technology for promoting sustainable development. In making capital allocation decisions, the private sector uses a methodology whose unintended short-term bias discourages innovative investments in sustainable development as well as in smart growth and new urbanism projects.

By necessity, the financial markets are conservative. As a result, the lack of a track record for projects comparable to newly conceived and proposed alternative developments means that the latter will experience difficulty in obtaining equity and debt financing. In addition, alternative projects appear to perform financially in a fundamentally different way than conventional developments. Applying conventional financing techniques to alternative projects is not only difficult but also compromises the ability of the projects to demonstrate that they meet the social, environmental, market, and, ultimately, financial goals of their sponsors.

Clearly, conventional financing poses barriers to innovative developments and ignores a rich source of financial return that would be highly valued by appropriate investors. Unfortunately, these investors lack the methodological means to evaluate alternative development opportunities; they are blinded by methodologies and a mindset that was created for—and therefore encourages and rewards—conventional development. For example, for the past 40 years, business schools have been teaching discounted cash flow (DCF) methodologies as a means of comparing alternative investments. DCF and its various derivatives, such as net present value (NPV) and internal rate of return (IRR), are measures by which different projected cash flows over time can be easily compared with one another to select the highest-yielding alternative.

The assumption behind DCF calculations is that a dollar tomorrow is worth less than a dollar today. The amount that a current investment dollar falls in value over time is a factor of the "discount rate," a rate (expressed as a percent) determined by the cost of capital (the interest rate charged by lenders) and an investor's expectations of financial return. A common discount rate employed by real estate investors is 15 percent; it assumes an interest rate on borrowed funds of 7 to 8 percent and an expected profit of 7 to 8 percent. The discount rate permits an evaluation of the projected cash flow of a potential investment. For example, with a 15 percent discount rate, a dollar received one year from now is \$.85 in "current" dollars, \$.44 after five years, and only \$.20 after ten years. The rate is a means of measuring the risk of an investment; the higher the discount rate, the higher is the probable risk.

Internal rate of return is a DCF methodology for determining a specific value of a projected cash flow (expressed as a percent). The IRR is the discount rate at which the cash flow would be equal to the initial investment in current dollars. It is the most common method of evaluating a real estate investment. For a real estate development of moderate risk, the acceptable range for the IRR is between 15 and 20 percent per year. For riskier investments, the IRR can rise to 35 percent. As the perceived risk of an investment increases, so does the IRR expectation. Most conventional types of projects, for example, have a long and well-documented track record and therefore need a relatively low expected IRR to obtain financing. A project with less of a track record would need a higher IRR; the resultant higher cost of capital could make the project infeasible.

Figure 4-2 shows two different types of projected cash flows evaluated by IRR. Figures for each year represent cash inflows or outflows for different hypothetical projects; the figure for the final year includes the cash flow for that year plus the sales price, estimated at ten times the annual cash flow. The first project is a short-term investment that sells after seven years while the second project is a mid-term investment that sells after 15 years. The amount of each initial investment is the same, but the short-term example shows more immediate cash flow. The mid-term example, in contrast, shows less attractive returns

in the first few years followed by significantly improved returns after the seventh year.

The short-term investment has a higher IRR than the mid-term investment and would be the choice of most investors because the mid-term return, when converted to current dollars, represents only a fraction of its value in year ten and beyond; the $23 income projected in year ten is worth only $4.53 in current dollars. Investors therefore have an incentive to favor projects that produce short-term cash flow regardless of the impact on mid-term cash flow.

Short-term bias has had an immense impact on the character and quality of America's built environment. We marvel at the architectural design and quality of construction in the great retail emporiums built before World War II. We treat those structures as if their builders were unknowable "ancients" blessed with immensely more wealth than we claim. In reality, of course, the country's per capita gross domestic product is three times higher today in real terms than in the 1920s. The difference is that real estate projects undertaken in the era before the widespread use of discounted cash flow were generally built for the ages and not for short-term returns.

By contrast, primarily because it views the world through DCF lenses, Wal-Mart is willing to enter a new market by constructing a 60,000-square-foot building with a predetermined expected life span of five years. After the market is "primed," Wal-Mart then constructs a 110,000-square-foot building down the street and abandons the "old" building whose roof and mechanical systems are approaching the end of their useful life. Similarly, investors encourage developers to build retail centers with the cheapest available systems and simple, repeatable designs unrelated to the local architectural style. This short-term bias is somewhat baffling in that the Internal Revenue Service requires most real estate investments to depreciate over 39 years, hardly a short-term time frame.

Examples abound of projects, both prewar and more recent, that represent real estate investment aimed at mid- and long-term returns. Prewar projects such as Country Club Plaza in Kansas City, Lake Forest and Riverside in the Chicago metropolitan area, and Nassau Square in Princeton demonstrate that tremendous value can be created and sustained by following what is now referred to as new urbanism design concepts.

Recent projects have also created and sustained value in excess of the competition's value, though the projects'

4-2

Short- and Long-Term Investment Income and Resulting Internal Rates of Return (IRR)

	Initial Investment (000)s	1	2	3	4	5	6	7	8	9	10	11	12	13	14	15	IRR
Example #1 (short-term investment	100	0	8	11	13	14	15	176									15.1%
Example #2 (mid-term investment)	100	-5	-5	0	5	11	13	14	17	20	23	25	27	28	29	330	13.7%

short-term performance was sometimes inferior to nearby conventional development. Examples include Mizner Park in Fort Lauderdale, Hyde Park in Tampa, Valencia Town Center north of Los Angeles, The Avenue northeast of Baltimore, Harbor Town in Memphis, and Seaside in Florida. Generally, they were all slow in generating the critical mass necessary to ensure success. Once they did, however, their returns increased impressively.

For example, Seaside began selling its one-eighth-acre lots in 1982 for $15,000 and sold only 20 of them in the first two years. However, as the human-scale streetscape of houses emerged in combination with retail uses located within walking distance of the homes, potential buyers could see the value of what was being created. When Seaside reached its critical mass around 1985, the new community appeared to be heading for success; accordingly, the sales pace and prices escalated. The last lot of the 300-lot town sold for $500,000 in 1999 while the downtown was appraised for $60 million in 1998. Given that the Seaside property was originally worth only a million dollars and that it is located on the so-called Redneck Riviera, the current value of the community's downtown is testament to the appeal of new urbanist development. Seaside is perhaps one of the most financially successful resort projects ever developed, and the reason for its success is undoubtedly its innovativeness. Yet, even today, obtaining financing for a Seaside would face significant obstacles. Conventional underwriters have little interest in the mid- to long-term value created by a community.

Fortunately, though, there are many different types of real estate investors with many different needs. For example, banks look to make construction loans for a short period of time or to package permanent loans for immediate resale to the secondary loan market.

Publicly traded real estate investment trusts have a short-, mid-, and long-term need for sustainable cash flow. Foundations, university endowments, insurance companies, and pension funds—collectively the largest single category of real estate investor—have well-defined, predictable, mid- and long-term forecasts of their cash flow needs. Yet, each one of these investor types and its business school–trained real estate advisers use the same DCF methodology and same list of "conforming" products to evaluate investments for their long-term potential.

The goal, then, is to match appropriate investors with the appropriate investment. One possible solution borrows a concept from the commercial mortgage-backed securities (CMBS) industry, a multihundred-billion-dollar secondary market for commercial loans. In the CMBS industry, various "pieces" of the debt of an individual project, so-called tranches, are divided according to the risk associated with each. For instance, the first-position loan (the A tranche) is the loan to be paid off before all others.

It carries the lowest yield and hence the lowest price because of its relative lack of risk. The mezzanine piece (the B tranche) is paid off next. It carries higher risk and is therefore priced with a higher yield.

As shown in figure 4-3, time tranches could be introduced to match investors with different investment horizons to the appropriate "piece" of an investment. Specifically, the various cost elements of a project are divided into three categories: building development (the vertical piece), land development and parking (the horizontal piece), and land. Each piece has a different cost associated with it and is itself associated with a different investment time frame.

Investors in the first tranche who want to get in and out within five years, for example, receive the bulk of the cash flow during a project's first five years. Given that they employ DCF methodologies, they probably do not value mid- to long-term cash flows. The percent of projected cash flow is determined by the amount required to achieve, for instance, a 20 percent IRR on invested equity.

Mizner Park. A new mode of successful investment modeled on old patterns of development.

Example of New Urbanist Time Tranche Cash Flow Distribution

Cost Elements	Cash Flow Distribution		
	1–5 Years	6–10 Years	11+ Years
Building Development (65%)	90%	20%	10%
Land Development and Parking (25%)	10%	70%	45%
Land (10%)	0%	10%	45%

Division of cash flow into early-, mid-, and long-term segments offers options for investment returns.

Source: Arcadia Land Company.

The advantage from an urban design perspective is that only 65 percent of the costs of a project are amortized over the first five years. As a result, a much higher-quality project can be built. The second time tranche pays off land development costs; mid-term investors receive most of the cash flow from year six and beyond. Finally, long-term investors, who are responsible for the land investment, receive most of their returns after the eleventh year.

The difficulty in evaluating mid- and long-term investments cannot be minimized; however, a current cash flow (CCF) analysis is feasible. Though requiring more judgment, such an analysis evaluates projected cash flows on a current dollar basis and accommodates cost and revenue increases driven by market forces when critical mass is achieved. Adding current—positive and negative—cash flows year by year to see the aggregate totals and judging whether the timing of the cash flows fits investor needs should be the criteria for evaluating one investment as superior to another.

Time tranches allow for an approximation of the method that the "ancients" used. Pre-DCF investors expected to subsidize a real estate investment dur-ing its first few years and then reap the benefits for decades. Historically, many of the great real estate fortunes were built this way, and today's private investors generally follow the same model. That approach also offers the financial stability that investors need to ride out the inevitable industry downturns. Clearly, time tranches reduce development risk and increase the quality of what is built.

Much needs to be done to gain access to financing for alternative developments. Tasks include more research into the performance of existing, innovative projects and the definition of a much broader array of standard product types. Most important, however, is helping investors with a natural need for mid- and long-term cash flows recognize that the conventional methods of evaluating real estate investment are not appropriate for them.

The investors most likely to reevaluate their approach to real estate investment are charitable foundations. Motivated by the environmental and social impacts of sprawl, many of the country's largest foundations, including MacArthur, Rockefeller, Surdna, Packard, Hewlett, Mellon, and Hines, are now focusing on the new urbanism, smart growth, and sustainable development. By bridging the gap between their money-making side and the programmatic side of grant making, foundations can make innovative real estate investments from their asset base. That is not to say that bridging the two sides of a foundation is not without its difficulties. However, instead of investing their assets in conventional development—that is, to earn short-term returns that are then invested in various smart growth initiatives, which, in turn, attempt to curb conventional development—foundations could make investments that are congruent with their mission. In essence, foundations can do well by doing good even as they earn superior mid- to long-term returns.

The above model is more than theoretical. Arcadia Land Company, for example, is involved in the redevelopment of downtown Albuquerque. Arcadia knew it needed mid-term investors, and it recognized that a minimum of three to five years would be necessary to achieve the critical mass that would make downtown Albuquerque viable. It turned to the McCune Charitable Foundation, the largest New Mexico–based foundation. As supporters of smart growth under the auspices of the foundation, both the executive director and board decided to invest $5 million of equity in the downtown Albuquerque effort, fully expecting to receive superior returns after year five. As a side benefit, the foundation began to redirect some of its grant making to organizations that support smart growth and downtown revitalization, such as 1,000 Friends of New Mexico. These grants will support the foundation's investment and are completely consistent with its programmatic mission.

Long-term financing, therefore, is a vital component of sustainable development. The initial conceptualization of sustainable development, smart growth, and new urbanism gave little heed to how the three development alternatives might be financed. It has now become evident that if these development paradigms are to succeed at the daunting task of changing how America builds, they must also fundamentally change how we finance real estate. In the end, alternative developments must provide mid- and long-term returns that exceed those generated by conventional development. Only then will investors take the risk of trying something different.

Fiscal Sustainability for Government Entities and Utilities. Now that the costs of sprawl are better understood, the entities that subsidized sprawl in the past are questioning why they should continue their old practices. When revenues and costs were buried in mounds of undifferentiated public cash flows, decision makers had little ability or incentive to allocate them properly. Such was especially the case with elected officials, who might ideologically and politically believe that all growth, no matter what form it took, was good. But when the ongoing operating costs of maintaining new streets and paying for new schools came due, it was not clear what forces led to cost increases; and, in any case, the elected officials who made the decisions that occasioned sprawl often were no longer in office and thus could not be held

Planned development will be assisted by "patient" investments by the McCune Charitable Foundation, which expects long-term benefits rather than immediate returns.

Source: Used by permission of Moule & Polyzoides, Architects and Urbanists, Pasadena, California.

accountable. Clearly, no system built on subsidies can be maintained forever.

Several regions are now evaluating the long-term fiscal effects of development as part of their strategic planning efforts, using methodologies unavailable until a decade or two ago and determining what future metropolitan form will lead to the most cost-efficient infrastructure delivery. For example, the Salt Lake City region considered two scenarios for its infrastructure requirements for the years between 2000 and 2020: the first is a continuation of sprawl-oriented development; the second is a cluster development option. The resulting cost difference was nearly 2:1 between conventional development versus cluster options. The difference involves literally billions of dollars and thus easily captured the attention of public officials.

Unfortunately, when confronted with the type of fiscal results that came out of the Salt Lake City exercise, the real estate community, which has long been the beneficiary of public development subsidies, tends to react ideologically. To some in the development industry, the issue comes down to growth versus no-growth, which just obfuscates the discussion. And given that the development industry tends to be the largest contributor to election campaigns at the local level, the ideological views of the very beneficiaries of public subsidies are often the views considered by elected officials. Thus, the Urban Land Institute's recent cosponsorship of "smart growth" conferences and workshops is a major step forward in the debate. In fact, the issue of fiscal sustainability has nothing to do with the issue of growth versus no growth, but it has everything to do with eliminating sprawl-inducing capital subsidies that local municipalities cannot afford.

There is yet another force on the horizon that will not allow the continuation of public subsidies in support of sprawl. Specifically, utility deregulation will encourage analysis of the actual cost of the delivery of electricity and natural gas to different parts of metropolitan areas. At present, virtually all households or businesses pay the same rate regardless of the actual cost of delivery as determined by location. In Chicago, however, preliminary cost analysis by Consolidated Edison shows that it costs three times as much to deliver electricity to the suburban fringe than to existing urbanized areas. As with publicly provided water, sewer, and road infrastructure, it is easy to understand that construction and operation of an electrical or natural gas system at a density of 20 dwelling units to the acre will be less expensive per household than at a density of two dwelling units to the acre. Certainly, the capital and maintenance costs of the system will be the same, but, in the case of sprawl development, they must be amortized over fewer homes. With profit-making utilities now entering a competitive world for the first time, the political arguments and campaign contributions of the real estate industry will have far less effect on development patterns than in the past.

Sustainability of the Real Estate Market. The 1990s seemed to mark a fundamental shift in consumer preferences. The evidence is only anecdotal as is always the case when basic, social change is just unfolding. It appears, however, as if the downside of the industrial version of the American dream is beginning to catch up with those who experience the daily traffic congestion, pollution, and diminished quality of life produced by conventional development. Like all markets that are not satisfied, consumers seem to be voting for change with their pocketbooks.

The first and most obvious piece of evidence is the apparent comeback of many American downtowns. Nearly half of our downtowns are viable or in the process of becoming viable; in other words, office rents are at or above replacement levels, a resale market for housing has materialized, and a critical mass of retail has brought people to the streets. Twenty years ago, only midtown Manhattan, San Francisco, Boston, and Chicago had viable downtowns. By the end of the 1990s, the number of viable downtowns extended to San Diego, Denver, Seattle, and Portland, among others. Even more impressive is the list of downtowns that are in the middle of the comeback process: San Jose, Phoenix, Dallas, Houston, Austin, San Antonio, Boise, Minneapolis, Memphis, Chattanooga, Nashville, Charlotte, Atlanta, Providence, Cleveland, Columbus, and Cincinnati, among many others. It is not unreasonable to say that, by 2010, most if not all American downtowns will be in the process of becoming or will already have become viable real estate markets.

The emergence of viable urban-density real estate markets is not confined to downtowns. Many of the "third-generation" metropolitan cores have begun to urbanize. These edge cities, which emerged in the 1970s but today are miles from the edge owing to continued sprawl, include West Los Angeles, Century City, Bellevue (Seattle), Buckhead (Atlanta), and the profusion of urbanizing suburban metropolitan cores around Washington, D.C., that emerged or reemerged with expansion of the Metro transit system (e.g., Bethesda, Chevy Chase, Ballston, and Court House).

Throughout the country, evidence points to pent-up demand for more urban and urbane housing. Surveys conducted by Robert Charles Lesser & Co. in Atlanta, Chattanooga, and Albuquerque asked consumers a series of tradeoff questions regarding

lifestyle preferences. The results organized consumers into one of three preferred housing markets: semirural, suburban, or urban. In all three surveys, over 30 percent of respondents preferred urban housing that would allow them to walk to restaurants, services, and work, even though they would have to accept smaller dwelling units and little or no lot. Interestingly, none of the surveyed metropolitan areas has a recent urban housing tradition; in other words, respondents who preferred an urban lifestyle did not refer to a local example.

The underlying reason for the shift in housing preferences is probably the aging of the baby boom generation. As they approach age 50, the baby boomers are becoming empty nesters, and many seem to be questioning why they should remain in suburban isolation. An urban lifestyle, according to the above research, may be just the alternative for boomers who expect to lead a far more active life than their parents. Even some Gen Xers prefer to live in an urban setting.

Throughout the country, the past few years have seen a relative price appreciation in homes located in the favored-quarter inner suburbs. Since the mid-1990s, housing prices in favored-quarter inner suburbs such as Bethesda, Buckhead, Bellevue, Palo Alto, and the Park Cities in Dallas have increased between 10 and 20 percent per year. In contrast, the price appreciation of the new housing built at the fringe of the favored quarter has barely kept up with inflation. People are voting with their pocketbooks; to avoid traffic congestion, they are locating in close-in neighborhoods renowned for their character as well as in third-generation metropolitan cores.

With the bosses just beginning to move back downtown and favored-quarter inner suburbs enjoying a renaissance, it is only a matter of time until jobs begin to return as well. In Seattle, many Gen X software developers who chose to live downtown likewise decided to move their places of business downtown. The emergence of households willing to pay $200 per square foot for a downtown loft in LoDo in Denver has created demand for office space, driving up commercial rents to over $30 per square foot. In addition, bosses in the traditional suburban executive housing concentrations now face traffic congestion whether they commute toward downtown or out to the fringe. Ten years ago, locating a place of business on the edge of the metropolitan area meant a reverse commute with little traffic congestion. Now, bumper-to-bumper freeway traffic in both directions is becoming the norm. In a perverse way, the end of reverse commuting has leveled the playing field for downtown and infill business locations.

What appears to be emerging is a more diverse version of the American dream, one that results in a greater range of choices for the consumer. Those choices include more pedestrian-oriented development types that require fewer automobile trips and less mileage traveled. As mentioned, reducing automobile trips may be the most productive means by which to produce more sustainable development. A new image of what constitutes desirable places to work, live, and play and that is inherently environmentally friendly is the best means for creating a sustainable future.

Business Sustainability to Attract Knowledge Workers. Knowledge workers, particularly Gen Xers, are demanding a high quality of life. No longer willing to put up with long commutes, knowledge workers are voting with their feet to work closer to where they live, possibly even in their homes. As a result, many large companies find themselves in a quandary. For example, General Motors is trying to make its Warren Tech Center more pedestrian-oriented to encourage more creative interaction between engineers and scientists. In what is a difficult challenge for a firm with a stodgy reputation in a metropolitan area not known for high-tech innovation, GM is attempting to attract more high-tech Gen Xers to the center. The final irony is that the Warren Tech Center was designed by Eero Saarinen, the well-regarded mid-century architect who conceived of the facility as the prototypical automobile-oriented business park. By today's standards, the place is sterile; its buildings are not within walking distance of one another; its image is that of an outdated version of the future. As a result, GM is redesigning the center to include pedestrian-scale mixed uses and improved circulation, possibly even a rail system, to encourage human interaction and to attract the new generation of knowledge workers.

Perhaps the most important issue for knowledge workers is how to capture more time. The loss of time to commuting is one of the most irksome issues for many knowledge workers. Conventional sprawl development is the antithesis of what more and more knowledge workers want, though most metropolitan areas offer only a few, albeit a growing number of, alternatives. Added to the demand of knowledge workers is the number of baby boomers entering the empty-nester stage. They are looking to take advantage of the flexibility offered by the next stage of life, and, for many, that means a return to downtown. Clearly, the market for households demanding a shorter commute in a more exciting, pedestrian-oriented environment is growing, growing, growing.

Conclusions

Sustainability is not just an environmental term that implies a better place for bunnies and birds, though that is certainly an important part of the picture. It is also about evaluating capital allocation in a manner that rewards real estate investors with mid- and long-term returns, not just short-term returns. It is about fiscally sound local governments that are not addicted to a heretofore hidden system of capital and operating subsidies that cannot be sustained. It is about providing for a more sophisticated consumer—as soon as the real estate industry expands its vision beyond a formulaic approach to development. And, finally, it is about providing public investments in education, open space, and urbane places to live and work.

Implementing sustainable development is the most efficient and effective means of economic development. There is no longer a tradeoff. What is good for the environment in the knowledge economy is good for the economy.

SOCIAL EQUITY AND SUSTAINABLE DEVELOPMENT
RULES FOR BUILDING BETTER COMMUNITIES[1]

Edward J. Blakely

One of the three interlocking circles of sustainable development is labeled social equity (or sometimes social opportunity or advancement). The three-circle concept recognizes that reconciling economic development with sustainable environmental qualities is not enough; the social needs of the human inhabitants of the land must also be part of the equation. For many Americans, that translates into quality-of-life factors—comfort, security, privacy, and access to common facilities for education and recreation. For many other Americans, however, their principal social concern is equity—equal access to opportunities for jobs, incomes, and education as well as to the benefits of livable communities.

This is not a new issue, of course. Improving the lot of society's poor and disadvantaged has been a continuing political and social goal. But in the context of shaping our communities to achieve sustainable development, the concern for social equity raises practical questions: How? When? Where? And to what extent should people engaged

in developing communities assume some responsibility for answering these questions?

Some years ago, concern for environmental justice sounded a warning about ensuring social equity in the process of achieving sustainable development. As more and more people became aware of the extent of unsafe and unwelcome environmental problems, many residents of lower-income neighborhoods and communities realized that they were residing amid those problems. They looked with heightened concern at the proximity of their homes to solid waste disposal or transfer sites, to industries spewing out malodorous and even toxic emissions as well as noise and glare, to contaminated industrial sites, and to polluted streams and ponds. They also noted the number of times that their neighborhoods were chosen as the site for jails, halfway houses, and other necessary but less-than-desirable land uses.

Some of these conditions resulted from economics-driven decisions that define good sites as cheap sites, especially for

facilities such as landfills that require large expanses of land. Not by coincidence, of course, many low-income neighborhoods develop in less desirable areas where inexpensive housing can be built on inexpensive land. Historically, working-class homes sprang up within walking distance of the factories, railroad yards, and warehouses where residents were employed. Historically, too, these neighborhoods have housed minority populations that have little political clout to influence the location of locally undesirable uses. As metropolitan areas expanded their reach, many older and poorer neighborhoods have found themselves stuck with the detritus of declining core cities as burgeoning suburbs furiously fend off new locations or relocations of undesirable uses.

The rising clamor over the inequities of these conditions resulted in President Clinton's signing Executive Order No. 12898 on February 11, 1994. The order directs each federal agency to "make achieving environmental justice part of its mission by identifying and addressing, as appropriate, disproportionately high and adverse human health or environmental effects of its programs, policies and activities on minority populations and low-income populations in the United States. . . ."[2] Federal agencies were enjoined to provide all populations with, first, the opportunity to comment before decisions are made on government programs and activities affecting human health or the environment and, second, the opportunity to share in the benefits of such programs.

The executive order is important because many of the environmental ills visited on our society can be addressed by existing statutes and regulations. Federal and state environmental laws, for instance, restrict noxious emissions and hazardous wastes associated with manufacturing, power production, and automobile use as well as other impacts on air and water quality. A famous controversy in Louisiana, for example, involved the governor's fervent desire to lure a Japanese polyvinyl chloride plant to St. James Parish, a heavily industrialized area near New Orleans. The area's surrounding residents, mostly black, fought the idea of another potentially polluting industry locating near them, especially because it would offer them few jobs. Eventually, the Japanese company pulled out of the conflict and moved to a different site, proposing a smaller plant and committing to restricted emissions. Clearly, residents' fears of potential pollution could have been allayed by evidence that the industry would meet official environmental standards, but Louisiana's record on that score was not sufficiently reassuring.

The Louisiana example, particularly as it affected a minority population, makes it clear that the cause of social equity is broader than the restrictive definition of environmental justice. It calls for treating all members of the community as equal partners with

equal access to job opportunities, healthy and safe living and working conditions, an array of choices for housing and transportation, and, not least, a long-lasting and renewing natural environment. Social equity in towns, cities, and metropolitan regions means creating and maintaining opportunities and choices for quality of life in its widest sense.

When we examine the communities under development today, we see that we have much yet to accomplish in achieving social equity in sustainable development. The discussion below probes the nature of existing circumstances, defines directions of socially responsible development, and lays out some new rules. Most drum beating for sustainable development focuses on sustaining the natural environment, with only a nod to the fundamental social concerns intrinsically wrapped up with environmentally responsible development of our communities. This discussion attempts, perhaps somewhat crudely, to direct more attention to the realities of social equity as an essential part of sustainable communities.

Where We Are

Today, the nation is engaged in a great internal debate, one of the most significant since the civil rights movement of the 1960s. And like that movement, the current debate will shape the future course of the nation. It concerns *how* we will grow, not *whether* we can grow, and is indicative of the curious point that the nation has arrived at in its growth cycle. Since the days of the Pilgrims, settling this vast nation has been a central concern of our society and economy. At the beginning of the 21st century, however, the question is not how to continue the settlement process but *who* settles and *where*. As with most of the developed world, the United States has reached virtually zero population growth, but we continue to grow through immigration.

Therein lies the rub. When the nation's growth was largely attributable to a Caucasian population, metropolitan growth patterns seemed to be of relatively minor importance. However, as the nation's population becomes less and less Caucasian and more and more nonwhite—by some estimates, so-called minority groups will be the majority by 2050—much of the Caucasian base population is pursuing an exit strategy. Millions of Americans are abandoning central cities, leaving them to the rising tide of foreign-born non-Caucasians and native-born blacks. Although "white flight" is hardly a new phenomenon, it has reached astounding proportions in recent decades. Our nation's separate geography has led to, among other things, over 9 million Americans living in secluded, gate-guarded subdivisions and neighborhoods. It also threatens the very economic and social structure of our society and, with that, our ability to sustain basic environmental qualities.

As noted in chapter 2, the decade of the 1990s witnessed dramatic growth in the ecological footprint of America's metropolises relative to population increases. To cite an example, Seattle's metropolitan population grew at a remarkable 38 percent while the region's urbanized area grew by a whopping 87 percent. Fewer people are covering more land. Clearly, this trend cannot persist. At its root, it is environmentally flawed and, relevant to this discussion, socially irresponsible. Our nation is growing apart, not together.

Where We Must Go

The nation's growth over the past few decades has yielded a legacy of choking smog and a deteriorating quality of life. We are absent from home more and more as we motor longer distances to work. We are less engaged in our communities as more and more of our time is focused on earning money to sustain costly homes that house fewer people and see less and less use as a sanctuary for family and friends. We will not be able to deal with this dilemma effectively unless we face several important truths. First, our nation is increasingly polarized in terms of race, income, and spatial location. Native Caucasians tend to live in neighborhoods of similar-income families. If African Americans sought to live in neighborhoods in the same manner as whites, nearly 70 percent would have to move. Similarly, over half of Latinos would have to move, although less than 30 percent of Asians would need to do so. Despite some gains in integrating our society, our neighborhoods continue to represent separate societies, creating a tinder box of racial animosity and discontent. As Vietorisz and others suggest, "When areas of the region are divided into rich and poor, low-income communities are at a disadvantage in paying for services. . . . [Thus] physical and social conditions in the core of the city deteriorate . . ., reducing attractiveness, . . . which in turn pushes those who are capable of paying out. . . ."[3]

Second, we must build our way out of this situation as we have built our way into it. We can start by recognizing that building high-quality, socially equitable communities is the key to salvation. We need to pursue a smarter and better strategy for community development. If not, the resulting social and environmental disaster will threaten the quality of life of future generations. The threat is real. Economic and spatial inequality is crippling America's competitiveness in the global marketplace. For example, the nation's 284 sprawling metropolitan areas require three times the level of expenditure for transportation as that required by smaller and denser European settlements. Transportation in the United States consumes almost 20 percent of the nation's GDP compared with only 9 percent in Japan. If we spent less on travel, we would have more money for education

and social spending that would improve the nation's competitive position in global trade. As the Asian nations expand trade, they add significant internal urban structures to accommodate growth; as for U.S. cities, they continue to sprawl and create a situation that, according to economists Sklar and Hook, "should be a matter of economic policy concern [because] no other industrialized nation has [such] decentralized employment and allowed cities to deteriorate to the same degree as the United States."[4]

In large measure, houses have fueled the remarkable expansion of the nation's metropolitan areas. Probably no single tax measure in U.S. history has had as profound an impact on development patterns as the mortgage interest deduction for home purchases. This tax break has helped support the largest middle class in the world. As a result, future decisions on how and where we house our growing population are inextricably linked to how and where our cities will grow. Therefore, the third truth is that the course to the future is a retreat to our past. We must somehow find a way to provide a safe and decent inventory of housing that is adequate to house coming generations while reversing the outward movement of housing investment. We must maintain what has been built and stop building more housing

for the few and none for the many. We must build homes rather than houses, neighborhoods rather than subdivisions scattered across the countryside, communities that house people near their work and near shopping and services. We must build communities that embrace diversity rather than exclusiveness. Communities that cannot house their own police and fire forces, teachers and secretaries, busboys and trash collectors are incomplete. They shunt the burden of affordable housing to other communities and reap the benefits of hidden subsidies that support their privilege.

What We Must Do

As the nation ages, the options for housing a growing population will undergo a remarkable transformation. Over the next decades, a substantial proportion of the young population cohort will consist primarily of under-educated minorities with skills suitable only for lower-paying jobs. They will not be able to afford single-family houses on half- to one-acre lots in distant suburbs. What housing will be affordable to such people? What about the millions of far-flung, large-lot homes produced today? We must plan now to produce affordable housing in places close to jobs and existing infra-

---

5-1

Creating a Livable Neighborhood in Baltimore

The Terrace development in Baltimore, pictured in chapter 2, includes both physical elements and socioeconomic programs to address neighborhood needs, including

- a mix of for-sale and rental townhomes of similar appearance;
- inclusion of a business center, retail shop, and community recreation and daycare center;
- recruitment and training of community residents in the construction trades; and
- the new Lexington Terrace Joint Venture, which has organized and manages a community support program, including case assessment and referral services, vocational training, educational services, career counseling and placement, employee assistance programs, daycare services, primary health care services, family support services, recreation and after-school programs, public safety and beautification programs, and housing management programs.

structure systems. We need to find ways to rebuild suburbs to give them a functional future.

More specifically, the first steps in crafting a housing strategy must address dysfunctional practices such as the following:[5]

- large areas zoned for low-density, single-family homes, in part to screen out low-income families;

- minimum house-size requirements, including minimum standards for numbers of rooms, for floor area, and for construction materials, all of which practically guarantee inaffordability for a substantial share of home seekers;

- prohibitions against multifamily or higher-density developments as exercised through zoning standards and "discretionary" permit review procedures;

- restrictions on mobile or manufactured housing, which is viewed as housing for unwanted people;

- high impact fees and other contributions to infrastructure that are calculated to discourage low-cost development;

- building codes that discourage retrofitting and rehabilitation of single-family housing for more efficient use;

- administrative burdens in obtaining project approvals;

- overly restrictive covenants that discourage affordable housing; and

- gated communities that erect walls to social interaction.[6]

The types of design and regulatory tactics identified above are the product of a paranoia over land use. Community residents and their leaders often believe that their community will become a dumping ground for undesirable people and housing. The only way to reverse current beliefs is to devise regional strategies that allocate resources equitably and generate revenues in ways that serve the housing needs of the entire population, not just the middle- to upper-income classes.

Rules for the New Game

The new intellectual and social paradigm for community development requires a set of principles to guide future actions. The ten principles briefly outlined below provide a starting point—admittedly a debatable one—for a way to a better future, one house at a time.

1. Grow from outside in. The national interest in growth issues seems to focus almost entirely on the most desirable form of new suburban building. But the suburbs is not where much of the action should be targeted; instead, it should be directed to "regrowing" existing cities and first-generation suburbs. Using urban structures already in place is less costly and more efficient in the short and long runs than just building better suburbs. Millions of acres of core-city and inner-suburban land are lying idle as a result of social problems, economic disincentives, soil contamination, and the like. The first order of business should be to develop new solutions for city ills before investing still further in creating suburban drains for city vitality. Governments today spend more money on upgrading suburban highways than on the cleanup and redevelopment of existing built environments.

The difficult problems of securing safe and attractive areas for rebuilding in cities are not insurmountable. Private developers in Chicago, New York, and San Francisco have helped create livable communities by constructing affordable, high-quality housing in inner-city developments. Civic will and state and national government support can help make it happen. One strategy calls for expanding tax credits for inner-city housing while removing code and zoning restrictions that limit the range of permissible housing types. Another is wrapping housing within a community development plan that ensures critical improvements in community amenities as new housing is developed. The Playa Vista infill project in Los Angeles (further described in chapter 6) and the conversion of the Presidio in San Francisco are excellent examples of how to plan and build large-scale, multiuse, mixed-housing communities within existing urban settings to achieve sustainable development goals.

2. Good schools make good neighborhoods. Most people understand that much of the flight to the suburbs is a quest for high-quality, safe schools. (Recent events around the nation, however, demonstrate that suburban schools are not immune from problems that seem to travel with the population.) One key to "regrowing" cities is improving older schools in both core cities and older suburbs. Money to upgrade the physical condition of schools is essential, but even more important is improving teachers, book collections, equipment, and, most of all, community expectations for schools. Chicago, Newark, and other cities offer models for success that focus on smaller schools, not just smaller classes. Federal matching funds could help promote the reuse of underused land for smaller schools as well as fund the cleanup of contaminated sites and incorporation of schools into infill and redevelopment projects. State codes should be evaluated to allow more private sector school construction and delivery of education.

However, rebuilding rundown neighborhoods may require more than good design and construction. The Anacostia community in Washington, D.C., once an isolated, dangerous, and dilapidated area, is being revived through the efforts of both for-profit and nonprofit developers who are organizing volunteer and public agency support to re-create a livable community. The William C. Smith Company, for example, has restored 900 rental apartments and is building 210 for-sale townhomes on a 54-acre site previously occupied by 1,400 rundown apartments, 60 percent of them vacant and boarded up. Aided by District of Columbia housing finance programs that make home prices affordable to local residents, and by equity funding from Fannie Mae's American Communities Fund, the townhomes are selling briskly. Even before beginning construction, however, the company fashioned a comprehensive, imaginative program to reestablish the residential values of the neighborhood. First, company staff worked with residents and police to make the area safe, including evicting tenants engaged in illegal activities or who refused to obey resident rules. The developer worked with local school officials and invested over $300,000 in the physical improvement of two local schools. Subsequently, the developer "adopted" five more schools and the local library; for the latter building, the company organized volunteer and staff efforts to relandscape the grounds, paint the building, and enlarge the book collection. Perhaps most impressive was the company's $1 million investment in a Splash Park water-recreation facility for local residents. Now the developer is leading efforts to fund a nonprofit cultural and recreational community center.

3. Regional planning as the backbone for supporting growth. The current crazy quilt of jurisdictions that govern the delivery of urban services is too fragmented to provide a coherent approach to housing or economic development at either the regional or local scale. A fresh

The Townhomes of Oxon Creek, Washington, D.C. With nicely articulated home design, and a vigorous, developer-led campaign to improve schools, recreation facilities, and the local library, the for-sale townhomes are attracting first-time homebuyers back to the Anacostia neighborhood, once a crime-ridden backwater of the District of Columbia.

approach is required to create a regional template for the development process. Regional planning efforts (not regional government, which is virtually unknown in the United States) should allocate commercial, residential, and industrial development within a framework of environmental constraints. Building construction should be promoted where it is needed, not where it is easiest to accomplish.

4. A regional tax structure encouraging "best use." Tax policies steer development. Current forms of taxation based on sales taxes and user fees as well as on property taxes promote forms of development that may meet fiscal criteria but are deficient in creating communities, including most forms of housing. Moreover, taxes on existing properties often treat land as a secondary value, reducing incentives for transfer to higher and better uses. Frequently, for example, a landlord finds it less costly to leave a building vacant than to rent it at rates lower than its presumed "market" rent.

Land should be taxed on the basis of its potential use rather than on its current nonuse or poor use, thus driving more rational uses of land for housing and other purposes.

In addition, states should collect and reallocate sales and similar taxes according to population and job growth rather than according to the point-of-sales mechanism so often employed. Such a policy would help correct the fiscal imbalances and irrational land use patterns caused by competition between jurisdictions for sales tax–generating commercial development. Taxation on land use potential coupled with state-level tax collection and reallocation would begin to make regional development work in favor of better housing for more people.

5. Housing development integrated with overall community development. Few communities have developed housing plans that indicate how different housing types could be designed and interrelated to form livable neighborhoods. Instead, most local officials wait to react to developers' proposals, frequently losing opportunities to link residential development with other housing areas as well as with commercial services and employment areas. What occurs too often is widespread development of certain housing types that age poorly and increasingly fail to serve changing housing needs.

6. Open space as essential green infrastructure in urban development. With few exceptions, the cities we build today lack well-designed open spaces and open-space systems. The deliberate hierarchy of parks and open space linked together throughout London is a major factor in that city's success as an urban living environment. By contrast, most American cities lack comprehensive approaches to providing open space as part of the urban fabric. Cities and suburbs need new breathing spaces that are accessible and functional and that open up developed areas to systems of preserved open spaces that reach throughout a region. In some cases, cities will have to refocus their attention on creating open spaces in already built-up areas. In other cases, cities and suburbs should plan to acquire and require, through the development process, open space for human needs. Open space—green infrastructure—should be considered just as important as any other system of infrastructure in supporting livable communities.

7. Streets that work for people and transit as well as for cars. As our suburban development patterns have shifted from serving people to serving automobiles, we have lost the ability to substitute walking, cycling, and transit for automobile dependence. The magic of the new urbanism's grid street system is that it is more welcoming to nonautomobile forms of travel. Although a strict grid is not an absolute requirement, our travel systems should incorporate sidewalks as a matter of course. They should provide for a network of streets that allow for several choices of access. They should accommodate bus transit through neighborhoods as well as convenient access to nearby rail stations. Such travel systems need not and should not require wide streets but rather more streets, more pathways to important destinations, and narrower and more pleasant streets that act as foci for community interaction.

8. Good-looking, intergenerational buildings. Well-designed buildings last for centuries. As distinctive contributions to livable communities, they are treasured, maintained, restored, and reused for several purposes over time. In too many communities, developers' proposals are treated as potentially interim uses that are expected to be replaced with something else after they wear out. Every community should proclaim design principles that build architectural value into homes and commercial structures. The principles should respect community styles—historic and otherwise—and preferences without stifling creativity. Good buildings make livable, sustainable communities.

9. Jobs as well as houses. Creating good jobs is as important for every community as saving the environment. Without a sound economic base, communities cannot expect to sustain a sensitive environment or maintain neighborhood livability. As communities address the imbalance between jobs and housing and generate adequate-income jobs for all citizens, crime and other social pathologies will decline.

10. Interjurisdictional collaboration to protect the environment. The environment—sensitive lands and features and water, land, and air quality—should not become a battleground over who saves what. Clearly, these features and qualities are protectable only when communities and their leaders adopt a regional or watershed view of the long-term value of natural resources in relation to needed development. With a regional outlook, citizens and policy makers can define and fashion approaches to protect environmental resources. However, a regional outlook requires collaboration between cities and counties and between public agencies and private sector interests. The results of that collaboration can guide the land use actions needed to ensure a sustainable future.

Conclusion

Adequate, affordable housing and livable neighborhoods are essential elements of sustainable growth. If we do not learn how to develop housing that reflects the hopes and aspirations of all Americans, we will continue our downward spiral toward an unequal and divided society. To house an increasingly diverse citizenry and to restore and sustain our communities, we need a new set of rules to guide development at both the regional and local levels.

Endnotes

1 This chapter was adapted from a presentation by Professor Edward J. Blakely at the conference, "Housing in the 21st Century," sponsored by the Urban Land Institute on March 29, 2000, in Washington, DC.

2 Executive Order No. 12898, signed by President Bill Clinton, February 11, 1994.

3 Thomas Vietorisz, William Goldsmith, and Joseph Grengs, "Air Quality, Urban Form and Coordinated Urban Policies," Working Paper No. 176, Cornell University Department of City and Regional Planning, June 1998.

4 Elliott Sklar and Walter Hook, "The Importance of Cities to the National Economy," *Interwoven Destinies: Cities and the Nation.* Henry Cisneros, ed. (New York: W.W. Norton, 1993).

5 This list was adapted from Vietorisz, Goldsmith, and Grengs, Working Paper No. 176.

6 For more discussion on this subject, see Edward J. Blakely and Mary G. Snyder, *Fortress America* (Washington, DC: Brookings Institution, 1997.)

SITE DEVELOPMENT PRACTICES
CREATING SUSTAINABLE AND PROFITABLE DEVELOPMENTS

Douglas R. Porter with Tom Cahill and Rolf Sauer

The preceding chapters describe the key principles that frame the context for achieving sustainable communities. The principles are summarized as follows:

- Use land wisely to minimize development impacts on land, water, energy, and other natural resources and to protect regional natural resources and environments that help sustain urban economies and societies.

- Weave a network of natural spaces throughout the urban and urbanizing fabric of developing communities to conserve valued natural resources and environments and to provide opportunities for human appreciation of and benefit from such features.

- Maintain and expand infrastructure systems cost effectively.

- Promote sustainable forms of economic activity and social interaction and advancement that satisfy the diverse needs and desires of community residents.

- Recognize and value, through modified real estate financing practices, the long-term nature of sustainable real estate investments.

This chapter narrows the focus from communitywide aspects of sustainability to the ways developers can apply the above principles to making decisions about the location, components, design, and community relationships of specific developments.

Human beings have long used ecological principles to design their habitats. The Greeks pioneered passive solar architecture, the Romans and Phoenicians used thermal mass to regulate temperature, and the desert cultures of the Middle East and pre-Columbian western America built structures that achieved natural ventilation and cooling. During the industrial revolution, however, society discarded many of the techniques for working in cooperation with nature. Increasingly, site and building designs depended on technological means to augment or even replace reliance on natural processes. In these circumstances,

living and working spaces lost their connection with the surrounding natural environment and even isolated their occupants from nature. Accordingly, site development and building construction came to consume enormous quantities of resources while the activities they set in motion consumed extravagant amounts of energy and disgorged large volumes of waste.

By contrast, the message of sustainable development is that economic growth fueled by increased consumption, especially of nonrenewable resources, cannot continue indefinitely. The challenge for developers is to find ways to adapt to changing expectations for reduced resource consumption. In fact, developers can promote sustainable development by pursuing a real-world process that integrates the built environment with the natural environment and that uses modern technology to enhance traditional development approaches. Yet, an emphasis on sustainable qualities of development need not require developers to sacrifice profitability. Applying the principles of sustainability in imaginative ways can yield competitive advantages in development costs and market acceptance.

This chapter describes site development practices that offer opportunities for meeting sustainability goals while satisfying investment objectives. However, many of the practices represent innovative and therefore potentially more risky approaches than typical designs and forms of development. Developers attempting to introduce unconventional technologies or designs should not expect ready acceptance by lenders, public regulators, or even consumers. Furthermore, developers must be prepared to compete in regional markets where conventional projects generate relatively little resistance. Even so, many sustainable development practices have proven successful in completed and profitable projects. And, as discussed in the next section, it appears that sustainable practices can appeal to many consumers, providing a marketing edge for developments that incorporate such practices.

Throughout the chapter, sustainable practices are described in terms that demonstrate their contribution to sustainable development, compare their advantages and disadvantages in relation to conventional practices, and assess the short- and long-range investment values of such practices for both developers and consumers.

The Market for Sustainable Development

Developers depend for their livelihood on accurately identifying and satisfying consumers' needs and desires. Many have been able to carve out special niche markets that respond to particular forms of development—from seniors' housing and artists' lofts to entertainment complexes and boutique hotels. Among niche markets are groups of consumers who crave features and forms of devel-

opment that promote sustainability. Such consumers include those who support sustainable development based on personal belief and others who enjoy the distinctive features that characterize sustainable development. They also include a host of consumers whose lifestyle and household needs vary from the norm as well as consumers with a growing awareness of the long-term investment value of sustainable development. John Laswick, the city of Tucson's project manager for Civano, Arizona, a 1,200-acre master-planned community under development according to sustainability principles, says, "We have found that our development has been attracting a substantial market share that appreciates the sustainable features of Civano."[1]

Surveys have found that a sizable share of the consumer market believes in sustainability principles and seeks products that promote sustainability. A 1996 study by American LIVES, Inc., a San Francisco–based market research firm, indicated that about 24 percent of the U.S. population, or about 44 million Americans, can be described as "cultural creatives" who support the ideals of ecological sustainability and value globalism, altruism, spirituality, a social conscience, women's advancement, and optimism. The cultural creatives comprise a market segment previously undefined and untargeted by the real estate industry. Another American LIVES, Inc., study found that 77 percent of Americans support the principles of sustainability.[2] In addition, surveys conducted for the public utility industry by American LIVES showed that 75 percent of respondents would be willing to pay somewhat more for electric power if the sources of that power were cleaner than coal. In fact, one survey found that 71 percent of respondents would pay up to 20 percent more for electricity generated by nonpolluting and renewable energy sources.[3]

Americans are also attracted by historically and architecturally interesting buildings and areas. Many older parts of cities and towns are undergoing revitalization as consumers increasingly appreciate distinctive urban living and working spaces. In places as varied as Portland, Oregon; Peoria, Illinois; and Baltimore, Maryland, old and often vacant industrial and warehouse buildings are being refitted for residences, shops, and offices. Adapting existing buildings for new uses brings life to older sections of cities, effectively recycling and thereby sustaining the built environment.

The traditional community designs of the new urbanism, which respond to many of the principles of sustainable development, have gained the support of governments, environmentalists, and the marketplace. According to a 1994 survey of the Tucson, Arizona, market by Market Perspectives of Sacramento, 83 percent of respondents found great appeal in the concept of traditional neighborhood development. Three-quarters of respondents said they would like to be able to walk to retail and other local destinations, thereby reducing daily automobile trips per household and mitigating traffic impacts on air quality.[4]

A 1998 survey of community preferences by American LIVES found that homebuyers were most interested in features such as smaller parks and green spaces located throughout the community. According to the survey:

> Most of the features buyers want involve making little improvements to the land. Items like natural open space, walking paths, and sidewalks are at the top of the importance list. These were the same items topping the list in 1994 and appeal to all respondents in this study, no matter what type of home they bought or what kind of community they live in.[5]

The evolving marketplace also reflects the widening diversity of households that can neither afford nor need the one-size-fits-all suburban tract house. According to U.S. census statistics, only one-quarter of current households fit the supposed "norm" of two married adults and two children, and in only 13 percent of households does a spouse stay home with the children.[6] Projections show a continuing increase in the share of the U.S. population that lives alone, or as a married couple or unrelated adults, or as a single-adult family with children. In fact, "nonfamily" households, which are defined as persons living alone or with nonrelatives, now account for 31 percent of all households.[7]

The U.S. population is also growing older. The baby boomers born in the 1940s and 1950s are approaching retirement age. Many of them are more attracted by the availability of affordable housing in an interesting neighborhood than by large houses in the suburbs. Young adults and retirees, in particular, appear more willing to trade off expansive lawns and access to regional shopping centers for urban amenities such as proximity to cultural and entertainment activities. In describing this phenomenon, a recent analysis of central-city housing markets quotes William Whyte's classic essay "Are Cities Un-American?":

> The people who choose the city, in sum, are of many different kinds, but they have one thing in common: they *like* the city. They like the privacy, they like the specialization, and the hundreds of one-of-the-kind shops; they like the excitement—to some, the sirens at night are music—they like the heterogeneity, the contrasts, the mixture of odd people.[8]

These attractions seem to be borne out by recent trends that show large-city

gains in home construction during the 1990s. A Brookings Institution analysis of housing construction patterns concludes that "despite the dominance of suburban home building, large cities experienced rapid gains in new housing construction between 1991 and 1998. The number of new housing permits in large cities more than doubled . . . , growing at a faster rate than that of suburbs and metropolitan areas in general."[9]

In 1999, the National Association of Home Builders (NAHB) conducted a survey of 2,000 randomly selected households and found that most disliked the idea of building higher-density housing in their neighborhoods and that 83 percent would choose to buy a detached home in a suburban area rather than a townhouse in an urban area. However, the other side of the ledger revealed the growing diversity of housing demand: 17 percent would prefer a townhouse in an urban area, and 32 percent would support the building of townhouses in their neighborhoods. (The results do not expressly identify the education and safety concerns that respondents may have reflected in their desires for suburban living styles.)[10]

Another survey by American LIVES, Inc., in 1995 sampled consumers who had shopped for or bought homes in large-scale planned communities. It found that 44 percent approved of a mix of housing for all types and ages of residents in the neighborhood. After analyzing the study results, authors Brooke H. Warrick and Paul Ray determined that over 20 percent favored the close-knit community design advocated by new urbanist designers, including higher densities, foot access to a town center and community gathering places, and the availability of public transit.[11] Results of both the NAHB and American LIVES surveys indicate that a significant market exists for neighborhoods that embody the goals of sustainability.

Niche markets are willing to pay more to live in communities that incorporate aspects of sustainability. Studies published in 1999 that examined purchase prices of new urbanist projects compared with nearby conventional projects in suburban areas found that homes in new urbanist environments were selling for price premiums up to 15 percent and that resale values were higher.[12]

Other surveys indicate that homebuyers are generally willing to pay more for projects where developers or builders stress an environmental theme. A 1997 study by Permar & Ravenel, Inc., showed that price premiums for frontage on lagoons and marshes in coastal golf-oriented developments were as high or higher than frontage on golf courses. Whereas interior lot prices averaged $92,000, lots with lagoon and fairway frontage averaged $101,000; lots with marsh frontage were priced at an average of $225,000 while water-frontage lots averaged $467,000. These types of price increases are typical of resort communities as documented by ULI's *Resort Development Handbook*. Environmental amenities such as cycle and walking trails and wildlife or forest preserves also attract buyers. The developer of High Desert, a 1,000-acre master-planned community in Albuquerque, New Mexico, for example, estimates that the project's location adjacent to the 8,000-acre Cibola National Forest, as well as a landscape design that minimized environmental impacts, dramatically enhanced lot sales and prices. Of the 79 lots listed in the first phase of development, 63 sold at prices 20 to 50 percent higher than the area's average. By 1998, about one-third of the planned 2,250 homes were built, with prices for homes at four to eight units per acre ranging from $160,000 to $650,000.[13]

It appears, therefore, that developers who incorporate sustainable features into their projects can tap consumer markets that heretofore have largely gone ignored. Moreover, as the principles of sustainability become more widely known and appreciated and developers learn to integrate sustainable features into development designs and marketing, we can expect an expanding market for sustainable development.

From Greenfields to Brownfields: A Range of Sustainable Approaches

Although sustainable development is a marketable commodity in general, developers of new projects must still identify specific strategies for applying sustainability principles that will spark the interest of consumers. For example, some professional land planners and designers, conservationists, and engineers have addressed sustainability by reconfiguring conventional designs for suburban "greenfield" developments. Increasingly, their plans for mid- to large-scale developments propose to cluster development within settings that respect the natural assets of a development site. Site designs emphasize conservation and restoration of landscape features (such as native vegetation, wildlife habitats, stream valleys, and terrain attributes) and recognition of natural hydrologic functions (including management of water supply, wastewater collection and treatment, and stormwater). The teachings of Ian McHarg and Randall Arendt, in particular, have inspired many designers to plan suburban and rural developments that function in close partnership with natural features.[14]

Still focusing primarily on reforming suburban development patterns, other designers have proposed a return to models of traditional neighborhood design (TND) and transit-oriented development (TOD)—both of which are combined in new urbanism notions of community development. TND and TOD revive older patterns of close-knit development that use land more conservatively and thereby preserve open space. They cluster a mix of housing types around community and neighborhood centers that enhance opportunities for social interaction and accommodate travel by means other than the automobile. Both TND and TOD respond to concerns for sustainable development but tend to focus primarily on creating livable built environments rather than on conserving natural resources.[15]

More and more developers have been attracted to infill and redevelopment projects in urbanized areas. Typical project areas, which might be termed infields as opposed to greenfields, include central business districts and their environs, business districts in older neighborhoods and suburbs, established residential areas, and former industrial sites. Many developers can point to demonstrated experience in reinventing and retrofitting the existing urban fabric—whether through adaptive use of historic or architecturally distinctive buildings, cleanup and redevelopment of contaminated brownfield sites, or development of vacant or underused sites. By recycling existing buildings and urban sites, making more intensive use of existing infrastructure systems, and revitalizing declining employment centers and neighborhoods, infields development makes important contributions to sustainable development.

All the above approaches to sustainable development are underscored by the smart growth principles championed by many community planners and designers. As observed in chapter 1, smart growth principles are general but seek, first, to direct more development to existing urbanized areas where infrastructure is already in place or can be readily extended and, second, to promote more sustainable forms of suburban development from the standpoints of efficient use of resources, optimization of public and private investments, and community livability. Smart growth advocates envision community development at somewhat higher overall densities than those associated with typical suburban development or with the nature-respecting development patterns espoused by many conservation-minded designers.

Traditional residential design in Prairie Crossing, Grayslake, Illinois.

Here is the conundrum: Advocates of sustainable development are divided on the issue of reconciling conservation of natural areas with compact development. Do we favor limited development within a setting of conserved and restored natural features that generally results in overall low densities, or do we favor higher-density development that is served by urban infrastructure and depends on conservation of extensive open spaces outside urban areas? The first approach—designing resource-sensitive but generally low-density development—appears most appropriate for small, isolated developments in rural areas. In the case of development in growing urban areas, however, the spread-out form of nature-respecting development would only continue to push suburban settlements into the countryside. The second approach assumes that natural resource losses within densely developed urban areas can be mitigated or offset by a combination of improved technologies and resource conservation within the urban setting and by greater protection and restoration of resources outside urban areas. Instead of attempting to balance all the needs of man and nature within individual sites, the second approach seeks a sustainable balance of compact urban development and resource conservation within a region or watershed. It must be observed that neither model takes adequate account of inevitable changes in the form and density of development as urban areas grow larger. And neither model offers a foolproof solution to achieving sustainable community—or project—development.

In their 1999 publication, *Sustainability and Cities,* Newman and Kenworthy discuss how the conflict between the two approaches is playing out among supporters of sustainable development. One camp is guided by the "rural commons" concept, which proclaims that "cities are too big and need to be broken down into little pieces that should

be substantially self-sufficient."[16] In other words, the best way to improve the environment and achieve livable cities is to create large lots that would permit local cultivation of food and trees; in addition, most work, recreation, and social interaction would occur locally as well. Cooperative ventures would provide for sharing food production, water and solar power, urban forest management, and the like. Advocates of the rural commons concept abhor density. Newman and Kenworthy, however, point to an important flaw in the self-sufficiency approach: it would maintain dependence on the automobile.

The other camp has adopted the "urban commons" concept, which views the city as a system that should "become more urban, not less, and rebuilt from within."[17] Not only would "urban commons" development reduce today's dependence on the automobile, but it could also foster innovative approaches to "greening the city" with greenways, urban forests, and even some agriculture and linked water/habitat/recreation systems. Newman and Kenworthy nonetheless suggest that the advocates of the urban commons approach seem to ignore the fact that compact, highly interactive, walkable centers of civilization such as central Paris or downtown Portland, Oregon, cannot be created in the absence of concentrations of impervious surfaces, some degree of river channelization, and considerable dependence on piped water supply and wastewater collection. A green infrastructure of trees, open spaces, streams, and ponds, along with protection of rural open spaces, will certainly offset some impacts of urban commons development, but not the full range of impacts.

Newman and Kenworthy observe that the supporters of the two opposing concepts of sustainability are engaged in continuing conflicts about how to make urban

areas more ecologically sensitive and sustainable. The plan for the acclaimed Coffee Creek Center development next to Chesterton, Indiana, shown in figure 6-1, demonstrates the interplay of pro-environmental and prourbanist tensions. Designed by ecologically minded William McDonough and developed by the Lake Erie Land Company (a subsidiary of a deep-pockets power utility), the 640-acre Coffee Creek Center will contain 1,200 residences and at least a million square feet of office and retail space. The new urbanist plan combines a modified grid street system with neighborhood greens and a mixed-use town center and employment district. A prominent feature is a 240-acre swath of parkland along the creek, including existing and constructed wetlands, restored prairie lands, and cycle and walking trails. The riparian corridor will handle stormwater runoff and wastewater treatment as well as provide a central open space for recreation.

The proenvironmental/prourbanist tensions relate to the site's locational attributes and design. On the one hand, the site is 50 miles east of Chicago in the Indiana Dunes, giving rise to issues of traffic generation and costs of new infrastructure. On the other hand, the relatively low land costs permit more attention to the protection of natural assets. Conservation of the central, natural corridor locates open space near most residents yet makes the town center less accessible to neighborhoods on the other side of the creek. Another developer concerned with building a walkable community might have placed the town center nearer the creek and added more creek crossings, but Kevin Warren, a project spokesperson, observes, "I don't see sustainability and new urbanism always hand in hand. There clearly are cases where a compromise must be struck."[18]

For developers, sustainability issues such as those outlined above must be resolved in practical ways as projects are concep-

Coffee Creek Center, near Chesterton, Indiana

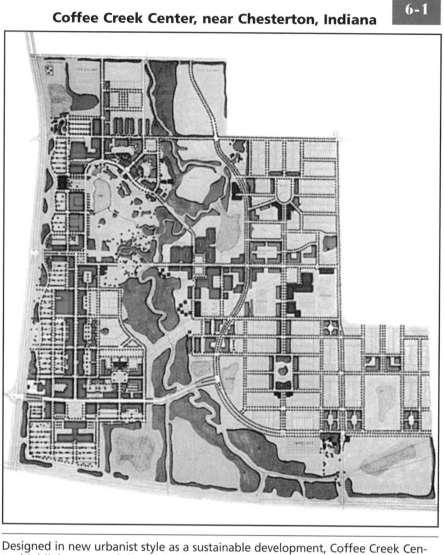

Designed in new urbanist style as a sustainable development, Coffee Creek Center highlights some of the tradeoffs often required between conservation and development.

At the other end of the scale, developers of lower-density suburban or small-town projects, business parks, and large planned communities usually can maintain and restore a site's natural features, particularly its hydrologic properties, and thus provide some needed infrastructure functions (such as storm drainage and wastewater treatment) while creating an attractive and beneficial setting for development.

Midway on the spectrum, we can imagine development of a 200-unit residential subdivision or a neighborhood shopping center that incorporates some elements of high and low levels of density, depending on the character and context of the site and the proposed development. At the mid-level scale of development, for example, some on-site aspects of landscape or hydrologic systems can be conserved while creating land- and energy-saving forms of development. Tolman Creek Shopping Center in Ashland, Oregon, a 94,500-square-foot neighborhood center, preserved existing trees, a stream, and bird habitat; reduced parking by providing bicycle and pedestrian access; and saved $40,000 a year in energy costs through energy-efficient design.

Clearly, the science and art of sustainable development is still evolving. The following section discusses a range of appropriate techniques for sustainable lower-density projects.

Sustainable Systems of Site Development

Potential development sites are often perceived as simply "the ground" upon which construction occurs. However, wise developers and their professional advisers recognize a site's inherent values and features when contemplating a plan for a new project. They begin by analyzing site conditions and aspects of the to-be-built environment that will affect or be affected by the magnitude

tualized. The character of a specific project—its building components, uses, overall density, and intended market—will define the demand for land, infrastructure, and amenities. A site's location in the region and community, its natural features, and the surrounding built or natural environment will suggest opportunities for leveraging site assets while limiting the magnitude of the development. High-density infill developments on small sites, for example, most likely will connect to existing infrastructure systems rather than attempt to meet water, sewer, and drainage needs independently. Infill developments must also

be designed to blend compatibly with adjacent development and thus encourage social and economic interactions with the neighborhood and community. Generally, in the case of infill projects, opportunities for restoring the natural landscape will be minimal and even antithetical to the concept of retrofitting development within compact communities. Developers can, however, integrate green building techniques into all their projects by, for example, adopting methods that conserve energy, improve air quality, and reduce impervious surfaces, as demonstrated in many of the examples cited in the next chapter.

and character of the proposed development. Frequently, developers conduct the needed analyses by ticking off a mental checklist as they consider how a development idea might fit a potential development site. The following, from ULI's *Real Estate Development: Principles and Process,* describes this process:

> While generating development ideas might often be thought of as unpredictable and intuitive, [the process] is just as frequently methodical and calculated. Developers need to *plan* future projects to keep their firms in business. Successful developers are rigorous in their planning but not so regimented as to lose the creative spark.[19]

Developer James J. Chaffin, Jr., offered the following description of his approach to conceptualizing the Spring Island golf/residential community:

> When I visited the island for the first time . . . , I was awed by its beauty and so frustrated to know that the original developer had approvals to build 5,500 homes on the island, that when the developer couldn't fulfill his options, we decided to grab it.[20]

In moving ahead with Spring Island, Chaffin operated from his "knowledge of the market and gut feeling." He set out to produce a high-quality project that would be sustainable and ecologically sound and provide an example for other developers.

Developers may formulate the overall development concept for a site—sometimes almost instantaneously—but their consultants are usually charged with the task of exploring the technical aspects of site conditions and devising preliminary designs. Consultants should consider all natural and human-made factors as a series of systems that intersect both on the site and with surrounding areas. Figure 6-2 on the next page highlights the natural and human systems that could be guided by sustainable principles.

Clearly, the systems are closely interrelated and cannot be analyzed individually in a vacuum. Moreover, on-site systems connect physically and functionally with systems beyond the site—whether immediately adjacent to the site, across the community at large, or even at the level of watersheds and ecosystems. The significance and interrelationship of systems vary from site to site and location to location. Large, master-planned communities on the outskirts of urban areas demand a comprehensive understanding of interlocking infrastructure systems supportive of the development planned for the site. At the other end of the scale, a small development at the edge of or within an urbanizing area, even with a mix of uses, depends on linkages to existing infrastructure and must be compatible with surrounding development.

Capturing the various interrelationships and connections is essential to building sustainable developments. An approach sometimes called "whole-systems thinking" or holistic design helps optimize the incorporation of sustainable features into planned developments while maximizing the benefits that make sustainability a worthwhile investment. The key to the approach is defining development and design solutions that, through tradeoffs and multiple benefits, address an array of problems. One such solution is designing narrower streets that reduce stormwater runoff and allow the use of infiltration swales rather than costly storm sewers, thereby creating more space for trees and walkways—amenities attractive to homebuyers.

Whole-systems thinking requires the simultaneous consideration of many eco-nomic, design, and regulatory elements at the outset of project conceptualization and planning, not after major decisions have been made. Thinking through the technical options and how they will interact both during and after construction may require more upfront investment in design, but that investment is likely to be repaid in long-term benefits. In retrofitting a 1970s suburban office building, for example, the design team for Continental Offices, Ltd., could not justify upgrading the mechanical systems unless it also upgraded the lighting system and improved the building's energy management devices. Continental's initial costs of retrofit were 8 percent greater than for a conventional renovation, but its energy costs dropped by 81 percent, substantially increasing the building's value. Similarly, many elements of environmentally sensitive design and green building have a higher initial cost than conventional development but frequently offer operational (life-cycle) cost savings that more than offset initial costs.

Sometimes the relationships are not obvious. Borrowing the marketing concept of "loss leaders," developers such as the Grossman Family Properties at Hidden Springs, Idaho, subsidized rents for the village center in order to sell homes more quickly and at higher prices and to cut vehicle trips. The developer further reduced the risk associated with its pioneering project by adding community amenities not offered by the competition.

Finally, incorporating sustainable features into a project can shorten the project approval process, thereby limiting risk and increasing return. Many of the most notable sustainable developments, such as Playa Vista and Prairie Crossing, were originally planned as traditional developments. After running into approval roadblocks at every turn, the communities were redesigned with sustainability principles in mind—protecting and restoring natural features

NATURAL SYSTEMS
CONDITIONS AND OPPORTUNITIES

Landscape
- Topography/Terrain
- Soils/Geology
- Vegetation/Species/Habitats
- Water Features

Hydrology
- Precipitation
- Surface Water Flows
- Water Quality
- Water Table and Aquifers
- Soil Filtration Characteristics

Energy Resources
- Availability of Renewable Energy Resources

Air Quality
- Ambient Air Quality
- On-Site Toxics (indoor air)

HUMAN SYSTEMS
CONDITIONS AND OPPORTUNITIES

Development
- Mix of Uses and Activities
- Intensity of Development
- Historic and Distinctive Buildings and Areas

Supportive Infrastructure
- Transportation Modes and Networks
- Water, Sewer, Drainage
- Community Facilities (e.g., schools and parks)

Economic Activities
- On-Site Employment
- Retail and Business Services
- Use of Natural Resources
- Proximity to Other Employment

Social Infrastructure
- Access to Health, Education, Other Services
- Social Interactions and Connections
- Recreational and Leisure-Time Activities
- Cultural and Religious Institutions

DECISION-MAKING PROCESS FOR LOCATION, SCALE, CHARACTER, DESIGN, AND FEASIBILITY

DEVELOPMENT PROJECT SYSTEMS: PRODUCT OF HOLISTIC DESIGN
Building and Use Patterns and Relationships
Transportation Choices
Water, Wastewater, Drainage Infrastructure
Open-Space Patterns and Uses (Green Infrastructure)
Other Community Facilities and Amenities
Place-Making Design Attributes
Incentives for Social and Economic Advancement
Resource-Conserving Building Designs, Materials, and Equipment
Recycling of Existing Buildings and Brownfields

and introducing energy-efficient design. Opponents of conventional development apparently are willing to back sustainable developments that offer superior products and greater conservation of resources.

This chapter focuses on major systems that form the building blocks of sustainable development: landscape, hydrology, the built environment, and economic and social interactions. The next chapter addresses the specific elements of green buildings, including energy, materials, and adaptable use of existing buildings.

Preserving and Restoring the Landscape: Developing Green Infrastructure

Developing a parcel of land—whether farmland, virgin woodland, or a former industrial site—requires a certain amount of disturbance to the landscape and associated water-related systems. In the past, development of greenfield sites sometimes meant a total reshaping of the landscape to meet the perceived needs for building. The result was a huge expense for earthmoving, destruction of the soil mantle, the loss of soil permeability for groundwater recharge, obliteration of topographic features and vegetation, and damage to streams and wildlife habitats. Some land developers refer to the practice of reshaping the landscape as "manufacturing sites"; some environmentalists call it "landscraping." The design of conventional suburban landscapes, for example, often calls for wide, treeless streets and large lawns. Shaping the terrain for such development disrupts existing natural systems while the resultant streets and unshaded lawns raise ambient temperatures as much as ten degrees above those in surrounding natural areas. In addition, the amounts of energy, both fossil fuel and human, used for lawn maintenance are usually much greater than the resources required for landscape management of meadows and woodlands.

Development regulations in many communities now tend to reduce the damage from such practices, but developers can still contribute to sustainability by preserving and even restoring landscape features as an integral part of their developments. After all, the natural terrain, native plant communities, and hydrologic patterns found on a site typically represent the fullest and most efficient use of natural resources. It is usually more expensive to disturb natural systems through extensive grading, drainage piping, and relandscaping with high-maintenance lawns than to acknowledge a site's natural functions and integrate them into a proposed design. For many sites, in fact, land development can be viewed as an opportunity to restore and enhance a site's natural vitality as well as that of the surrounding environmental community. At the same time, natural features command price premiums and result in a more marketable development.

[An excellent source of ideas and guidelines for protecting trees during construction has been prepared by the National Association of Home Builders and the American Forests organization. Entitled *Building Greener Neighborhoods: Trees as Part of the Plan*, it is available from American Forests, P.O. Box 2000, Washington, D.C. 20013 (202-955-4500).]

Developers should also consider that their projects will become part of the regional and local ecosystems within which they are built. Therefore, developers should design their projects to be as least disruptive to such ecosystems as possible. Identifying and understanding the natural systems functioning on a site as fragments or connections to larger systems will lead to design strategies that conserve functioning systems and heal damaged systems.

Landscape elements can be viewed as the "green infrastructure" of a develop-

ment that is just as important to future occupants as the traditional infrastructure of streets, drainage lines, schools, and so forth. In addition, by integrating natural and cultural resources into site design, developers can preserve and enhance the "uniqueness of place."

An example of the extent to which natural systems can be interwoven with human needs both on and off the site is the development plan for a 280-acre campus in Monroe, Michigan. A religious order wanted to consider an ecologically sound development plan that would sustain the order and promote both spirituality and ecological health. Beyond renovating existing facilities for elder care and creating a sustainability institute, the plan calls for developing agricultural fields into a community-supported agriculture and organic gardening operation intended to supply healthy fruits and vegetables to the order and the surrounding community. The plan also provides for on-site composting of wastes, preservation of existing woodlands, and conversion of many acres of lawn to meadows. A proposed ecovillage would house and train participants in the facility's agricultural and food processing operations. A handicapped-accessible path system would allow elderly residents to tour the preserved open space, meadows, and agricultural fields as a part of their living experience on the campus. Thus, the campus is designed to perpetuate valuable natural features while expanding human use of the site.

To accommodate the continued functioning of natural features during and after construction, an inventory of site features allows developers and their consultants to become familiar with a site's natural assets and understand their interrelationships. The process advanced by Ian McHarg in the 1960s synthesizes scientific information and mapped overlays of site features to determine areas in need of conservation and protection.[21]

Design professionals have widely adopted McHarg's system as a starting point in the development process for identifying and understanding natural features.

Designers of large-scale planned communities have been employing McHarg's approach for decades—conducting site analyses of natural resources and features, designating sensitive areas for conservation, and identifying features that can add to the attractiveness of a proposed development. To be most sustainable, the functional areas of a proposed development—buildings, roads, and parking—should be adapted to the given landscape patterns. In other words, the "green infrastructure" system becomes part of the overall infrastructure of site development.

The Woodlands master-planned community outside Houston is a notable example that directly involved McHarg himself. The comprehensive ecological inventory of the 25,000-acre site included scientific examinations of the site's geology, subsurface and surface hydrology, limnology, soils, plant ecology, wildlife, and climatology. The inventory revealed that a high percent of the site's soils were poorly drained and that local streams experienced low base flows and high peak flows, resulting in extensive and shallow floodplains. Once the design team understood that conventional development patterns would reduce groundwater recharge, generate land subsidence from lowered water tables, and increase downstream flooding, it focused the site planning effort on both protecting permeable soils to reduce runoff and erosion and protecting natural vegetation and wildlife habitats. The general plan for the Woodlands therefore preserved stream corridors and other ecologically valuable areas, called for the construction of major roads on ridge lines away from drainage areas, clustered higher-density development on impermeable soils near roads, and used minor residential streets as berms

to impede water flow over excessively permeable soils.

Elaborate studies also determined degrees of permissible site clearing and coverage for each soil type to maintain the water balance. For the pilot development phase, grassed and planted trenches, swales, and berms collected runoff and encouraged groundwater recharge. As development has proceeded (10,000 acres have been developed), wetlands mitigation efforts have established natural reserves of uplands, natural wetlands, and constructed wetlands. In his recently published autobiography *A Quest for Life*, McHarg identifies the plan for the Woodlands as one of his "proudest accomplishments."[22]

Even small subdivisions can benefit from a landscape evaluation that defines sensitive areas in need of special treatment as well as natural qualities that can add interest to the future residential setting. Except for the occasional large parcel, infill sites are less likely to retain significant natural features, and/or the density of proposed development may limit opportunities for conservation of open lands. Even on these sites, however, some landscape qualities (terrain, stands of trees, surface water drainage ways, and so forth), small parks, or other "special places" can be accommodated within the development.

The following guidelines suggest an approach to sustainable landscape design for both large and small sites:

- Respect the existing natural landforms and landscape features; understand the historic and current ecosystem, its natural processes, and the stresses that adjacent development place on it.

- To the degree possible, take advantage of a site's natural assets by preserving the existing landforms and vegetation that define its natural structure and character.

- Create landscapes that can be sustained as a permanent, ongoing natural environment, plan to restore the site's landscape character and vegetative palette, and use native plant species that require as little water and maintenance as possible for those portions of the site that will remain undeveloped or be designed as natural open space.

- Refrain from breaking up or promoting intrusion into contiguous expanses of sensitive habitats and wildlife movement corridors, especially those of threatened or endangered species.

- Avoid construction in washes and other watercourses.

- Ensure that landscape improvements enhance the daily life of residents and workers; landscapes should define spaces, create places for varied activities, and reinforce the expression of relationships between buildings and landforms.

Reinventing the landscape. In many cases, landscape-sensitive designs for development can connect fragments of and/or restore natural site systems. Reconnecting landscape fragments establishes networks both within and beyond the site by taking advantage of the natural succession of landscapes and plant communities. For example, restoring the drainage network on a site and allowing swales and stream corridors to reestablish woody vegetation along their length can reconnect forested fragments along watercourses to adjacent woodlands. Introducing meadow buffers along hedgerows or woodland edges also provides habitat areas for wildlife and allows woodland vegetation to expand over time. On disturbed sites, establishing meadows instead of lawns can foster a higher level of natural diversity and can lend itself to more economical management.

The primary maintenance task in managing natural vegetation is to limit the proliferation of exotic, or nonnative, invasive vegetation. Japanese bamboo, kudzu, Japanese honeysuckle, and the Norway maple are examples of invasive plants that can overwhelm native plant communities.

In his new book, *The Nature of Reston*, developer/photographer Charles Veatch demonstrates how this approach succeeded in the new town of Reston, Virginia, which was planned in the 1960s but is still developing. Reston's planners clustered development to preserve natural areas but also created lakes and streams, reforested pasturelands, and built woodland trails. Residents of Reston have extended the surrounding intact elements of nature into their gardens, restoring and enhancing native vegetation. Today, Reston's natural environment is a robust example of Virginia's natural landscapes. Says Veatch, "Reston's principles [can] be followed on a smaller scale by other enlightened developers and builders who will go to the effort of setting houses into existing hills instead of grading the land flat, keeping and protecting mature trees, and planting natural landscapes that then give home-owners a framework for their own naturalistic gardens."[23]

In several developments of recent vintage, developers have carefully removed and stored trees for later replanting. The Civano project in Tucson, Arizona, for example, salvaged 3,000 cactus and other plants that were used in landscaping completed sites.[24]

If clearance, landfills, roads, and other activities have already disturbed portions of a site, it is often advisable to develop those areas first rather than further disturb the site's natural systems. Even sites that have been extensively disturbed, however, may evidence a few remaining fragments of natural landscape. To

Before restoring landscape features. Decrepit parkway edges and old cycle paths along a heavily traveled highway in Brooklyn, New York. Compaction, dumping, and neglect were damaging adjacent shoreline habitats.

After restoring landscape features. Six miles of parkway, with a new protective guard rail, was planted back into shoreline meadows and incorporates a renovated cycle path. [Landscape Architects: Andropogon Associates, Ltd.; Project Director: Rolf Sauer.]

develop a better understanding of how the site functioned before it was disturbed, design professionals might be able to deduce the profile of the original landscape by analyzing the remaining landscape of adjacent sites or undertaking a historical review based on old photographs or surveys of the site. In some cases, regrading can restore the original topography (assuming no extensive landfills injurious to plant growth), and existing drainage pipes can be removed to reintroduce surface water flow and infiltration. Restored landform and drainage can create a better foundation for reestablishing a sustainable natural system of plant communities.

The development underway on Tryon Farm in Michigan City, Indiana, demonstrates how landscape features can be restored to foster a more sustainable natural environment and, at the same time, provide a beneficial setting for new homeowners. Developer/designer Tom Forman of Chicago Associates proposed to develop an environmentally sensitive residential project on a dairy farm in the urbanizing suburban area of Michigan City, which is the terminus for the electric interurban trains that run into Chicago and South Bend.

Forman began with a landscape analysis that not only identified existing features but also probed historical records to determine earlier landscapes disturbed by the century-old farm. The site evaluation revealed 30-foot-high dunes thick with oak, maple, pine, and beech trees, some over six feet in circumference. It also identified wetlands and former prairie areas. Forman organized the residential development plan around these features, renewing the wetlands to function as wastewater treatment areas, restoring the prairie habitat for migratory birds and ground animals, retaining major wooded areas, and setting aside pastures for continued farming—120 acres in total. The plan also calls for restoration of the century-old farmhouse and construction of 150 houses, lofts, and cabins in eight clusters occupying about 160 acres. As of early 2000, of the 18 units in the first phase, 14 sold quickly and work has begun on a second phase.

The developer leveraged benefits from the conserved farmland by entering into a barter agreement with an adjoining horse stable—free pastures for free rides—while the croplands planted with alfalfa and sorghum are maintained by the grandson of the dairy farmer in return for crop profits. The developer also struck a bargain with the U.S. Fish and Wildlife Service to underwrite most of the costs of restor-

Tryon Farm at Michigan City, Indiana. The development of Tryon Farm features clusters of housing among farmlands, woodlands, and restored prairie, plus use of constructed wetlands for wastewater treatment.

ing three wetlands in exchange for cooperating in the mitigation program. In addition, Michigan City is helping to fund the restoration of two wetlands in order to solve mitigation problems associated with other sites.[25]

Respecting the Hydrologic Cycle to Achieve Sustainable Development

Water is one of the resources essential to sustaining all life and, through its interaction with geology, soils, topography, vegetation, and wildlife, is a major ingredient in achieving sustainable development on every parcel of land. Managing water supply, wastewater disposal, and stormwater drainage are therefore primary and interlocking concerns in land development. Over the past century, in particular, developers have tended to address hydrology needs by contriving technological solutions that serve immediate needs but too often generate unwanted long-term impacts on the natural resource base. Many environmental problems such as

floods, erosion, landslides, aquifer depletion, and even loss of biodiversity and climatic change can be traced to our tendency to use technology as substitutes for, instead of working with, natural hydrologic systems.

Water enters a development site as rainfall and through surface and groundwater flows. Some evaporates or transpires through the vegetation it feeds. Some infiltrates the soil to join subsurface flows and to recharge the water table before flowing out through wetlands, streams, and rivers. The constancy of these cycles of flow keeps the earth green and alive.

Land development too often ignores and interferes with the hydrologic cycle, most significantly by regrading the topography, removing ground cover, building impervious surfaces, and creating inhospitable landscapes that deflect water flow off instead of into the land. Runoff from construction sites, roadways, and parking lots carries sediments, greases, and oils while water draining from manicured lawnscapes conveys excess fertilizers and pesticides. Typically, pipes intercept runoff and carry it away from a development site and dump it into detention basins and/or streams. Stormwater discharged into waterways during storms raises and drops water levels precipitously, scouring banks and generating widespread erosion and flooding. The reduced infiltration of water into the soil and groundwater lowers the water table and starves vegetation of needed nutrients. Detention ponds typically hold water for too short a time to have any significant impact on the consequences of runoff.

Reconfiguring dysfunctional hydrologic cycles to reintroduce natural systems to the development process is a chief objective for conservation-minded landscape architects and engineers. In fact, science-based experience has demonstrated workable alternatives to conventional pipe-dependent approaches. Those approaches not only get the hydrologic job done in ways that prevent unwanted consequences but also add value to a development. Even on small sites and infield sites dependent on pipe systems, developers can adopt measures that significantly reduce impacts on areawide hydrology.

Natural and Disrupted Hydrologic Cycles. The pursuit of a sustainable land resource requires a clear understanding of the natural water cycle and how it functions on undeveloped land (see figures 6-3 and 6-4). Whatever the climatic conditions or amount of rainfall in a given physiographic region, much of the annual precipitation returns immediately to the atmosphere as evaporation or as transpiration from vegetative systems. Where woodlands exist, they are the most significant hydrologic feature on the landscape; the role played by woodlands in the terrestrial ecosystem can be appreciated if trees are pictured as a water pump that operates when the weather is wet or dry. The pump mechanism accounts for about half of annual rainfall. A relatively small fraction of annual rainfall runs off from the land surface under natural conditions, and more than twice as much soaks into the soil mantle to become the base flow of groundwater.

The rate at which rainfall percolates into the soil is controlled by the physical composition, thickness, and topologic form of the soil mantle. In most areas, soil is the result of thousands of years of weathering of the underlying bedrock. Rainfall drains slowly through the upper layer of the earth by the force of gravity until it reaches the zone of saturation called the water table. In the layer of subsurface soil and weathered bedrock, which is defined as an aquifer, the water moves slowly downgradient as seeps, springs, or streams toward surface discharge points. A few days after a rainfall, a small stream flowing in a valley is made up entirely of groundwater discharge. This process is essential to

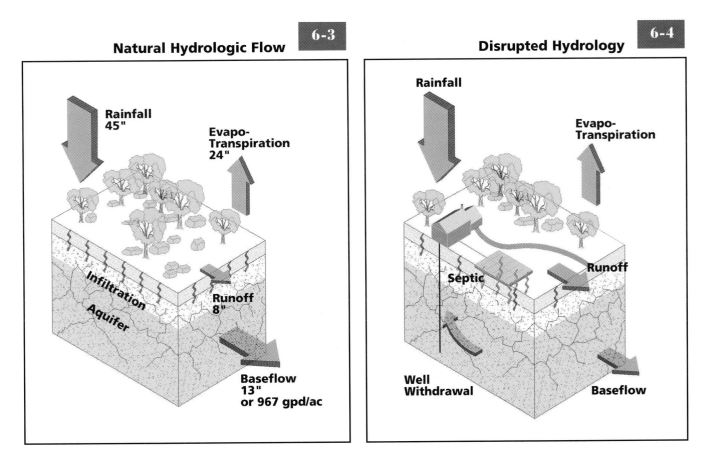

6-3

Natural Hydrologic Flow

Rainfall
45"

Evapo-
Transpiration
24"

Infiltration

Aquifer

Runoff
8"

Baseflow
13"
or 967 gpd/ac

6-4

Disrupted Hydrology

Rainfall

Evapo-
Transpiration

Septic

Runoff

Well
Withdrawal

Baseflow

natural stream flows and, in most regions, accounts for the entire flow for much of the year. (In the Piedmont region, estimated base flows are about 15 inches per year, or about one-third of typical annual rainfall.) A single raindrop may take weeks or months to reach a stream, but the displacement of groundwater is a constant process. If we disrupt the flow by reducing the amount of water that enters the soil mantle in the upland, we threaten the entire stream system, particularly the stream water quality and the ability of aquatic life to sustain itself.

On developed land, rainfall continues to initiate the hydrologic cycle, but disruption of the natural landscape substantially alters water pathways through the site. Figure 6-5 is based on the annual average rainfall for the Piedmont Physiographic Region of the Eastern United States, but the net impact of impervious surfaces is the same anywhere on the planet. With the soil mantle largely covered with rooftops and impermeable pavement, rainfall on a unit of land surface is transformed into direct runoff. Whereas rainfall on a naturally vegetated soil surface would generate eight to ten inches of direct runoff in a given year (a relatively small fraction of an annual total rainfall of 45 inches), impervious surfaces transform almost all rainfall into runoff, dramatically increasing the volume of stormwater runoff and decreasing percolation into the soil mantle and thus recharge of the groundwater system. To handle the runoff, we build elaborate and costly systems of inlets, storm sewers, and swales to channel the water to the nearest stream as quickly as possible.

The tremendous increase in runoff volume and loss of groundwater recharge from developed lands can significantly affect the hydrology of an entire watershed. The net result of numerous impervious surfaces is alteration of the water balance to the point where the water resource is reduced in both quantitative and qualitative value. Clearly, the potential impacts of development on the hydrology of a site, and ultimately an entire watershed, have significant implications for achieving sustainable development.

Stormwater Management. Normally, the development of new impervious surfaces affects water resources in three ways.

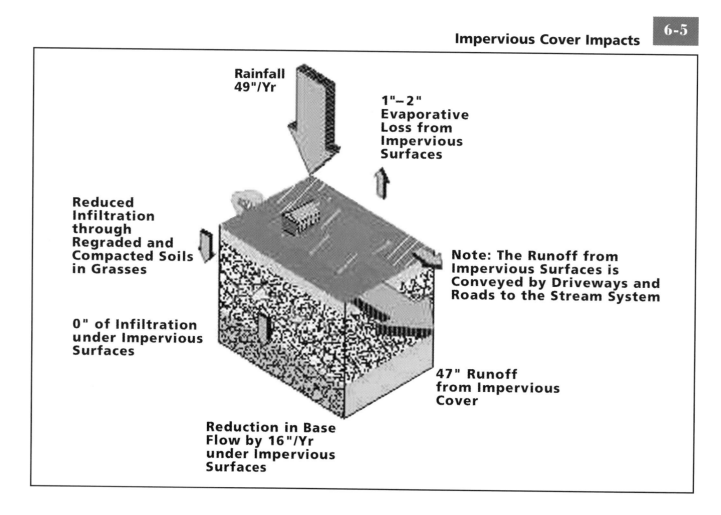

Rainfall 49"/Yr

1"–2" Evaporative Loss from Impervious Surfaces

Reduced Infiltration through Regraded and Compacted Soils in Grasses

Note: The Runoff from Impervious Surfaces is Conveyed by Driveways and Roads to the Stream System

0" of Infiltration under Impervious Surfaces

47" Runoff from Impervious Cover

Reduction in Base Flow by 16"/Yr under Impervious Surfaces

First, pavements and structures produce a dramatic increase in the volume of stormwater runoff. Second, impervious surfaces lead to a loss of groundwater recharge and a subsequent reduction in the base flow of local streams. Third, land pollutants scoured from the surface during runoff, known as nonpoint source (NPS) pollution, adversely affect water quality. Such runoff contains nutrients, sediment, petroleum compounds, and a turbid soup of other pollutants. The effects of pollutants on water resources provide one of the strongest arguments against urban development as we know it.

Since the 1970s, experts have recognized the problems posed by runoff of sediments from developed land. Largely under the leadership of the U.S. Soil Conservation Service (now the Natural Resources Conservation Service, or NRCS), the conventional farm pond of the 1950s has been adapted for use in suburban development. Situated downstream of areas disturbed by site clearing and grading, earthen ponds are designed to capture runoff and release it slowly to waterways at a peak rate no greater than before development. Combined with a series of on-site erosion control strategies and the use of geotextiles and other innovative materials, detention basins significantly reduce sediment loss and associated stream pollution.

Over the past two decades, use of detention basins, though more practical for large rather than small sites, became the basic means of controlling stormwater runoff. The technique has been incorporated into virtually every municipal land development ordinance and is described in elaborate detail in design manuals used by practicing civil engineers. Increasing recognition of water quality impacts and the decline in groundwater recharge has led to numerous modifications to the design of the basic detention basin along with the emergence of other stormwater management techniques—all grouped

An impacted stream bed. Runoff, increased by upstream impervious surfaces and the mowed-grass floodplain, erodes the streambed and degrades water quality.

under the heading of Best Management Practices. None of these approaches, however, significantly lessens the increased volume of stormwater runoff from new impervious surfaces. Nor do detention basins significantly reduce the nonpoint source pollution generated from new development. Moreover, for small sites with a high proportion of impervious surfaces, detention basins may be infeasible and runoff therefore more problematic.

As an alternative, it is possible though challenging to develop a parcel of land while still maintaining the natural hydrologic cycle. The evolving solution calls for systems and materials that mimic natural processes. Thus, for a given site, the design process begins with an examination of how the hydrologic cycle works—how various land and water features control the volume and quality of runoff, infiltration, and recharge—and how these factors will be altered by the proposed introduction of new impermeable surfaces. The process

then considers how—short of diverting runoff to a nearby mitigation site—the water balance can be maintained.

The guiding principle for sustainable stormwater management is to design for stormwater recharge rather than for detention. There are a variety of techniques, including temporary storage of runoff in large pipes, drainage swales, and woodland berms, that slow runoff to permit its infiltration into aquifers. Some projects have used constructed wetlands to collect, clean, and allow recharge of runoff. Studies of such wetlands demonstrate that they can effectively remove pollutants from runoff, although factors such as the size and volume of the wetlands system, rates of runoff and sedimentation, and flow volumes generate highly variable results in removal efficiency.[26] Detention ponds in series that discharge slowly into wetlands also work well. Generally, environmentalists frown on the use of natural wetlands for pollution control; the pollution removal efficiency of natural wetlands is less predictable than that of wetlands engineered for such a function.

The use of wetlands for stormwater management is demonstrated at Prairie Crossing, a 667-acre conservation community in Grayslake, Illinois, 45 miles northwest of Chicago. Stormwater is managed through a natural, sequential system of stormwater swales, restored upland prairies, created wetlands, and lakes. This treatment train reduces the rate and volume of runoff and increases lag time to allow greater water infiltration and evaporation. Swales and prairies remove 60 to 90 percent of suspended solids, phosphorus, and metals. Wetlands play the principal role in denitrification of the runoff, thus preventing surplus nitrogen from reaching the lake and nearby creeks and marshes. In addition to improved water quality, Prairie Crossing's natural system of stormwater management reduced infrastructure costs by more than $1 million compared with a conventional curb, gutter, and storm sewer system.

The stormwater management plan for Playa Vista, a 1,087-acre, mixed-use infill development in Los Angeles, was required to demonstrate no net increase in stormwater pollutant loads to Santa Monica Bay. To that end, as depicted in figure 6-6, the program called for significant expansion and restoration of the saltwater marsh near the ocean as well as for the redesign and restoration of the freshwater marsh and riparian corridor along the southern edge of the site. The freshwater wetlands system is designed to control periodic flooding; filter runoff pollutants, including those from off-site flows; and provide for rehabilitation of the natural aquatic habitat. The design also allows for occasional flushing of the saltwater marsh. Finally, the plan included a pollution prevention program of street sweeping, car-washing facilities, a survey of off-site illicit connections and dumping, and use

of native landscaping requiring little irrigation and chemical treatment.

Despite demonstrated successes with mitigating the hydrologic impacts of impervious surfaces in conventional developments, designers are increasingly turning to the reduction of impermeable surfaces as a means of expanding a site's capacity for infiltration, thereby reducing the volume of runoff. (A recent study estimates that proportions of impermeable surfaces greater than 10 percent throughout a watershed

Constructed wetlands at Prairie Crossing, Grayslake, Illinois. Wetlands filter stormwater and recharge aquifers while providing attractive views for nearby homes.

Restored wetlands at Prairie Crossing. Prairie Crossing's designer retained and restored large natural areas to provide a sustainable environment.

induce more runoff than can be handled on site.[27]) However, two of the three solutions for reducing the proportion of impermeable surface in developments illustrate the tug-of-war between the goals of on-site conservation of natural resources and the development of more compact communities. The first strategy calls for limiting the proportion of impervious surface by spreading development over larger land areas, such as single-family homes on three-acre lots—a development pattern that hardly fosters sustainability. A second approach reduces impervious surfaces by shrinking building footprints and downsizing roads and other paved areas. Certainly, constructing more multistory structures (such as two-level rather than one-level homes) shrinks the footprint per individual dwelling, but it usually results in

Wetlands under restoration at Playa Vista, Los Angeles, California.
Degraded saltwater and freshwater wetlands and a riparian corridor are being restored as part of the major infill development taking place at Playa Vista.

6-6

The Plan for Playa Vista

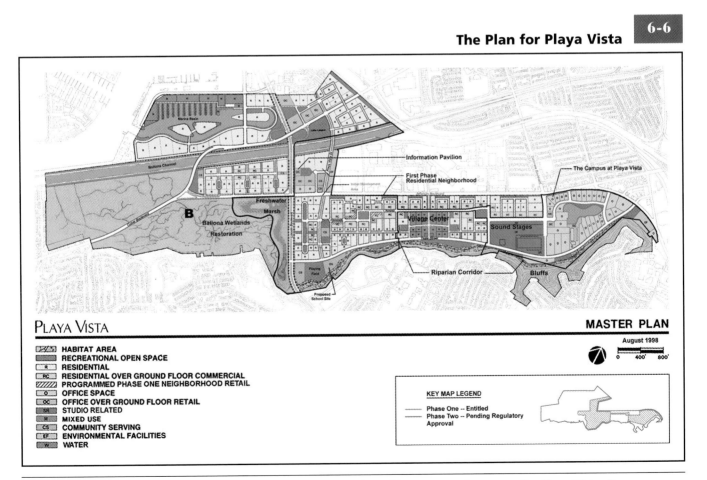

Tight clusters of housing and commercial uses allow conservation of large natural areas on the Playa Vista site.

higher-density development that itself increases rather than decreases the percent of impermeable surface owing to the addition of sidewalks and alleys. The third approach, recognizing that only habitations are required to be impermeable, is to make pavement areas more permeable either by using new materials in the pavement or underlying paved areas with infiltration beds.

Making pavements more permeable raises several problems that have been addressed in experimental projects over several decades. A major technical breakthrough in materials that occurred during the mid-1970s allowed the Franklin Institute in Philadelphia to develop porous asphalt concrete. The material is the basic asphalt concrete mix but omits the two smallest aggregate sizes, producing a strong wearing surface that permits water to pass through rapidly into a deep stone bed for storage. The stormwater then soaks slowly into the soil mantle beneath the bed. After installation of several prototype designs, the surrounding soil filled the stone beds, greatly reducing the beds' storage capacity; thereafter, the material found little application in new development.

In the late 1970s, as geotextiles became available, engineers discovered that a fabric liner beneath the stone bed prevented the bed from filling with soil and preserved the integrity of the recharge system. The addition of several other design features, including open edges and trench drains of various types, ensured operation of the bed in the event of pavement sealing. One design team of landscape architects and environmental engineers produced 40 designs, largely in the eastern mid-Atlantic region, that use porous asphalt concrete pavement and groundwater recharge beds. Subsequently, several designs constructed in Maryland were inundated by sediment-laden runoff and became clogged,

giving rise to the local perception that the design was flawed. Nonetheless, experience with several parking lot designs (see figure 6-7) indicates that the combination of porous asphalt concrete and recharge beds is a feasible alternative stormwater management system. A recent study of four types of permeable pavements concluded that the alternative systems dramatically decreased runoff compared with impervious surfaces. Nevertheless, their appearance and ability to handle high traffic volumes differ from conventional systems and therefore should be evaluated by designers for specific project use. In addition, their long-term performance in terms of durability, infiltrability, and water quality has yet to be fully determined.[28]

Despite assertions to the contrary, the study noted above concluded that costs for permeable pavements are substantially higher than for traditional asphalt. Typical asphalt paving for parking lots over a prepared base runs from $0.50 to $1 per square foot (1997 estimates); equivalent costs for permeable pavements range from 25 percent to over 300 percent more depending on material and assumptions about volume decreases. However, total costs for permeable pavement actually may be *lower* than for conventional asphalt pavement if costs are discounted for the drainage facilities needed to handle runoff from impervious surfaces. Permitting jurisdictions too often fail to accord full credit to the runoff reduction capabilities of permeable pavements. Therefore, in many jurisdictions, developers interested in using such pavements will have to argue their case for not constructing expensive drainage facilities.[29]

One alternative to permeable pavement materials is to design runoff and filtration to underlay large paved areas such as parking lots. Given that most Americans are unlikely to abandon the automobile any time soon, parking areas will

continue to consume sizable proportions of development sites. A series of distribution pipes can drain stormwater from inlets and roof drains to recharge beds beneath paved parking areas.

Systems that promote infiltration in these ways are designed to different standards than detention basins. Historically, the 100-year storm has been the standard for the engineering design of bridges, culverts, and detention basins. Detention basins are usually sized to attenuate the peak rate of runoff flow from a 100-year event; they are designed for a storage volume of about 63 percent of the increased runoff volume and thus require an enormous hole in the ground. The design standard for infiltration, by contrast, is a rainfall of two-year frequency, which represents 95 percent of the total rainfall experienced in a given region. Storage volume in a recharge system's stone beds is designed to be equal to the two-year storm increase, with outlet controls for major storms. A recharge system based on the two-year standard also mitigates the peak rate of flow for large storms, usually satisfying most jurisdictions' regulatory standards.

Irrespective of stormwater management method, preserving the integrity of the soil mantle during site development is important not only for maintaining water quantity but also for maintaining the quality of stormwater runoff. The soil should be sufficiently thick to allow construction of the recharge bed several feet above any seasonal water table or bedrock. Preferably, the soil should fall into Hydrologic Group B, although many Group C soils can be used with care. In any event, the soil mantle plays a critical role in the hydrologic cycle; it is responsible for the operation of a significant pollutant removal and reduction process whereby a community of microbes and physical-chemical

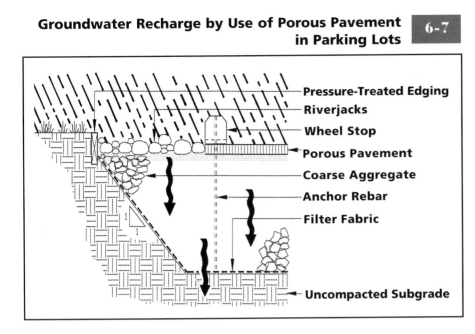

Pressure-Treated Edging
Riverjacks
Wheel Stop
Porous Pavement
Coarse Aggregate
Anchor Rebar
Filter Fabric

Uncompacted Subgrade

Porous-pavement parking lot aids stormwater management.

processes treat the NPS pollutants applied on the land surface.

To summarize the several approaches discussed above, all emphasize capturing and allowing infiltration of stormwater on the site through the use of swales, protected open lands, constructed wetlands, ponds and lakes, surface and subsurface infiltration beds, reduction of impervious surfaces such as rooftops and

paving, and permeable paving. These techniques are most effectively applied in low- to moderate-density developments on substantially sized lots where natural systems can be retained, restored, or constructed at costs at or below those for conventional piping and detention ponds. Moderate- to higher-density projects with smaller sites may not be able to incorporate open spaces and wetlands of sufficient size to filter run-

off; if so, such projects may need to increase the use of permeable paving and subsurface infiltration beds. At some level of density, it may be necessary to resort to piped removal to adjoining or, as in conventional development, distant streams and water bodies. However, current studies are underway to develop "low-impact development" or microscale methods of stormwater management intended for small, intensively developed sites. The newer methods emphasize integration of stormwater retention into many components of the built environment, including streetscapes, buildings, sidewalks, parking lots, alleys, green spaces, tree boxes, and pipes—all of which compensate for the loss of hydrologic function due to development.[30]

Wastewater Management. For the past 80 years, wastewater has been handled in an increasingly elaborate fashion. Engineers long argued that natural streams and rivers had a natural "assimilative capacity" for treating wastewaters discharged to them in reasonable amounts. This operating rule broke down during the middle of the 20th century when hydrologists finally recognized that most surface waters had long ago lost the natural capacity to complete the treatment process. In effect, many rivers had become all but open sewers. Subsequently, to avoid discharging sewage effluent to small streams, public authorities in many regions have invested heavily in regional wastewater collection and conveyance systems that pipe wastes to large treatment plants on major rivers or water bodies. Such systems gained popularity during the 1960s and 1970s when substantial federal funding encouraged their development, the increasing cost of which has led communities to seek local solutions for wastewater treatment.

The emergence of the concept of sustainability has spurred a reconsideration of the "interceptor sewer" approach not only because of its enormous costs but also because the long-distance conveyance of wastewater makes little sense when the same result can be achieved on the development site. On-site wastewater systems are designed to serve a limited number of residences or other uses. Small-scale systems rely on applications of the effluent to the soil mantle to complete the treatment process and, in so doing, return the effluent to the groundwater.

Various types of on-site wastewater treatment systems, including the ubiquitous individual septic tank, have been installed in existing and new developments of all types. Most systems substantially reduce key pollutants—as much as 95 percent of solids and organics—but none removes all pollutants. The final treatment is provided by the physical and biochemical processes that occur in the soil mantle and by the community of microbes that thrives in moist soil.

Regrettably, on-site systems are not without other limitations. As septic fields age and maintenance becomes a sometime

thing, systems can begin to have a major impact on subsurface water quality. According to one estimate, the 22 million septic systems in the United States introduce over 1 trillion gallons of waste per year into subsurface aquifers (see chapter 2). That waste includes nitrogen, phosphorous, bacteria, viruses, detergents, solvents, and other chemicals that, at too high a density, can contaminate groundwater and affect water quality in freshwater and saline lakes, rivers, and ponds. Nitrogen transported in high concentrations to groundwater supplies of drinking water can cause serious health hazards for newborns.

Most current wastewater treatment technologies emphasize effluent application either to the land surface or in a shallow system of lines. Application takes many forms, from spray and drip irrigation systems (see figure 6-8) to variations on the concept of a recharge bed. Again, the dual goals of recharge and pollutant removal are achieved in the soil mantle while any woodlands on the parcel benefit from the process as well. The treatment systems tend to be

biological in process but unconventional in form. For example, the use of wetlands plantings in containers and beds of greenhouses known as Living Technologies has found appeal in some installations. In another approach, conventional septic systems are outfitted with recirculating filter units used in combination with outdoor wetlands treatment systems (see figure 6-9). Whatever the basic treatment system, the common factor with respect to sustainability is the return of water to the land.

Technologies increasingly favored for sustainable development include freewater and subsurface-flow constructed wetlands and solar aquatic systems. Constructed wetlands—artificial marshes—purify water by breaking down pollutants through a combination of physical, biological, and chemical processes before returning the water to the ground. Such systems can save as much as 30 to 50 percent of construction and operating costs compared with conventional systems, and they offer the added benefit of detaining and purifying stormwater runoff (as discussed in the stormwater

Wastewater Treatment by Drip Irrigation 6-8

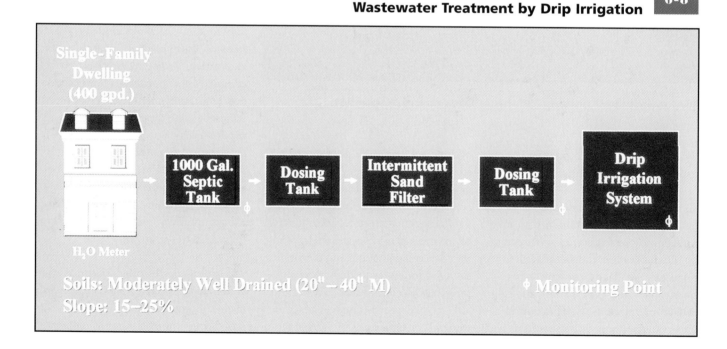

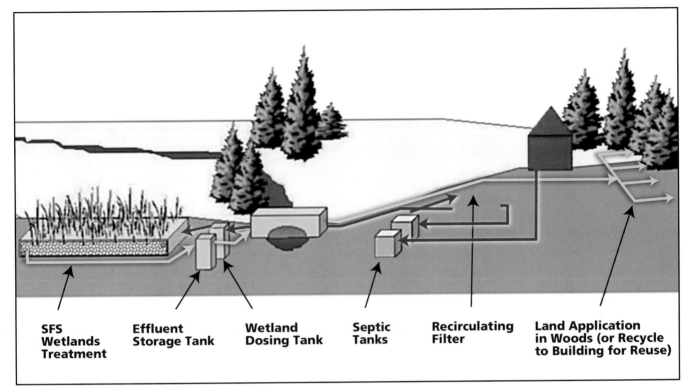

SFS Wetlands Treatment | **Effluent Storage Tank** | **Wetland Dosing Tank** | **Septic Tanks** | **Recirculating Filter** | **Land Application in Woods (or Recycle to Building for Reuse)**

section). The Tryon Farm development discussed in the landscape section uses a series of small constructed wetlands to process wastewater, with each wetlands serving nine to 12 houses. The wetlands clean wastewater in seven days as oxygen seeks the roots of tuber plants and nutrients feed the plants. The cleaned water is pumped onto on-site hay fields for irrigation and return to the aquifer. The first wetlands cost $30,000 to restore, a figure about equal to sewer service. The second wetlands, designed to serve houses in a woodland, cost a similar amount; however, sewer service would have cost as much as $100,000. Developer Tom Forman believes that he has achieved significant cost savings in installing innovative wastewater collection and treatment systems while enhancing natural assets.

A smaller development in Long Grove, Illinois, a suburb of Chicago,

Tryon Farm. A wetlands constructed to treat wastewater.

95

provides another example of on-site wastewater treatment. The 160-acre Fields of Long Grove is a community of 87 custom homes that originally sold from $425,000 to over $700,000. About 75 percent of the site is preserved as open space that includes wetlands, 45 acres of restored prairie, water retention ponds, a wastewater treatment lagoon, and agricultural land. Sewage is pumped to a central comminutor where it is pulverized and sent to the bottom of a storage lagoon covered with 13 feet of aerated water. Aeration keeps the lagoon from freezing in winter and permits aerobic biological action to oxidize organic materials. In summer, treated wastewater is pumped from near the top of the lagoon and disposed of by a circular spray irrigation system on an adjacent alfalfa field. Chlorination of the pumped water is possible but has been unnecessary. Sludge from the bottom of the lagoon will need to be removed about every 20 years. One drawback to the system, which allowed cluster development on smaller lots than could be served by septic systems, is that it requires the full-time presence of operating personnel experienced in managing wastewater systems.

The suspicion with which some public works departments greet innovative systems is best demonstrated by the experience in Hidden Springs, a developing community near Boise, Idaho. Its designers developed a system to carry wastewater from each development cluster to a series of ponds (or "cells") where it would undergo intensive aeration and natural filtration before it was pumped out to irrigate farm fields and common areas and returned to the aquifer. The designers intended the ponds to function as a visual amenity for surrounding homes. The local public works department, however, required a high fence, black liners, and setbacks around the ponds, thus negating their amenity value. The experience at Hidden Springs illus-

trates the problems that developers may encounter in attempting to apply innovative techniques.

Another technique, solar aquatic systems, uses sunlight, water hyacinths, fish, algae, and snails in a series of indoor tanks to purify sewage through natural processes. The purified water meets effluent standards without the use of chlorine or other toxics and is safe to drink. Aquatic systems have been used successfully in office projects since 1990.[31]

Water Supply. Every development must have access to an adequate supply of potable water. For the most part, it is taken for granted that a public or private local water purveyor exists and can deliver the required service at a reasonable rate. As development extends farther beyond the suburban fringe, however, public delivery of water may not be feasible. In such event, the development must tap an independent supply, usually a groundwater source, from within or near the development. Surface diversions from impoundments may offer an option in some locations, but the primary on-site water source is generally the subsurface aquifer.

Sustainable design principles suggest that water extracted from a subsurface aquifer should be returned to the aquifer within the same watershed or, even better, within the extraction site itself. As discussed in the previous sections, a net extraction of groundwater directly affects the capacity of an aquifer to feed small streams during a dry period. Even when water is recycled by means of soil filtration of wastewater effluent, some net loss of water still occurs, particularly when water is used in manufacturing processes. This so-called consumptive loss, usually in the range of 10 to 20 percent of the extracted water, must be weighed in achieving a sustainable hydrologic system. Some recent studies set the allow-

able consumptive loss for a given parcel at a percent of the local base flow in accordance with the size of the tract. Whatever the design criterion, a given development's net impact on local water sources determines the upper limits of that development.

Of equal importance to the hydrologic balance on a given parcel is the location of the water supply source. On the one hand, if the water source is derived from the site through groundwater extraction and then discharged to surface waters as treated effluent, a substantial loss of base flow will occur. A more serious concern arises if wastewater derived from water extracted from the site is discharged far downstream or into another watershed. In this case, which occurs more frequently than generally recognized, extraction can significantly deplete the base flow in the stream system. Such depletion is one of the factors contributing to degradation of surface streams in urbanizing watersheds. In fact, the combination of water depletion and an increasing proportion of impervious surfaces produces the well-recognized phenomenon of streams that function primarily as open sewers. On the other hand, if the water supply is imported from off site, then land application of wastewater adds to the water balance. In either case, the hydrologic balance can be significantly altered.

In the absence of standards, effluent returned to the aquifer by filtration can lead to serious deterioration of groundwater quality. Well-recognized water quality criteria are available to guide system design to ensure that water quality is sustained over time. The best indicator of wastewater pollution is the level of nitrate (NO_3), a soluble pollutant that does not respond to treatment by conventional septic systems. In response, federal and state health officials have set the water quality standard for allowable nitrate concentrations at 10 mg/l for water supply sources. In designing a site's hydrology system, design engineers can estimate the potential increase in groundwater nitrate levels under different treatment technologies and formulate designs to ensure that groundwater supplies remain adequate and potable for long-term use.

Taking a cue from the principle of conserving and recycling resources, developers can reduce water supply requirements—and therefore wastewater volumes—by adopting water conservation measures and reusing water on site. In addition, water shortages and declining groundwater reserves have motivated many public water agencies and authorities, especially in the arid Southwest, to initiate water conservation programs, some voluntary and others that involve regulatory and pricing mechanisms.

A typical American home consumes more than 90,000 gallons of water each year. The use of high-efficiency faucets, fixtures, and appliances can reduce that rate of consumption to less than 52,000 gallons a year with no perceptible effect on quality of life or convenience. Low-flow showerheads alone can save 14,000 gallons a year, front-loading (horizontal-axis) washing machines reduce washwater consumption from 24,000 to less than 9,000 gallons a year, and water-efficient toilets cut annual water consumption from 20,000 to 9,000 gallons a year. Education of residents and workers about water consumption can also significantly lower water use.

In many suburban communities, as much as one-third to one-half of water consumption goes for irrigating landscapes, including the lawns so beloved by Americans. Greater use of drought-resistant vegetation, soil treatment, and mulches combined with water-efficient irrigation systems can sharply cut water demands. "Graywater" systems that

reclaim water from household sinks and showers for landscape irrigation have been used successfully since the 1970s. A four-person household typically generates enough graywater to irrigate 900 square feet of turf, plus shrubs and trees. Graywater systems offer the additional advantage of increasing local groundwater recharge and reducing drainage needs. Another technique is to collect rainwater from roofs in cisterns for irrigation; in many cases, this old method supplies nearly all irrigation needs at little or no cost. Anyone who has used rainwater for bathing, drinking, and cooking is familiar with its softness, cleaning ability, and friendliness to plants and water-using equipment. Of course, designing smaller lawns, especially in combination with smaller lots, and retaining natural woodlands and meadows as part of the

community landscape, will also save substantial amounts of water.

Clearly, sustaining the water balance on a parcel of land, both quantitatively and qualitatively, requires careful consideration of all three water-related aspects of land development—water supply, wastewater, and stormwater management. While no formula covers all the possible situations faced in land development across the country, a set of general guidelines, shown in figure 6-10, identifies applicable management practices.

Designing a Sustainable Built Environment
An evaluation of a site's landscape features and hydrologic functions as described in the foregoing sections

| Sustainable Design Guidelines for Water Resources Management | 6-10 |

Stormwater
Prevent any increase in stormwater runoff volume for the two-year frequency storm
Recharge all stormwater generated by impervious surfaces
Avoid/minimize new impervious surfaces through footprint reduction
Design permeable surfaces for site needs
Avoid detention basins unless recharge is not feasible
If detention is used, provide additional NPS pollutant removal treatment processes
Minimize stormwater conveyance and use perforated piping in beds

Water Supply
Limit consumptive aquifer withdrawals to preserve base flow in streams
Protect aquifer quality by limiting surface chemical applications
Minimize water use and prevent consumptive use
Avoid irrigation systems except with wastewater effluent

Wastewater
Recycle effluent for flushing use
Avoid direct stream discharge of wastewater effluent
Use land application systems for effluent
Use nitrate reduction technologies where required to protect aquifer
Avoid export of wastewater from drainage area
Use nonchlorine disinfectant systems

helps establish a menu of opportunities and objectives for on-site conservation and restoration of natural resources. The menu defines options for providing basic water supply, wastewater disposal, and stormwater infrastructure and identifies a variety of natural areas that may protect resources while benefiting future site residents. Still to be considered, however, are other important components of the infrastructure system, particularly transportation and community facilities and the desired pattern of buildings on the landscape. The choices that developers make regarding the latter components of development can, in combination with the use of a site's natural resource systems, contribute to a project's overall sustainability.

Broadening Travel Options to Promote Sustainable Development. Achieving more sustainable development by improving the interplay between land use and transportation is a central theme of sustainability as well as of the smart growth and new urbanism movements. Many of the ills blamed on current forms of development stem from the perceived overdependence on the automobile for meeting daily travel needs. Transportation experts Newman and Kenworthy have long studied the interaction between transportation and land use and cite overdependence on the automobile as "a fundamental cause of unsustainability in cities." Such dependence, they assert, comes at a great cost and involves "an almost open-ended supply of transportation infrastructure that caters to exponential growth in demand for travel," with consequent impacts on global resources and city environments "and a whole array of unforeseen social costs such as isolation, destruction of community, and degradation of the public realm."[32]

Reducing dependence on the automobile will necessitate long-term modifica-tions to urban development patterns and people's travel behavior as well as significant shifts in both public policies and private development practices. But the starting point is obvious: an expanded range of opportunities and incentives that encourages residents and workers to choose alternative means of travel. For example, sustainable development principles and those of smart growth speak of increasing residents' and employees' access to public transit, walkways, and bikeways and encouraging more efficient use of the automobile through carpools and other arrangements. Broadening access to travel options means, first, making alternatives physically available and, second, shaping development to make the alternatives accessible to more people.

To be most successful, transportation alternatives require actions at the community and even regional levels; developers, however, can design developments in ways that expand travel options without adding significant costs to a project. Developers can measurably enhance project sustainability by planning an attractive network of pathways, assuring residents and workers of convenient access to existing or future transit ways, and designing the built environment to encourage use of these travel modes.

In many ways, the simplest means of expanding travel options is to make it easier for people to walk or cycle to their destinations—designing walkable communities at a human scale. Designing at a human scale means, among other things, reordering priorities in the automobile/pedestrian relationship to give pedestrians an even break. One of the earliest community designs that responded to problems created by increasing dependence on the automobile was Henry Wright and Clarence Stein's 1929 new town, Radburn, New Jersey. Radburn's organizing principle is complete separation of pedestrian and automobile traffic. The automobile is kept in its place with the use of short culs-de-sac that provide access to clusters of homes; the homes in turn face open spaces in the interior of large blocks. Pathways lead from the homes through interior green spaces to schools, playgrounds, and shopping. Some aspects of Radburn's plan, the cul-de-sac in particular, came into extensive use in the 1960s, 1970s, and even the 1980s, but without many of the other design elements that made Radburn a success.

In 1973, designers/developers Michael and Judy Corbett revitalized and improved on the Radburn concept when they developed Village Homes in the university community of Davis, California. At Village Homes, the houses are likewise oriented away from the street and toward green spaces that incorporate natural drainage areas, parks, community gardens, and orchards. Pedestrian traffic is completely separated from automobile traffic, and the pedestrian/cycle path is the primary circulation grid. Village Homes is designed to take advantage of passive solar energy and makes efficient use of natural resources. Today, homes in the community sell for $10 to $25 per square foot more than nearby comparable homes, turnover is low, and houses resell quickly.[33] Although Village Homes, like Radburn, was ahead of its time, its success in the market demonstrates the benefits of pedestrian-oriented and ecologically sensitive development.

Radburn's designers tended to treat the automobile as a dangerous machine to be relegated to a domain beyond the community's living areas. By contrast, today's advocates of livable communities have embraced the automobile as a vehicle that is here to stay but that can be put in its place. Instead of turning development away from the street and its traffic, proponents of livable communities view streets as valuable public spaces that can be made attractive for pedestrian as well as vehicular travel. Their designs emphasize interconnected street and pathway systems that knit the neighborhood together both functionally and visually. While leaders of the new urbanism movement proclaim the benefits of grid street systems as a unifying element, most land designers prefer street designs that respond to a site's terrain, even including curved streets and culs-de-sac. The essential quality for land designers is the interconnection of streets and pathways to maximize convenience and travel options. The importance of interconnections also carries across site boundaries to the street and walkway systems of adjacent developments.

Walkable (and bikeable) communities require just a few—albeit fundamental—changes to conventional development design, including the following:

- the provision of sidewalks or pathways linking residences to common destinations such as schools and parks, shopping and services, public transit stops, other residential areas, and even employment locations;

- pathways designed to be attractive, convenient, and safe;

- clustering several often-used destinations; and

- shortening overall walking distances by increasing the overall density of development.

In addition to sidewalks along streets, a common design treatment favored by developers of many planned communities is pathways through neighborhood and community open-space systems such as greenways. By far the most important stimulus to walking and cycling, however, is reducing distances between important destinations, a function of compact and interconnected development.

Developers can also widen travel choices by making their developments transit-friendly. Ideally, they can develop sites along existing or planned rail and bus lines and concentrate a mix of housing, jobs, retail shops and services, and public facilities at stations or stops. If well designed with attractive pathways connecting to transit lines, such development can spur transit ridership and reduce dependence on the automobile. Developments most supportive of transit service generally demonstrate the following characteristics:

- locations within ten minutes' walking distance of transit lines;

- a mix of uses, including a compact urban core of public, commercial, and residential uses;

- a mix of housing densities, types, prices, and ownership forms;

- a street and pathway system easily understood and interconnected, converging on core areas; and

- building orientation toward the streets.

Many transit agencies are working with developers to generate transit-friendly forms of development by publishing guidelines for transit-friendly development and sponsoring public/private ventures on transit properties.[34]

In the San Francisco Bay region, communities and the transit agency are using a combination of powers and incentives to promote transit-oriented development. Redevelopment powers expedite land assembly; assessment districts provide infrastructure financing and density bonuses; and reduced parking requirements help make development feasible. Proximity to Bay Area Rapid Transit (BART) stations is becoming a primary factor in attracting tenants to downtown office buildings. Employers have discovered that it is easier to recruit workers when convenient transit service is available.

Transit-focused development in Bethesda, Maryland. At the Bethesda Metrorail stop in Bethesda, collaborative planning by the transit authority, Montgomery County, and developers spurred a mixed-use development above the rail and bus stations. The central public plaza is enlivened by a kinetic sculpture and fountain. Bethesda Metro Center is flanked by almost a dozen other office, mixed-use, and residential projects built over the last 12 years.

Similarly, the Washington Metropolitan Area Transit Authority (WMATA) has worked with developers and local jurisdictions to promote over 30 public/private ventures at or near Metrorail stations. In Bethesda, Maryland, for example, WMATA cooperated with the Montgomery County Planning Board to promote development at the station, which is located in the heart of the Bethesda business district. The board drafted design guidelines for WMATA's use in reviewing development proposals for the site. WMATA selected a local firm to develop a mixed-use development over the station, along with a related bus terminal. Access to rail service permitted a reduction in on-site parking requirements. At many other Metrorail station areas, developers have negotiated deals with WMATA to gain direct access to the stations for development.

Another example of a suburban city taking advantage of rail station–related development opportunities is Evanston, Illinois, south of Chicago. The Arthur Hill company negotiated an agreement with the city and Northwestern University to develop long-vacant properties located between rail stations on the Metra commuter and Chicago Transit Authority rail lines, near the university and in the heart of downtown Evanston. In fall 1999, ground was broken for Church Street Plaza on a seven-acre site, shown in figure 6-11. Under construction is the Pavilion, which will house a cineplex with retail and restaurant uses. In addition, a 160- to 180-room Hilton Garden Inn has been announced, and construction drawings are in preparation for a high-rise residential building with about 250 rental units. A 1,400-car municipal parking garage will serve both the project and downtown stores and offices. With all these uses within a few steps of both rail stations, the development is expected to increase transit ridership and benefit from multimodal travel access.

Development sites in the path of planned extensions of transit lines can be designed to respond to eventual opportunities for transit service. In the case of rail transit, projects can take the form of higher-density, mixed-use development focused around a proposed station site and even reserve land for a future station. In addition, development can be designed along a proposed line with future train movements in mind. The cost of planning for potential rail connections is likely to be more than offset by the escalation in development value that follows the introduction of transit service. In any case, a well-designed, mixed-use development can deliver satisfactory profits on its own, as demonstrated by recent experience in Pasadena. The Janss Company, active in southern California for many years, developed Holly Street Village in downtown Pasadena, a $56 million mixed-use project with 384 apartments and 11,000 square feet of retail space. An internal pathway network links housing

Another Transit-Oriented Development: Church Street Plaza, Evanston, Illinois 6-11

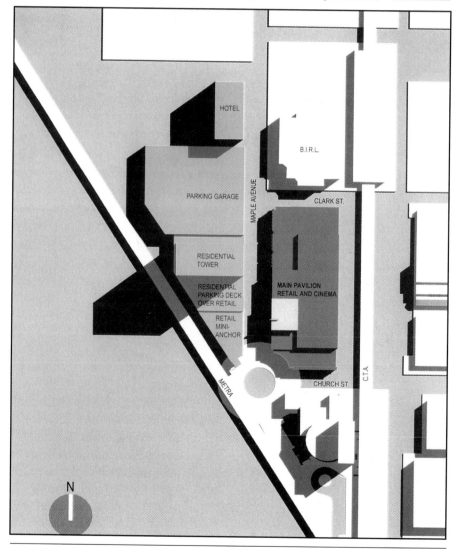

Located between two rail transit lines, the mixed-use Church Street Plaza will strengthen downtown Evanston and serve the Northwestern University campus while boosting transit ridership.

to retail shops and the village square. With the expectation that the Metropolitan Transit Authority of Los Angeles (MTA) will extend the light-rail Blue Line to a station within the development over the next few years, the project was built in cooperation with and with financial assistance from the Pasadena Redevelopment Agency and a light-rail line MTA. Upon the introduction of rail service, the city will benefit from higher property tax receipts and the transit agency from greater ridership; the developer will benefit as well from the rail access, although the project is successful as it now stands.[35]

Designing development for eventual bus service is somewhat less complicated and simply calls for the provision of adequate street widths, turning radii, and stopping points along arterial streets designated as likely bus routes. Projects designed for planned bus service should also consider the possibility of incorporating a multimodal center (for buses, taxis, and kiss-and-ride and park-and-ride facilities) in or adjoining a mixed-use community center and providing convenient pathway connections to future stops.

Development sites not in proximity to rail or bus routes can still encourage access to transit by establishing shuttle bus service in association with park-and-ride facilities.

In addition to shaping development to promote a variety of travel options, many developers have established or participated in traffic management programs intended to reduce peak-hour congestion. They work with employers to schedule a range of arrival and departure times, to promote telecommuting (home-based work) for a given proportion of the labor force, and to encourage workplace-based employees to use forms of travel other than single-occupant automobiles. The last approach can include

arrangements such as vanpool and carpool programs and paying for part or all of employees' use of transit.

Developers can organize such efforts themselves or in partnership with other developers or public agencies, or they can even contract with a firm that specializes in providing those services. Grossman Family Properties, developing Hidden Springs near Boise, Idaho, for example, commissioned a traffic management plan to reduce potential traffic impacts on highway links to the city. The plan set forth a goal of reducing vehicle trips associated with Hidden Springs from an estimated 12 per household as in a conventional development to eight per household. The plan proposed several elements to achieve that reduction, including the following:

- development of commercial and community features that contribute to a relatively high degree of self-sufficiency on the site, including retail services, a post office, parks, play areas, cycle trails for recreation, a community school, and a working farm that operates a produce stand to serve the community;

- an information center providing a rideshare matching service, information on cycle and pedestrian routes, and delivery and shuttle services available from vendors;

- a "partial grid" street pattern that provides direct pedestrian routes to the commercial and community center;

- pedestrian and cycle pathways that offer convenient routes through the development;

- a park-and-ride lot for both work and nonwork trips to encourage carpooling;

- advanced wiring in all dwellings to support telecommuting and home-based work; and

- appointment of an on-site transportation coordinator, issuance to all new residents of an orientation package describing transportation options, participation in any future areawide transportation management association, and periodic promotional events and mailings.[36]

Traffic management programs are not new. The developers of Hacienda Business Park in Pleasanton, California, strongly supported the drafting of a trip reduction ordinance to deal with the area's growing traffic congestion. In 1984, the developers formed an association of property owners and lessors to implement a trip reduction program. The program's design guidelines for the business park specified that new developments must provide preferential carpool parking, install bicycle racks, and appoint transportation coordinators to help workers find new ways of commuting to the site. In addition, the developers began to balance the jobs/housing mix by rezoning some parcels and developing them for high-density residential use.[37]

These and many other developments demonstrate the value of designing projects that offer a range of transportation options. Not only do such options attract occupants, but they also help mitigate traffic congestion that might otherwise further degrade air quality and lead to public limits on development.

Community Facilities and Open Space. Sustainable development incorporates the public services and open space essential to creating livable, interactive, and healthy communities. Developers of large-scale planned communities have decades of experience in planning and constructing community facilities and open space as necessary and attractive components of new neighborhoods and communities. They go to great pains to determine appropriate sites for schools,

101

libraries, fire stations, and the like and occasionally design and build them as well. They also lay out elaborate open-space systems of small parks and playgrounds, larger sports facilities, greenways, and conserved woodlands and wetlands. Even in smaller residential and business park developments, developers frequently provide a well-designed amenity package—usually a central park or a recreation center in an attractively landscaped setting—that establishes the identity and tone of the development. In addition, developers of smaller projects are careful to identify and provide access to major community facilities in the surrounding neighborhood that can benefit project residents. Not only do these facilities enhance a development's living and working environment, thereby encouraging sustainability, but they also become an essential aspect of project marketability.

Site designers frequently use open-space systems as "organizers" of the built environment and as the setting for commonly used facilities. Working from the type of landscape analysis described earlier, designers identify site features—terrain, meadows, woodlands, and other natural assets—that can be conserved, restored, or enhanced to create a special character or identity for the development. At the same time, landscape features provide passive and active recreation opportunities for site residents.

The Del Webb Company designed its 5,856-acre, mixed-use development north of Phoenix to fit within the site's ridges and washes in the foothills of Daisy Mountain. Called Anthem, the development retains over a third of the site in open space and for recreational use. About 290 acres of hillsides above the 15 percent slope line remain untouched, offering a wonderfully scenic backdrop for residential areas. Walking and riding trails extend along the washes and a 63-acre central park adjoins a multiuse community center. Together with three golf courses

(designed within the state's acreage limits on irrigated fairways), the open spaces provide both recreation opportunities and a pleasant setting for Webb's traditional active-adult market and the extended market of families and individuals targeted by the development. Although some opposed the development of Anthem as a leap-frogging form of sprawl, the community's mix of uses, overall density, and conservation of open space are far more sustainable than the scattered one- and two-acre lots preferred by project opponents.

Smaller developments also benefit from preservation of open space. Developer Robert Engstrom set out to design an environmentally sensitive alternative to the large-lot subdivisions so common in the Twin Cities area of Minnesota. The Fields of St. Croix (see figure 6-12) in the city of Lake Elmo allocates more than 60 percent of the 226-acre site to permanent open space, which comprises farmland, horticultural gardens and a

Anthem master-planned community, Phoenix, Arizona. Anthem clusters homes to retain views of the hills and provide recreational open spaces throughout the community.

tree nursery, wooded slopes, two ponds, and restored native prairie. Over three-quarters of the 45 home-sites in the first phase sold in six weeks after sales began in 1997; a second phase is now complete. Lots were priced in the affordable range of $44,500 to $150,000.

The farmland conservation allowed by clustered homesites in Engstrom's development is echoed in a number of large and small projects in other parts of the nation. The Qroe Companies, based in Nashua, New Hampshire, has developed several New England properties that blend development with working farms. One example, shown in figure 6-13, is Pardon Hill, a 177-acre site on which 22 homes have been developed on one- and two-acre lots, leaving 83 percent of the site—including 60 acres of dedicated farmland—in open space. Hidden Springs near Boise, Idaho, has set aside 85 acres to continue operation of a working farm. Over 60 varieties of fruits and vegetables produced by the farm are sold at the adjoining farmers' market and in the development's general store. The developer, taking every opportunity to remind residents of the site's farmland past, planted a large field of pumpkins and corn in the village center on a vacant parcel planned for future retail use. These deliberate touches and the location of a working farm in proximity to consumers reflect sustainability principles and, not incidentally, provide residents with a distinctive and valued amenity.

Smaller developments can promote sustainability by designing preserved open spaces linked to adjoining natural systems. The on-site inventory of landscape resources should identify connections to the natural systems of the larger watershed or ecosystem so that open space in individual developments functions as part of the whole system, not just as an isolated fragment. Developers can identi-

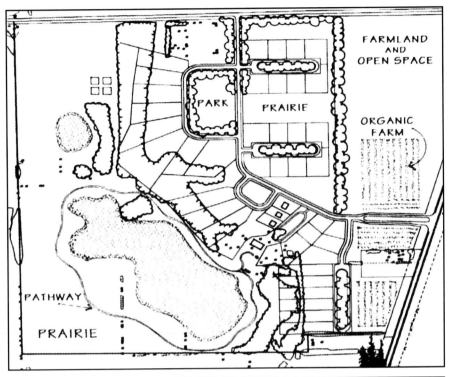

Almost two-thirds of the 226-acre site is retained in permanent open space, including restored native prairie lands, farmland, ponds, horticultural gardens, and wooded areas.

The Fields of St. Croix, St. Elmo, Minnesota. The development preserved farm fields that continue to be cultivated for crops and also function as valued open space for residents.

fy opportunities for linked systems by consulting community conservation plans that might have been developed by local planning offices. Coordination avoids scattershot patterns of open-space conservation that sometimes evolve from conservation efforts on individual properties and thus are far less effective in maintaining natural resource lands than large connected systems. In Lincoln, Massachusetts, for example, the town's program for promoting cluster development in concert with related open-space conservation was greatly enhanced by the adoption of a long-range conservation plan that demonstrated how developers' incremental conservation efforts could link into greenway and other open-space networks.

Trees and woodlands are an important part of every sustainable development, offering cooling shade in summer, absorbing stormwater, filtering harmful air pollutants, furnishing mini-habitats for birds and other creatures, and providing value-increasing landscape greenery. Trees, either along a street or clustered around homes and businesses, use solar radiation to transpire 100 gallons of water per day, the equivalent of five air conditioners running for 20 hours.[38] A comparative study of air quality along two streets found that the street with trees had less than 3,000 dust particles per liter of air while the street without trees had from 10,000 to 12,000 dust particles per liter.[39] Trees not only take up water as it seeps into the ground, but the foliage shields erodable ground from heavy rains and acts much like a drip irrigation system after rains. The stormwater management capabilities of existing tree cover are estimated to be worth $305 million in Milwaukee and $883 million in Atlanta, according to the American Forests organization. That organization has established desired goals for tree canopy (tree coverage) of 15 percent for business districts, 25 percent for urban residential areas, and 50 percent in suburban areas.[40]

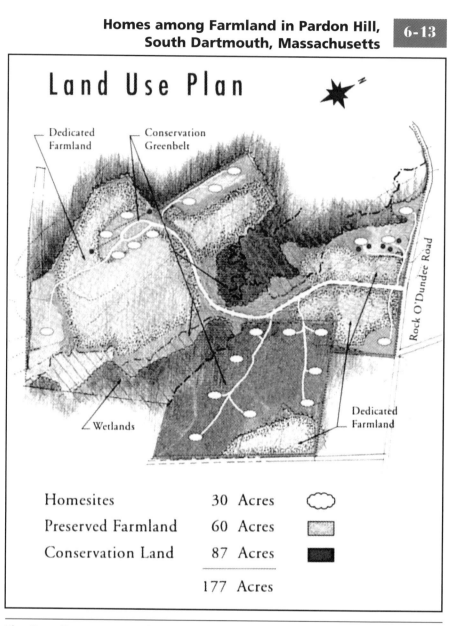

Land Use Plan

Dedicated Farmland

Conservation Greenbelt

Rock O'Dundee Road

Wetlands

Dedicated Farmland

Homesites	30 Acres	
Preserved Farmland	60 Acres	
Conservation Land	87 Acres	
	177 Acres	

The Qroe Company specializes in developing homes in a natural or farmland environment. Pardon Hill includes 22 homesites and maintains 83 percent of the site in open space.

One issue that often arises in restoring or capitalizing on landscape features is reconciling the potentially conflicting goals of conserving natural qualities and allowing human use. Preserved wildlife habitats and wetlands often may lure site residents who wish to enjoy a walk through nature's wonders. These visits, however, may damage vegetation, habitats, and erodable terrain, gradually diminishing an asset's viability as an environmental resource.

Thus, in the case of Playa Vista in Los Angeles, for example, plans for the restored saltwater wetlands will deliberately exclude walkways or other facilities that could attract visitors, although the wetlands will be visible from developed parts of the site. In some developments, walls and fences have been required to protect habitats and wetlands; in others, occasional visits by hikers, bird watchers, or school classes are expected and welcomed.

Hidden Springs, near Boise, Idaho. Homes in Hidden Springs were clustered to retain the hilly landscape as a visual and environmental asset.

The effectiveness of such conservation measures depends on the specific character of the resource, its location in relation to nearby development, and the effectiveness of the management program established for resource conservation. Naturalists have discovered, for example, that the Least Bell's vireo, an endangered bird, thrives in the vegetation bordering golf fairways. In at least one habitat area, coyotes were introduced to discourage cats from nearby homes from preying on native birds. (After losing a few pets, residents now keep their cats indoors.) In any case, on-site conservation in proximity to development calls for a well-designed resource management program, including educational programs for site residents (discussed later).

Although most infield developments contribute to sustainability primarily by taking advantage of existing systems of community facilities and open space, they too can incorporate elements that add to the mix of amenities available to the neighborhood and community. For example, mixed-use projects and regional shopping centers sometimes incorporate community meeting or event rooms as well as outdoor spaces that function much like community parks. Even attractive landscaping adds value to and helps create an identity for the neighborhood.

Many studies have established the value-added quality of open space for development. Other studies have shown that lots with trees can be sold for 5 to 18 percent more than lots without trees. A 1986 Gallup survey determined that across the nation landscaping adds almost 15 percent to the value of a home.[41]

Community facilities and open space, then, provide essential community-making elements for any development. If linked to larger facility and natural systems, these elements become even more important in providing regional settings for sustainable development. Ultimately, they help establish the livability of places that contributes to long-term sustainability.

Buildings on the Site: Patterns and Relationships. Landscape resources and open space, hydrologic systems, and transportation and community facilities establish the broad parameters of a development's design; for developers, though, the ultimate goal is to provide building construction sites. (The next chapter discusses how individual buildings and linked groups of buildings can incorporate "green" elements that promote sustainability.) In considering overall design approaches to site development, developers need to recognize that the patterns and relationships between buildings and the land and among buildings themselves play a significant role in achieving sustainable development. In particular, development designers can site buildings in ways that minimize disruption of the natural landscape, reduce energy requirements, and create a sense of place for the development and larger neighborhood.

The landscape analysis described earlier will identify areas most suitable for building and the landforms that should be preserved. To conserve a property's natural systems and features to the extent possible, developers should site buildings in patterns that minimize earth cuts and fills. Accordingly, buildings should be grouped on parts of the site least susceptible to erosion or already disturbed by clearing and cultivation or previous development. Buildings can be designed in clusters that use less land than typical subdivision lots, leaving more of a site in its natural condition and reducing transportation and utility costs. Building more densely—up rather than out—can reduce impervious surface and thus stormwater runoff.

Forms of development that make efficient use of land have long been espoused by leading development and environmental organizations. The Urban Land Institute, the American Planning Association, and the National

Association of Home Builders, for example, in addition to the U.S. Department of Housing and Urban Development, have promoted clustered, land-saving development since the 1930s. Over the decades, their publications have, first, demonstrated the cost and conservation economies that can be achieved through more efficient use of land and, second, described several projects that achieve those goals successfully.[42] The Coffee Creek Center, Pardon Hill, and Tryon Farm developments described earlier indicate that developers know well the techniques of land-saving clustering; too often, though, they have to "fight city hall" and neighboring residents to obtain approvals for building such projects.

Building patterns (along with individual buildings as discussed in the next chapter) can also be planned to conserve energy. To optimize energy efficiency across a site, developers must integrate a project's land planning, building design, and building components during formulation of the initial project plan. Streets and lots can be laid out to maximize access to solar energy but must also respect other landscape and hydrology considerations. A typical cul-de-sac plan, for example, leaves only about 20 percent of lots usable for passive solar energy. Minor revisions to the street layout can increase that figure to up to 80 percent. Laying out streets and buildings to conserve existing trees and allow extensive tree plantings takes advantage of trees' shade-giving cooling power and windproofing and warming properties while reducing energy requirements for heating and air conditioning. Clustering buildings on interconnected streets to encourage walking and cycling and thus shorten distances between uses cuts down on the amount of fuel consumed by automobiles.

Whether a project is large or small, development designers can group buildings to create a special identity and sense of place. Buildings can be arranged to form a perceivable and hospitable public realm, to create recognizable central places, and to preserve and enhance landmarks of all types. A development's architecture can establish a distinctive identity for the community while the themes and variations of building placement and design can mark the community as a welcoming and enjoyable place.

Town centers—in towns, suburbs, and large-scale new developments—are one expression of place-making. At the planned community of Reston, a 7,400-acre development near Dulles International Airport in Northern Virginia, the town center was designed and developed as an urban place to respond to a market that had matured over decades of community development. The 22-acre first phase consists of 220,000 square feet of retail shops, a 514-room hotel, and 530,000 square feet of office space as well as several parking structures. It centers on a "main street" of retail and office buildings grouped closely around pleasant pedestrian spaces. Since opening in 1990, the project has also become an entertainment destination; today, the center is expanding with the development of hundreds of residential units and additional office towers.

At a smaller scale, the Haile Plantation Village Center is part of a 1,700-acre planned golf community in Gainesville, Florida. Developer Robert Kramer decided to create an "authentic" small-town main street. Over the course of eight years, he has built 30 buildings, each about 2,000 to 3,000 square feet, on 15 acres of the 51-acre site. The remaining acreage is under development as a traditional residential village focused around a village green, shown in figure 6-14.

The redevelopment of the town center in Smyrna, a city of 30,000 amid Atlanta's urban sprawl, is a notable case of reestablishing a distinctive identity for a downtown in deep decline. Sizemore Floyd Architects, commissioned to plan and design a new library and community center for the town, recommended that the public buildings be used to leverage the creation of an entirely new downtown center. To that end, the city assembled a 29-acre site

Creating a big-city town center in Reston, Virginia. The new town of Reston, under development since the 1960s, has matured enough to warrant a prominent place-making center.

Haile Plantation Village Center

The heart of Haile Plantation's Village Center is the green bordered by shops, offices, townhouses, and community buildings, as depicted in this drawing.

Recreating a suburban center: Smyrna, Georgia. Smyrna stimulated private redevelopment in its town center by the artful design of new community buildings.

just a block off the main street. The plan incorporated most of the town's civic and community buildings, a town green, a three-acre park, and a site for private high-density commercial and residential development. The public buildings were designed in a distinctive style, and design guidelines were adopt-

ed to guide other development. The 1991 completion of the community center and library sparked the development of 22 cottage houses, which sold immediately, and 40,000 square feet of retail and office space. A second phase, including a city hall, public safety facility, and seniors' center, has been completed, followed by private development of space for several shops and services. Plans for additional public and private development were drawn up in 1999.

Another approach to place-making is illustrated in the design of Northpark, a 350-acre village within the enormous expanse of the Irvine, California, development. The design focused on the creation of a strong landscape character to achieve a special identity for the community. To remind residents of the site's natural heritage, the design called for retaining existing windrows of eucalyptus trees and the views of the foothills. A trail system that follows the region's arroyos promotes connectivity within and beyond the village. The street system also provides a continuous walkway system that links to open spaces and community facilities. All of these features contribute to Northpark's sense of place, but that sense is heightened by the design of the buildings along the streets and around the open spaces. The rhythmic interrelationship, individuality, and human scale of the buildings enrich the pedestrian experience.[43]

Even small developments can establish a style and distinctiveness in building placement and design that complement rather than compete with adjoining developments. As Edward Blakely points out in chapter 5, too many community designers depend on guarded gateways to mark a development's identity. Careful siting of buildings around central open spaces, in well-designed clusters, or along attractive streets can stimulate a civic consciousness of place that is sustainable without being exclusionary. Preservation of historic or architecturally interesting buildings can also provide a distinctive identity for a development. The Victorian farmhouse preserved in the Tryon Farm development in Michigan City, Indiana, and the old barns retained in the Hidden Springs development near Boise, Idaho, add place-making character to their respective developments.

Infield Development: Profitable Place-Making. Many infill (or infield) projects capitalize on the sense of place and distinctive architecture of existing buildings and neighborhood surroundings to create a unique identity, as in a sensitively designed project in Charlottesville, Virginia, shown in figure 6-15. Charlottesville is the home of the University of Virginia, whose expanding student body adds to a growing demand for housing. Kellytown, a neighborhood established by freed slaves after the Civil War, is a single-family area near the university with some large undeveloped parcels and many old trees. After a developer purchased two parcels in Kellytown, he participated in a 16-month collaborative planning process to prepare a place-sensitive site plan. Following many meetings and the consideration of several design concepts, the developer agreed to honor the neighborhood's heritage by retaining the original structures still standing; preserving a large forested area as a wildlife habitat that would also mitigate the possible flooding of Kelly's Creek, which runs through the neighborhood; integrating new development into the existing community; and designing small lots and narrow streets in order to retain open space. On the first parcel, 32 houses and ten accessory uses were planned on 40-by-50-foot lots. As of late 1998, 12 houses had been constructed at prices ranging from $120,000 to $170,000.[44]

Many communities view infill development as an essential tool for revitalizing aging neighborhoods and business centers and curbing sprawling fringe-area development. Development of infield sites can reduce the need for investment in new infrastructure, restore declining areas, and improve tax bases and local economies. Infill sites may include vacant lots and tracts, abandoned properties, and underused parcels whose potential value outweighs the value of existing uses. (Chapter 7 discusses infill by reuse of vacant buildings.) In many cases, infield development can be combined with renovation of adjoining properties to stimulate broader neighborhood redevelopment.

By their very nature, infield sites have problematic qualities that sometimes offset any locational advantages. Zoning restrictions or parcel size and shape may restrict development opportunities. Terrain conditions such as steep slopes, poor drainage, and questionable subsoil may increase potential development costs. Removing obsolete structures may add to development costs while ownership conflicts or tax problems may cloud use of the properties. The condition of surrounding land uses and local infrastructure systems may dissuade potential developers. Outdated or overly restrictive local codes and regulations may drive up development costs. Any or all of these possibilities can increase the costs and risks attendant to infill development and thereby reduce the marketability of an infill site.

From a financial standpoint, infill developments pose issues of risk and nonroutine deals. Site prices per unit or square foot are frequently higher than those in urbanizing fringe locations, and the customized design required for virtually every product typically adds to development costs. Moreover, market responses to proposed products are less certain and project approval processes often more tortuous than in the case of suburban greenfield development.

One of the most significant obstacles to many infield projects is neighborhood opposition. Infill development necessarily affects adjoining property owners and residents. Sometimes, neighbors welcome new investments that may shore up their property values or even improve the neighborhood. Sometimes, however, they react fearfully to infill proposals that may "change the character" of the area or bring new residents to old neighborhood. As ULI's book on infill housing put it,

> [E]xisting residents may object even if the development will improve the neighborhood. [They] may fear gentrification, displacement, and change; they may want to preserve vacant property as open space; they may be concerned that community facilities will be overloaded by the influx of newcomers . . . .[45]

Indeed, most cities that have initiated effective infill policies and programs (including, for example, Portland, Oregon, and San Diego) have experienced resistance from neighbors who dislike the appearance, higher density, or other impacts of new development.

Overcoming these obstacles to infill housing typically requires extraordinary efforts by developers and local governments as well as a supportive real estate market. Infill succeeds in communities with strong growth rates and economies, where developers are actively looking for opportunities, and where potential returns on investments can absorb higher risks. Particularly in areas of need, infield development succeeds where the financial resources and project management skills of committed organizations can be brought together to focus on stimulating development. To spur infield development, many local governments and nonprofit organizations have initiated or partici-

New Development in an Old Neighborhood in Charlottesville, Virginia: New Homes Designed to Be Compatible with Existing Residences

6-15

The site plan and photo of houses under construction demonstrate the careful manner in which new homes were inserted into a historic neighborhood. Photo by Lucie Vogel.

pated in redevelopment projects and rehabilitation programs, including land assembly, financial assistance, and infrastructure development. Nonprofit groups such as community development corporations have organized fix-up campaigns and provided channels for financial assistance.

Developers must expect to customize infield projects to the particular conditions and limitations of the site, neighborhood, market, and local regulations. Compared with typical greenfield development at the urbanizing fringe, infield development demands close attention to individual site conditions and requires the design of products highly tailored to niche markets. In fact, developers of

infield developments have learned to shape their products carefully to ensure compatibility with neighborhood needs while meeting the demands of the marketplace. They expect (and usually enjoy) the challenge of finding the right design for the right product for the right site versus developing yet another suburban subdivision.

The gestation of the Uptown District mixed-use development in San Diego exemplifies the collaborative and creative challenges of infield development. In 1986, the city acquired the 12.5-acre site of a defunct Sears shopping center in the Hillcrest neighborhood north of downtown. Business and civic groups worked together to craft an overall plan

for the site; the plan called for a reduction in retail space but development of a supermarket much needed by area residents. Meanwhile, a development and design group assembled by the development partnership of Oliver McMillan/Odmark & Thelan initiated a strategy of land acquisition and community involvement to formulate a community- and market-responsive plan for redevelopment of what was by then an expanded 14-acre site. Ultimately, the city accepted the plan through a competitive selection process. The plan called for 144,000 square feet of retail space, a 3,000-square-foot community center, 318 residential units, and 1,200 parking spaces. A central feature is a supermarket sited behind smaller stores to provide a continuous street facade along University Avenue. A boulevard through the residential portion of the site is part of the pedestrian-scale street grid, and a central courtyard adjacent to the community center is the focal point of the entire development. The three-story residential buildings are clustered around courtyards built over underground parking and street-level stores. Michael Stepner, then city architect, observed, "Uptown District has broken new ground, placing dense development on an infill site in a way that is acceptable

and maintains community character. This project takes a giant step toward making Hillcrest an urban village that works."[46]

A smaller but still complex residential development in an already developed area likewise employs courtyards and underground parking. Developed entirely by private interests, Madison Place provides 125 townhomes on a six-acre site in Northern Virginia in a previously declining neighborhood of single-family bungalows just 20 minutes from downtown Washington, D.C., as shown in

figure 6-17. Five groups of townhomes are clustered around highly landscaped courtyards. Below the courtyards, driveways lead to the homes' underground garages. Despite the project's infill location, the developer was required to upgrade roads and stormwater systems in the area. The townhomes, priced at $220,000 to $240,000, have sold well.[47]

Brownfields as Infield Development Sites. Sites that encompass brownfields present a special case with respect to the natural landscape. The U.S. Environmental Protection Agency (EPA) defines

The Uptown District: A Mixed-Use Development Replaces a Shopping Center 6-16

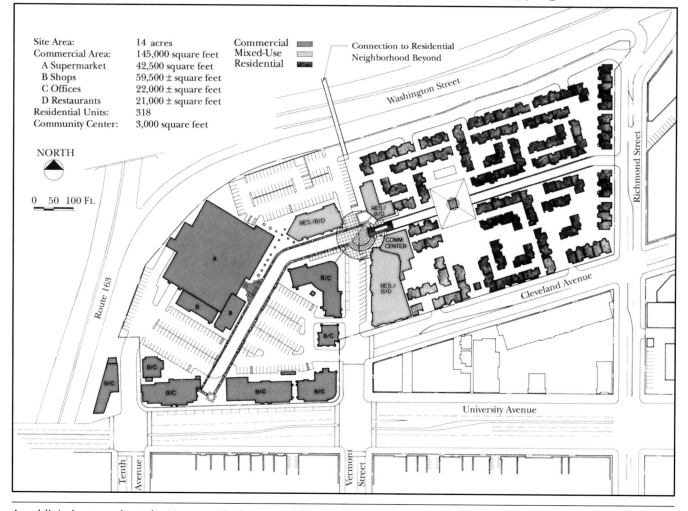

Site Area: 14 acres
Commercial Area: 145,000 square feet
 A Supermarket 42,500 square feet
 B Shops 59,500 ± square feet
 C Offices 22,000 ± square feet
 D Restaurants 21,000 ± square feet
Residential Units: 318
Community Center: 3,000 square feet

Commercial
Mixed-Use
Residential

Connection to Residential Neighborhood Beyond

A public/private project, the Uptown District exemplifies a development designed to be compatible with and supportive of the surrounding neighborhood.

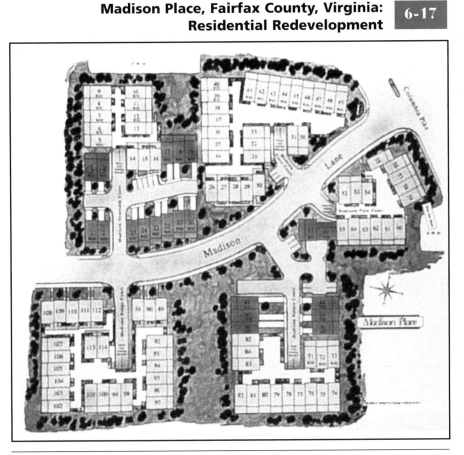

On a six-acre infield site, 125 townhomes replaced a declining low-density residential area.

brownfields as "abandoned, idled, or underused industrial and commercial facilities where expansion or redevelopment is complicated by real or perceived environmental contamination." Even though the EPA has pruned its Superfund list to about 1,200 sites, some estimates claim that 400,000 to 500,000 brownfield sites exist, ranging from closed gasoline stations and dry cleaners to abandoned railyards and steel mills. Many, but not all, are located in urbanized areas and are especially prominent in inner-city areas where large-scale manufacturing occurred for up to a century or more. In many cases, the sites' size and location make them prime candidates for redevelopment; many states and municipalities favor the economic revitalization that can flow from investments in brownfield cleanup.

Developers, however, have learned to approach the development of brownfields with great caution. Not only are many sites located in areas considered commercially undesirable, but federal laws governing cleanup may also require massive and frequently unexpected investments by current and past property owners. Ironically, the liability provisions of the Superfund law—the Comprehensive Environmental Response, Compensation, and Liability Act of 1980, known as CERCLA—discourage redevelopment and even encourage abandonment to avoid cleanup liability. Thus, brownfields or sites incorporating brownfields may prove to be risky investments that drive off lenders.

Nonetheless, several trends are helping to enhance the potential for brownfield

development. First, evaluations of site cleanup needs often reveal that contamination, although suspected, is either absent or not sufficiently widespread or dangerous to require expensive remediation. As part of its Brownfields Pilot Program, for example, the city of Chicago conducted environmental audits of several former industrial sites desired as expansion sites by adjoining industries. While the sites had become dumping grounds and eyesores, the city found no significant contamination or only a minor need for remediation, thereby making the parcels available for reuse.[48] Second, Congress amended the Superfund law in 1997 to hold lenders harmless when financing redevelopment of brownfield sites; in addition, at least 35 states have enacted legislation to limit cleanup liability. As a result, insurance companies are now writing policies to limit developer liability and financial institutions are making loans for brownfield development.

Third, state and local agencies have become more knowledgeable about cost-effective cleanup approaches and are frequently willing to provide tax incentives for, and reduce the liability risks associated with, cleanups. Fourth, as changing demographic and economic factors begin to favor central locations, inner-city brownfields are becoming increasingly desirable development sites. The last two trends are exemplified in the development of Washington's Landing, located on Herr's Island two miles from downtown Pittsburgh. The former heavy industrial site required a two-year environmental cleanup financed by state and city agencies. In 1995, builders Montgomery and Rust initiated construction of upscale townhomes and an office park flanked by a rowing club, tennis courts, and a marina. By early 1999, 65 townhomes had been completed and sold at prices ranging from $139,000 to $560,000; by the end of 1999, the project had moved into

Brownfields reused for Washington's Landing, Pittsburgh, Pennsylvania. Townhomes and a mix of commercial and office uses recycled a former industrial site in an attractive center-city location.

its final phase. The Pittsburgh Urban Redevelopment Authority, in addition to managing the predevelopment planning and cleanup efforts, constructed basic infrastructure systems, a public park, and a riverside pathway and helped finance the development.[49]

On sites where contamination is suspected, the landscape analysis should include testing for the presence of toxic wastes. If significant contamination is found, the developer will need to work with state and local agencies to determine cleanup needs and potential financial assistance in meeting remediation requirements. Ideally, testing for toxic wastes should occur before the developer's final acquisition of the site.

Developing for Economic and Social Enhancement

Sustainable developments are not only concerned with a site's natural features and the arrangement of buildings, streets, and open spaces; they are also focused on the people who will live and work in the developments and the adjoining neighborhoods. To be sustainable, physical systems must mesh with and enhance the economic and social fabric of the development and its host community. As stated in the Urban Land Institute's *Trends and Innovations in Master-Planned Communities,* "[P]lanning for the future can no longer simply involve issues of land use and density . . . . For future communities to be truly competitive they must provide quality of life for the community's residents."[50]

Providing opportunities for citizens' economic and social well-being is an essential responsibility of government, but developers can advance the principles of sustainability by attending to such concerns in planning and managing development. In particular, devel-

opers can contribute to sustainable social and economic activities by carefully specifying project components that support stimulating activities and by connecting on-site facilities and activities to the broader community. In addition, developers can work to link economic and social activities to the conservation of natural resources.

Broadly stated, initial determinations of the components of a proposed development should consider possibilities for advancing social and economic opportunities. Plans for large residential developments routinely recognize the need for schools, parks, playgrounds, religious buildings, and other community facilities and amenities—all supportive of a sustainable society. In fact, developers are increasingly aware of the competitive edge they may gain from providing top-quality educational opportunities in new developments. Many times, local school districts are unable to finance the timely construction of needed schools. For this reason, developments such as Hidden Springs near Boise, Anthem near Phoenix, and Westin in Broward County, Florida, built schools during the initial phases of development. Some developers have even taken the next step of launching programs to enhance the quality of local education. For example, the Grupe Company's Brookside Community employs a teacher full time on its community association staff and lends the teacher to the middle school to help establish goals and benchmarks for student achievement.

A survey of existing facilities around a proposed development may identify needs and opportunities that can be satisfied on the development site. Even a relatively small development, for example, can host a branch library or child care center or provide space for adult education. Haile Plantation's village center, for example, provides these types of services. Especially if wrapped into a central mixed-use activity center along with shopping, office, and school facilities, space devoted to community services can help create the beneficial sense of place already described. At the same time, a survey of existing facilities may reveal opportunities for meeting the needs of on-site residents by connections to off-site facilities. One of the advantages of the Village Green development (low- to moderate-income housing in Los Angeles) is access to a transit station and an adjoining child care center just across the street from the development.

Developers also look for opportunities to provide retail shops and related services that benefit site and neighborhood residents. Depending on the size of the development, possibilities can range from major shopping malls to small spaces within residential buildings. One of the first buildings completed in Hidden Springs was a general store that offers convenience supplies for new residents; it also accommodates an informal eating space (to be converted later to a fire station), a central mail pickup point, and the sales office for the development, which will eventually be converted to general office space. The 30-unit Knickerbocker Lofts, an adaptive use development in New Rochelle, New York, incorporates 3,000 square feet to be used for neighborhood retail services. A southern California developer, Alexander Hagen, has focused on constructing neighborhood shopping centers, typically anchored by Ralph's supermarkets, aimed at underserved African American and Hispanic neighborhoods in south-central Los Angeles.

Including job-creating businesses in development also helps support the founding and expansion of local firms while widening employment opportunities for local residents near their homes. Business, industrial, and mixed-use developments can include incubator space to nurture new compa-

nies and expand local employment. The Can Company development located in a revitalizing neighborhood east of downtown Baltimore, for example, adapted a historic industrial complex to create neighborhood-supporting retail uses, along with jobs for local residents. It also provides incubator space for new businesses that are expected to create new jobs in the area. The project was encouraged by community leaders who saw the need for neighborhood-serving activities to support regeneration of the historic residential area. As for outlying sites, developers can work with large employers to incorporate telecommuting centers that are available to local residents who wish to reduce long-distance commuting a few days each week.

In addition, many developers can work with public agencies and labor unions to offer job opportunities both during and after construction. For infield developments in particular, nearby residents can learn new skills for later use in the employment market. Developers may also help support local business

development by working with public agencies to spur "access-to-jobs" programs that provide transportation and related job counseling. These efforts benefit both unemployed workers in central-city labor pools and suburban businesses that need to fill jobs.

Developments may also advance social opportunities by offering a range of housing options, including affordable housing for moderate- to low-income occupants. In many cases, projects are eligible for public financial assistance that makes possible discounted home prices.[51] The Village Green development in Los Angeles, featuring single-family homes targeted to a moderate-income market, has arranged for a partial rebate of construction loan interest, thereby reducing by almost half the income requirements for purchase of some of the development's 186 homes. RiverStation, a multiphase residential development in Minneapolis, offers opportunities for middle-income owners and renters—a market ill-served in the past—to live near downtown. The 360 condominium apartments in

A can-do project: The Can Company in Baltimore, Maryland. Leveraged by city and state funds, the Can Company development transformed a vacant industrial complex in a reviving residential area into a neighborhood-friendly retail and office center.

113

the first phase and 232 rental units in the second phase are expected to encourage revitalization in the immediate area. The Minneapolis Community Development Authority, which assembled the property and sold it to the developer for $1, is providing below-market mortgages that will allow families with incomes as low as $36,000 (compared to the Minneapolis median of $57,300) to purchase homes in the development. In the initial phase of Rancho Santa Margarita's development, 65 percent of the residential units were priced to meet Orange County's (California) affordable housing standards.

Infield developments that may displace existing residents should not ignore residents' housing needs, especially in the case of low-income occupants who may find alternative housing difficult to obtain. Where displacement will occur, developers should plan ahead by arranging for relocation assistance if necessary and even for affordable rehabilitation rather than demolition of existing homes.

Development of open space and recreational amenities also serves social goals. As discussed earlier, the provision and layout of parks and recreation areas in developments should take account of the different needs of residents and, if possible, should link to open-space systems around the development. Rancho Santa Margarita's 2,500-acre open-space system, for example, connects to O'Neill Regional Park. Such facilities and connections will improve social interaction both within the development and with adjoining neighborhoods.

Social and economic concerns also focus on safety, a continuing worry for many Americans. Developers who plan to do away with gates to maintain connections to the larger community can turn to other measures for ensuring safety. Site and building design is a primary consideration. Techniques such as designing for high levels of activity on streets and in public areas, installing appropriate lighting in those spaces, and carefully designing other open spaces to ensure their visibility from adjacent buildings can stifle opportunities for crime. Laying out small, distinct neighborhoods can encourage residents to watch out for each other. In larger developments, privately hired security patrols have been successful in limiting crime. The Woodlands in Houston reduced crime and increased social interaction by using highly visible horse patrols.

Finally, developers can help educate site occupants to appreciate and maintain the sustainable features of their homes and work environment. Raising residents' awareness of the environmental values of a site's natural qualities helps affect occupant behavior—what Dewees Island developer John Knotts calls "building institutional memory"[52]—and protect those qualities. Some developments sponsor interpretive nature walks or make on-site features available as laboratories for school programs. Dewees Island has gone further, creating partnerships with local schools to sponsor environmental programs that include class instruction as well as field trips to the island throughout the school year. Other projects such as Shenoa Retreat and Learning Center in Mendocino County, California, and Rancho San Carlos in Carmel, California, marketed land stewardship as a primary lure for buyers willing to pay premiums to preserve open space and support sustainable practices in community and building design. Guests at Shenoa, for example, are educated about the food grown in the center's organic garden. The food is then served to the visitors and the surplus donated to a food bank. The ecotourist resort, Harmony at Maho Bay in the Virgin Islands, showcases innovative building technologies. Closer to home, developments can make community gardens available for cultivation by residents and hire local farmers to teach the basics of successful food production, thereby reducing needs for importing food.

Conclusion

This chapter identifies numerous paths and approaches to investing developments with sustainable features. Many are feasible and applicable to a variety of developments; others are most useful in particular locales, climates, terrains, and markets. Developers and their consultant teams can map out paths to sustainable development through their initial decisions on development locations and specific sites; their subsequent determinations of the program of uses and activities to be developed, the green infrastructure to be preserved and restored, and other community facilities and infrastructure to be developed in support of the built environment; and their judgments on the place-making and livability qualities of that built environment and the economic and social factors that can be satisfied and enhanced through the planned development. Developers do not make these decisions in a vacuum; they must be supported by community policies and programs and private market practices that make it at least as easy to apply the principles of sustainability as to produce another conventional project.

1. Presentation by John Laswick at the October 1999 annual meeting of the Urban Land Institute in Washington, DC.

2. Paul H. Ray, "Toward a Winning PCSD Strategy," research paper prepared for American LIVES, Inc., 1997.

3. "Hometown Connections, Residential Survey," table from Appendix C: Question 10D, p. 13 (prepared by RKS Research, Consulting).

4. *Nations Building News,* December 1994.

5. "Community Preferences: What the Buyers Really Want in Design, Features and Amenities," American LIVES, Inc., in cooperation with Intercommunications, Inc., February 1999.

6. William H. Frey, "America's Demography in the New Century: Boomers and New Immigrants as Major Players," in *Housing in the 21st Century, A Symposium Report* (Washington, DC: Urban Land Institute, 1999), p. 11, figures 4, 5, 6.

7. Ibid.

8. William H. Whyte, Jr., "Are Cities Un-American?" in *The Exploding Metropolis,* William H. Whyte, Jr., ed. (Berkeley: University of California Press, 1993; original edition, 1957), pp. 23-52. Cited in Robert E. Lang, James W. Hughes, and Karen A. Danielsen, "Targeting the Suburban Urbanites: Marketing Central-City Housing," *Housing Policy Debate,* Vol. 8, Issue 2, p. 437.

9. Alexander von Hoffman, "Housing Heats Up: Home Building Patterns in Metropolitan Areas," Center on Urban & Metropolitan Policy, Brookings Institution, December 1995 Survey Series.

10. National Association of Home Builders, *Smart Growth: Building Better Places to Live, Work and Play* (Washington, DC: NAHB, 1999), pp. 14-16.

11. 1995 New Urbanism Study by American LIVES, Inc., in cooperation with InterCommunications, Inc., San Francisco, summarized in newsletter of the Real Estate Center of the University of Colorado at Boulder, 1997.

12. Mark J. Eppli and Charles C. Tu, *Valuing the New Urbanism* (Washington, DC: Urban Land Institute, 1999).

13. George B. Brewster, *The Ecology of Development: Integrating the Built and Natural Environments,* Working Paper No. 649 (Washington, DC: Urban Land Institute, 1997), p. 26; updated by Michael Horst.

14. See, for example, Ian L. McHarg, *Design with Nature* (New York: John Wiley & Sons, 1992), reprint of the 1967 edition; and Randall Arendt, *Conservation Design for Subdivisions: A Practical Guide to Creating Open Space Networks* (Washington, DC: Island Press, 1996).

15. See, for example, Andres Duany and Elizabeth Plater-Zyberk, *Towns and Town-Making Principles* (New York: Rizzoli, 1991); and Peter Calthorpe, *The Next American Metropolis* (Princeton: Princeton Architectural Press, 1993).

16. Peter Newman and Jeffrey Kenworthy, *Sustainability and Cities* (Washington, DC: Island Press, 1999), p. 258.

17. Newman and Kenworthy, p. 258.

18. Robert Steuteville, "New Urban News," [reprinted from *In Business*], posted on the Web by the Florida Sustainable Communities Center at sustainable.state.fl.us.

19. Mike Miles, Richard L. Haney, Jr., and Gayle Berens, *Real Estate Development: Principles and Process,* 2nd Edition (Washington, DC: Urban Land Institute, 1996), p. 189.

20. *Real Estate Development: Principles and Process,* p. 192.

21. See McHarg.

22. For more on the Woodlands development, see D. Scott Middleton, "The Woodlands: Designed with Nature," *Urban Land,* June 1997, pp. 26-30.

23. Charles A. Veatch, *The Nature of Reston* (Reston, VA: Charles A. Veatch Co., 1999); and Adrian Higgins, "What Reston Did Right for Gardeners," *Washington Post,* February 17, 2000, pp. G1, G10.

24. Laswick, note 1.

25. Information supplied to the author by Thomas A. Forman, Chicago Associates, Chicago, Illinois.

26. See Eric W. Strecker, "The Use of Wetlands for Storm-Water Pollution Control," *Infrastructure,* Vol. 1, No. 3, pp. 48-66, 1996.

27. Center for Watershed Protection, "The Importance of Imperviousness," *Watershed Protection Techniques,* Vol. 1, No. 3, Fall, 1994.

28. These conclusions are presented in a report on a recent analysis of permeable pavements, which included a survey of findings from previous studies as well. See Derek B. Booth and Jennifer Leavitt, "Field Evaluation of Permeable Pavement Systems for Improved Stormwater Management," *Journal of the American Planning Association,* Vol. 65, No. 3, Summer, 1999, pp. 314-325.

29. Ibid.

30. Information supplied to the author by Neil Weinstein, executive director, The Low Impact Development Center, Inc., Rockville, MD, in December 1999.

31. American Institute of Architects, *Environmental Resource Guide,* April 1993.

32. Newman and Kenworthy, p. 64.

33. Rocky Mountain Institute, *Green Development* (New York: John Wiley & Sons, 1998), p. 192.

34. For more information on development opportunities in rail station areas, see Michael S. Bernick and Robert B. Cervero, *Transit Villages in the 21st Century* (New York: McGraw-Hill, 1996); and Project for Public Spaces, Inc., *The Role of Transit in Creating Livable Metropolitan Communities* (Washington, DC: National Academy Press, Transit Cooperative Research Program, 1997).

35. Bernick and Cervero, *Transit Villages in the 21st Century,* p. 242.

36. TDA Inc., "Hidden Springs Transportation Management Plan," July 16, 1997.

37. Robert Dunphy and Ben C. Lin, *Transportation Management through Partnerships* (Washington, DC: Urban Land Institute, 1990), p. 125.

38. Brewster, *The Ecology of Development.*

39. William R. Nelson, Jr., "Trees in the Landscape: A Look Beyond the Obvious," *Journal of Arboriculture,* Vol. 1, 1975, pp. 121-128.

40. American Forests, *Urban Ecosystem Analysis Reports,* 1996, summarized in *State of Our Urban Forest,* 1997.

41. Elizabeth Brabic, "Trees Make Cents," *Scenic America Technical Information Series,* Vol. 1, No. 1, 1992.

42. For example, see Lloyd Bookout et al., *Residential Development Handbook,* Second Edition (Washington, DC: Urban Land Institute, 1990), pp. 144ff; American Planning Association, *The Cluster Subdivision: A Cost-Effective Approach,* Planning Advisory Service Report #356 (Chicago: APA, 1980); and National Association of Home Builders, *Land Development* (Washington, DC: NAHB, 1994).

43. Presentation by Robert N. Elliot, senior vice president for urban planning and design for the Irvine Company, at the Urban Land Institute annual meeting in Washington, DC, October 23, 1999. Also profiled as one of ULI's Awards for Excellence in *Urban Land,* July 1998.

44 Lucie Vogel, "Collaborative Planning for Infill Development," *Planner's Casebook* (Chicago: American Institute of Certified Planners, 1998).

45 Diane R. Suchman, *Developing Infill Housing in Inner-City Neighborhoods* (Washington, DC: Urban Land Institute, 1997), p. 43.

46 Janice Fillip, "Uptown District, San Diego," *Urban Land,* June, 1990, pp. 2-7.

47 National Association of Home Builders, *Smart Growth: Building Better Places to Live, Work and Play* (Washington, DC: NAHB, 1999), pp. 17-18.

48 City of Chicago, *Brownfields Forum Final Report and Action Plan,* November 1995, p. 8.

49 National Association of Home Builders, *Smart Growth: Building Better Places to Live, Work and Play,* pp. 18-19.

50 *Trends and Innovations in Master-Planned Communities* (Washington, DC: Urban Land Institute, 1998), p. 5.

51 For more information on affordable housing programs, see Michael A. Stegman, *State and Local Affordable Housing Programs: A Rich Tapestry* (Washington, DC: Urban Land Institute, 1999), which profiles over 100 affordable housing programs that might be employed in developments; and Tom Jones, William Pettus, and Michael Pyatok, *Good Neighbors: Affordable Family Housing* (New York: McGraw-Hill, 1995), which highlights 85 case studies on affordable housing design and development.

52 See Rocky Mountain Insitute, *Green Development* (New York: John Wiley & Sons, 1998), p. 372.

chapter 7

SUSTAINABLE BUILDING

Susan Maxman with Robert Hotes, Muscoe Martin,
Don Prowler, George Brewster, and Douglas R. Porter

This chapter describes methods of constructing human shelter in the most sustainable way. Buildings reflect a culture's values and knowledge while their physical form helps shape our outlook and behavior. But buildings also consume vast amounts of materials and energy, both in initial construction and subsequent operation. The architecture and site orientation of buildings, the materials used for construction, and the selection of building lighting, heating, cooling, and ventilating systems all affect the ways in which buildings use resources. If we make informed choices, we can design buildings to conserve rather than consume resources, support and restore rather than destroy natural systems, and mitigate rather than exacerbate the impacts of development on the environment.

Sustainable building, or "green architecture," looks beyond the realization of a physical shell made up of foundations, walls, and roofs to view building design as part of the natural environment and human, economic, and social institutions. To be sustainable, building

design must evolve from concerns for environmental impacts, human needs, cultural vision, and social remediation. "Green" buildings are designed to conserve resources but, in the end, must also inspire, inform, and motivate their occupants to think differently about their relationships to each other and to the environment that surrounds them.

Unfortunately, too many people equate "green" building with "green" dollar bills—that is, building green means building expensively. It is true that initial costs for some elements of green building can exceed the costs of conventional approaches. Life-cycle costs, however, are lower, with the payback frequently occurring within five years. It is also true that with resourceful design, green building, when considered as a whole, can save money at the outset—what Amory Lovins calls "tunneling through the cost barrier." Porous paving, for example, a more costly material than regular paving, eliminates the need for more expensive independent drainage systems. So-called "super windows" are so well insulated that

they can preclude the need for perimeter heating, thereby generating additional energy savings. Use of highly efficient lighting, at no greater cost than conventional lighting, can reduce air-conditioning tonnage. "Green architecture" therefore is not necessarily more costly if design solutions are integrated to realize savings in one area as a result of conservation in another.

Another potential stumbling block in undertaking green building is fear of the unknown. Development clients often ask for proof of savings, for a record of experience over time, for assurance that a proposed design is not a radical departure from accepted practice. Most people are reluctant to be part of an experiment. They want to have confidence that a green product or solution has a proven track record. When our firm suggested incorporating a raised floor system into a renovated building to allow flexibility in distributing both the electrical and HVAC systems, the client first rejected the design as too innovative and unproven. In fact, this design approach has been used for many years in Germany and for several years in the United States. When, however, we demonstrated that the design would also negate a requirement for leveling the existing floor slab and eliminate duct work, the client decided to be "experimental."

The same arguments hold for reusing existing structures. Often the costs associated with rehabilitating existing structures are a deterrent to reuse. If true costs were assigned (such as costs for infrastructure extensions and environmental degradation), new construction would be seen to be more costly. The embodied energy of existing materials and reuse of land and infrastructure make building restoration a superior choice for achieving efficient use and preservation of natural resources. In addition, building reuse often stimulates revitalization in the surrounding area.

When, however, the decision is made to build a new structure, the first question is why a building in Boston should look and function like a building in Houston or Phoenix. Why should the building site and landscaping look the same in Atlanta and San Diego given the large variation in climate and availability of water. Yet, over the past few decades, buildings have become homogenized statements of the current trend. Designers pay little attention to the character of the place or microclimate that might be reflected in building designs. More important for sustainability, many designers are neither interested in nor encouraged by their clients to look for ways to reduce resource consumption through choice of design, materials, equipment, and siting.

Students of "indigenous" architecture—buildings constructed without the use of an architect—know that those edifices evolved out of necessity and practicality. They demanded a respect for the culture of the community and the specific character of the climate, site,

and place. Indigenous designs are beautiful because nothing about the architecture is arbitrary. They are sensitive designs based on the availability of local resources. Montezuma's Castle in New Mexico is a great example. It merges beautifully with the spectacular natural setting; its orientation welcomes the warming winter sun but shades the structure from the hot summer sun. Adobe wall construction uses local materials from the desert. The elegant simplicity of the structure flows from its design response to local conditions—the definition of "green" architecture in its most fundamental sense.

Designers of indigenous architecture did not have the luxury of importing materials from across the globe. The materials they used were locally available and suitable for their use. Buildings in Boston were constructed of timber, taking advantage of the region's plentiful wood that also provided excellent insulation for the wintry climate. Adobe wall construction in the Southwest accommodates the extremes of heat and cold in that region; it absorbs sun during the day and radiates heat during the night.

Today, with easy access to all parts of the world, architects think nothing of specifying materials that must be imported from great distances. The energy used in transporting those materials can, however, be tremendous. Consider the use of energy in quarrying granite in North Dakota, sending it to Italy for processing, and then bringing it back to New York to clad a building—a common practice in construction. Architecture that demands heavy investments of energy for transportation or fabrication compromises designs for energy efficiency within a building.

Some communities have taken steps to require greater consideration of local materials and conditions in the design of buildings. In Nantucket, all houses

must be constructed of wood weathered to the natural gray of the adjoining woodlands, celebrating the New England tradition of using local materials and minimizing the visual impact of buildings on their setting. In Bermuda, all buildings are constructed of masonry with stepped, white roofs to reflect the hot sun, collect rainwater, and survive hurricanes. Both Nantucket and Bermuda claim some of the most highly valued real estate in the world. People seek out the two islands for, among other attributes, their distinctive regional architecture. In other locations as well, designers can infuse their designs with the concept of sustainability by understanding the local and regional culture and climate, the availability of local materials, and the character of a site.

Designers make many choices to help ensure that buildings "tread lightly on the earth," minimizing the impact of buildings on the natural environment. One important choice is to build only the amount of space actually needed. Skillful designs can meet project goals and still minimize building size. Other choices about siting, materials, and equipment must be considered in light of the particular limitations and influences of the building's use and location.

All of these issues must be approached holistically with "whole-system" design thinking. Norman Kurtz, a mechanical engineer in New York, explains the strategic design approach to energy-efficient buildings by comparing the energy consumption of a sailboat to a motor boat. Due to its careful design, a sailboat needs only the smallest of motors to propel it through the water, whereas a power boat of the same size needs a much larger motor. Similarly, buildings designed to achieve optimal energy efficiency must be designed from the beginning with this aim in mind. A decision to employ a highly efficient HVAC system is not enough to save substantial amounts of energy. The building's orientation to the sun, the design of the building's "skin," and the selection of glazing methods are also important in achieving that goal. Designing the 24,000-square-foot Women's Humane Society building in Philadelphia, for instance, involved the skills of many consultants who merged their knowledge from the initiation of design to achieve annual energy savings of more than $40,000 over a conventional design. The interdependence of the design effort mimics the natural environment, the elements of which are all interdependent. Sustainable design takes the arbitrariness out of the design equation, providing an integrated response to the design problem. Designers must remember the Native American adage: We do not inherit our land from our ancestors, we borrow it from future generations.

This chapter describes how traditional building practices can be combined with current technologies to create buildings that work in harmony with nature and provide better places in which to live, work, shop, and be entertained. Environmentally responsible buildings provide a foundation for future generations to build upon rather than leaving behind a legacy of burdens and waste. The following sections of this chapter describe approaches to energy conservation, material choices, and reuse of existing buildings that will help achieve green buildings and sustainable development.

Energy Efficiency

Reducing building energy consumption may be the single most important aspect of sustainable development. But what constitutes an energy-efficient building? Unfortunately, the answer is not a simple one. The amount of energy a building consumes depends critically on many factors, including local climate, square footage, functional use,

architectural design, and the selection of mechanical systems. Some of these factors, such as design and systems selection, are within the control of the developer while other factors, such as climate and use profile, provide the framework within which alternative decisions must be evaluated. Still, as has been suggested, "The challenge in every modern building is to close the gap between the climate that it naturally generates and the one people expect with a minimum of environmental damage."[1] The goal for energy efficiency in buildings is to emulate natural systems, which function on renewable energy sources and minimize the generation of waste. That goal can be achieved through thoughtful integration of the energy-saving opportunities available from sunlight and by taking advantage of landscaping, site attributes, and materials.

According to the Lawrence Berkeley National Laboratory (LBNL), world energy use for buildings will grow at a compounded rate of approximately 2.4 percent annually through 2020 if current consumption patterns persist. This rate can be reduced to about 1 percent by applying off-the-shelf technology, although LBNL estimates that the application of advanced solutions can reduce the rate to zero.[2] Today, most of our energy comes from nonrenewable sources such as coal, oil, and gas. Before the industrial revolution, these resources seemed virtually inexhaustible. However, with a burgeoning population consuming an ever-greater amount of resources, our "inexhaustible" supply of fossil fuels will invariably begin to dwindle. Furthermore, use of fossil fuels generates air pollution that is difficult to control and—most scientists agree—slowly leading to global climate change.

Largely due to building code changes resulting from the 1970s oil crisis, today's new buildings are much more

energy-efficient than those constructed just a few years ago. Nevertheless, new homes, offices, and other buildings constructed to current standards could be even more energy-efficient with just minor changes in their design and the specification of materials and equipment. According to the U.S. Department of Energy, for instance, homes incorporating simple passive solar principles generally require about 30 percent less energy for heating than equivalent code-conforming homes. The use of well-insulated and tightly constructed building shells in conjunction with passive solar design and energy-efficient mechanical systems can save 75 percent or more on residential utility bills as well as reduce initial HVAC equipment costs. The opportunities for energy conservation in commercial and institutional buildings are on the same order.

Though building energy requirements vary dramatically, it is possible to make some generalizations about energy use that can guide conceptual decision making. Of course, like all rules of thumb, any generalization must be applied with caution and a healthy respect for the uniqueness of every project.

How Buildings Use Energy. From an energy perspective, most buildings can be characterized as either *skin-load dominated*—also called envelope-load dominated—or *internal-load dominated*. In skin-load dominated buildings, energy consumption is determined primarily by heat flow through the building envelope as driven by the exterior climate. In other words, when it is cold outside, occupants must purchase a lot of heating energy to keep warm; when it is warm outside, occupants must purchase a lot of cooling energy to keep cool. The primary example of a skin-load dominated building is a single-family detached house, but many small, freestanding commercial and institutional buildings (of, say, 5,000 square feet or less) behave thermally in a similar fashion.

By comparison, the energy consumption in internal-load dominated buildings is more heavily influenced by the demands of electrical and mechanical equipment, including the lighting system, the ventilating system, and computers and other business equipment—often called the plug load. Examples of internal-load dominated buildings include large office complexes, department stores, and hospitals. In these cases, lighting, ventilating, and computing requirements drive energy consumption patterns more than climate. For example, during winter, many office buildings in temperate climates actually consume more energy for cooling than heating because of the need to compensate for the waste heat generated by lights, people, and plug loads. In internal-load dominated buildings, annual cooling requirements usually exceed heating requirements on an energy or cost basis.

Most large-scale developments are composed of buildings of both thermal types. Accordingly, it is important for developers to appreciate that the design approaches to saving energy in different buildings types vary significantly.

Skin-Load Dominated Buildings.
Single-family homes and other small buildings consume energy in different ways in cold versus hot climates. For a skin-load dominated building in a cold climate, most cost-effective/energy-reduction strategies involve techniques and investments for reducing heat loss.

Improving envelope design. In cold climates, minimizing energy use begins with optimizing the efficiency of the building envelope. The performance of the building envelope can be increased by reducing the building perimeter, providing high insulation levels, reducing air infiltration, eliminating thermal bridges

(short circuits through the building envelope, such as uninsulated perimeter slabs or continuous building framing), and optimizing window selection.

Insulating walls for optimum energy efficiency usually means providing R-values higher than the minimums required by building codes. Infiltration should be reduced to 0.35 to 0.5 air changes per hour (ACH) through improved construction quality and detailing. Decreasing infiltration, however, must be considered in conjunction with potential indoor air pollution problems, moisture build-up, and proper ventilation. When buildings are very tight, interior materials, finishes, and furnishings must be selected carefully and adequate fresh air provided for occupant health.

In homes, windows can account for up to 25 percent of a building's heat loss and 30 percent of its cooling load. In cold climates, window design and materials should vary according to the direction they face. South-facing windows can take advantage of solar energy to help heat the building while north-facing windows can lose a significant amount of heat in winter in almost any climate. Large east- or west-facing windows increase heat gain unless shaded for at least part of the day. It is easier to decrease window areas on east and west exposures than to design adequate shading.

Using high-performance glass. In recent years, many residential window manufacturers have dramatically improved the thermal performance of their products largely with the application of low-emissivity (usually referred to simply as low-e) coatings. These coatings retard the flow of heat in and out of glass due to temperature differences, effectively increasing the thermal resistance—or R-value—of the window assembly.

What is less well understood is that not all low-e coatings are the same. Some

are designed for hot climates and some for cold climates. Low-e coatings designed for northern climates reduce temperature-driven heat loss while still permitting a large percent of desirable solar heat gain to pass through. Low-e coatings designed for southern climates again reduce temperature-driven heat loss but also reduce the transmission of solar heat gain to lessen cooling requirements.

In addition, inert gas fills such as argon and krypton can be added between panes of glass to reduce heat loss further. In fact, some large residential window manufacturers now provide low-e glass with inert gas fills as standard practice. In some cases, triple and quadruple glass units combined with multiple low-e coatings have been coupled with highly energy-efficient frames to produce "super" windows whose insulating effect rivals those of insulated walls. While these windows come with a high cost premium, part of their first cost can sometimes be recovered by the elimination of perimeter heating systems in some types of buildings.

Employing passive solar heating. The use of solar energy in all its various forms should be considered for all buildings—whether located in cold or warm climates. The term passive solar heating may conjure up images of geodesic domes to some, but the techniques developed in the 1970s under oil embargo conditions have been highly refined over the years. They are now used in many everyday applications with outstanding results.

A typical passive solar-heated residence orients a larger-than-typical area of glass within 30 degrees of due south. The solar energy admitted through the glass heats up—or "charges"—thermally massive building surfaces that are enclosed within the building's insulated envelope. The surfaces may be constructed of concrete block, brick, stone, and even encapsulated water. The heat captured by these building elements is slowly released into the interior during the night and other sunless periods.

Studies by the U.S. Department of Energy indicate that a conventional frame house meets about 10 percent of its heating needs from passive solar heat that enters through the normal allotment of south-facing windows; the balance is supplied by energy from other sources. Optimizing the building envelope and increasing insulation increases the amount of heat load supplied by solar heat to 15 percent of the total. Expanding the amount of south-facing glass and coupling it with adequate mass can increase the solar contribution to between 25 and 75 percent depending primarily on climate and window area.

Optimizing orientation and site planning. From an energy perspective, it is usually best to elongate small buildings in an east/west direction. Such an orientation increases the area of the south facade and encourages the addition of south glass for passive solar heating. At the same time, it minimizes the area of east and west glass that is difficult to control in terms of glare and unwanted summer heat gain.

Other aspects of site design can have a significant impact on energy consumption. For example, compact planning can maximize the use of party walls and other shared surfaces that reduce heat loss (and gain) to the environment. And pedestrian-friendly communities can save energy by reducing automobile traffic.

For the design of a skin-load dominated building or complex in a warm climate, much of the same guidance applies, but it should be supplemented by strategies that reduce unwanted summer and swing-season heat gain through windows, walls, and roofs.

Improving window orientation and shading. When possible, the area of east and west windows should be limited. Given that the sun is relatively low in the sky in the early morning and late afternoon, it is impossible to shade east- and west-facing glass efficiently with simple overhangs or other fixed shading devices. East- and west-facing windows must be shaded by more complex devices such as vertical fins, canted egg-crates, or operable louvers.

At most North American latitudes, windows located on the south side of buildings can be well shaded with simple horizontal overhangs. For most of the day, north-facing glass in most American climates sees limited direct sunlight and therefore generally requires little or no shading.

Optimizing envelope performance. As in cold climates, it is important to design and construct tight building

Passive solar heating. South-facing windows provide passive solar heating in this attractive, single-family home in Colorado.

envelopes, particularly when a building is to be mechanically air conditioned. In many residences, the infiltration of unconditioned air into the dwelling represents the single largest contributor to cooling loads.

In hot climates, roofs should receive special attention because of their capacity to absorb or reflect heat from the high summer sun. Typical dark-colored asphalt shingles on homes or tarred roofs on commercial buildings soak up solar radiation, convert it to heat, and then transmit the heat to the interior of the building over time.

According to the Florida Solar Energy Center, attic temperatures can be reduced by as much as 30 degrees Fahrenheit by using reflective roof surfaces such as light-colored metal roofing. White painted metal is preferable to bare metal, which absorbs a relatively high percent of the solar energy that hits it.

Encouraging passive cooling through natural and fan-assisted ventilation. The careful placement of windows, doors, skylights, and other openings makes it possible to achieve considerable cooling through cross-ventilation, particularly in swing seasons. A room at 82 degrees Fahrenheit with a ceiling fan has the same comfort level as a room mechanically cooled to 78 degrees. In some climates, the use of ceiling-mounted paddle fans and attic-mounted whole-house fans can significantly increase the portion of the year when mechanical cooling can be avoided at the expense of small amounts of electrical energy. In other words, on a square-foot basis, ceiling fans typically consume about one-twentieth the energy of mechanical cooling systems while whole-house fans might require one-tenth the amount.

In some dry climates with cool summer evenings, coupling nighttime natural ventilation with thermal mass is an excellent strategy for reducing cooling requirements for the next day. The thermal mass of a structure is a measure of the capacity of the structure to absorb and store heat. In general, the greater the density of the materials, the better the materials store heat. Due to its "massive" construction coupled with fan-assisted ventilation, a demonstration house built by the Pacific Gas and Electric Company in its 1993 Energy-Wise program maintains 68- to 70-degree interior temperatures during the Napa Valley's 100-plus-degree summers without any air conditioning or mechanical ventilation.

For skin-load dominated buildings in all climates, efficient mechanical systems should be installed. As a rule of thumb, builders should specify and install air-conditioning systems with SEER ratings and heating systems with AFUE ratings that are in the upper quartile of available equipment. These systems will prove cost effective, with simple payback periods of less than ten years in nearly all utility districts. When not provided as standard equipment, upgrades to more efficient equipment should be offered by developers and actively encouraged through marketing campaigns and incentive programs.

But the installation of efficient mechanical equipment does not guarantee that a system will be properly operated. To optimize system performance, heating and cooling equipment should be controlled by advanced thermostats that provide for automatic and easily programmable winter setbacks and summer setups. "Easily programmable" is the key term. In households where the VCR is blindly blinking the time, there is no reason to believe that setting the thermostat properly will be any easier to master.

Efficient home appliances should also be specified. Refrigerators are now available that deliver energy savings of nearly 50 percent compared with five-year-old conventional models, and they no longer use CFCs as refrigerants or in their foam insulation.

A new generation of horizontal-axis washing machines and dishwashers that require less water to operate is also becoming widely available. Though currently more expensive than standard models, the cost of the equipment is expected to drop significantly in coming years. Even now, however, the models pay back handsomely on a life-cycle basis with dramatic annual savings in water, energy, and detergents.

Internal-Load Dominated Structures. In the case of internal-load dominated structures, effective energy-saving strategies tend to focus on reducing artificial lighting, ventilating, and mechanical cooling requirements.

Optimizing electrical lighting design. In many older commercial and institutional buildings, lighting energy accounts for as much as half of all energy consumption on a dollar basis. For this reason, it is crucial in a sustainable building that efficient fixtures and lamps are specified as part of an integrated lighting solution. The results can be impressive—a decade ago offices routinely required installed lighting levels of two to three watts per square foot (kW/ft^2); today, high-performance offices can be constructed with installed lighting levels of 1 kW/ft^2 or less.

Results like these have been achieved by using several strategies, such as substituting compact fluorescent sources for incandescent sources whenever possible; employing task/ambient lighting design with reduced ambient footcandle levels; and providing automatic or easy-to-use manual lighting controls, including occupancy sensors and on/off scheduling.

The Energy Policy Act of 1992 stated that, after October 31, 1995, conventional T-12 fluorescent lamps would no longer be produced in or imported into the United States. Instead, thinner T-8 fluorescent lamps have become the norm. Combined with parabolic reflectors, dimmable electronic ballasts, and occupancy and ambient-light sensors, a new generation of T-8 fixtures can yield significant energy savings.

The substitution of compact fluorescent for incandescent lamps is also becoming standard. For example, five Red Lion hotels in Portland, Oregon, retrofitted nearly 3,000 old-style incandescent light fixtures with compact fluorescent lights in all corridors, lobbies, and exteriors. They cut energy use for lighting by at least 80 percent. The same technology can be applied to domestic use. Compared with incandescent bulbs, compact fluorescent lights can reduce energy use in the home by 75 percent while reducing operating costs over their lifetime by 51 percent.

Incorporating daylighting. Another approach to reducing energy consumption for lighting is daylighting. Daylighting is the controlled admission of natural light to building interiors by using light "shelves" and other reflecting and diffusing surfaces to permit energy-consuming artificial lighting systems to be dimmed or turned off. Daylighting is possible only if natural light does not contribute to excess cooling loads and does not create glare or uncomfortable contrast. Good daylighting is not, however, as simple as adding more windows.

Properly implemented, daylighting has a dual benefit. It saves the electrical energy that would have been required to run the lights as well as the cooling energy that would have been required to extract the waste heat given off by the lighting. But remember—the benefits of daylighting can be harvested only if adequate lighting controls are in place

and functioning properly. Depending on space use, criticality of task, and other factors, appropriate control choices include photosensors, occupancy sensors, and timers.

The Norm Thompson Outfitters building developed by the Trammell Crow Company in Portland, Oregon, integrated natural daylighting, high ceilings, and reflective surfaces and colors to increase available light and reduce energy demand. Fixed metal "light shades" inside and out help reduce glare and heat gain and bounce light into the building's interior. Compact fluorescent bulbs, computer-controlled dimmable ballasts that adjust lights in response to daylight levels, and "light sweeps" that turn off lights at night also add to lighting efficiency. All these measures cut utility bills by 40 percent, saving $122,000 per year and offsetting the extra costs of other green measures.

Natural light has also been shown to benefit worker productivity and health. The design for a new Lockheed Corporation office building for 2,700 employees in northern California stressed nat-

A daylighting technique. A light-reflecting "shelf" bounces daylight onto the ceiling of a perimeter office, allowing the electric lighting system to be dimmed.

ural daylighting. The design reduced lighting costs by 75 percent and overall energy costs by 50 percent, but it also contributed to a decline in absenteeism of 15 percent.[3] With a similar goal in mind, some European countries now require a third or more of a building's interior light to come from natural sources.

Specifying glazings carefully. In many large buildings, a significant percent of the heat that finds its way inside on a sunny day results from through-glass transmission. Fortunately, a new generation of high-performance glazing products—sometimes known as super windows—permits designers, engineers, and consultants to control such transmission. Low-e coatings can be combined with specific tints to produce spectrally selective glass that differentiates between light and heat. For example, it is now possible to specify glass that admits adequate levels of visible light for daylighting while blocking heat from the infrared portion of the solar spectrum. By varying the glazing according to solar exposure, the transmission of natural light can be maximized or minimized to prevent glare and solar heat.

In commercial construction, spectrally effective low-e windows cost slightly more than conventional windows, but they can reduce solar heat gain through windows by as much as 50 percent with a minimal reduction in daylighting. Depending on the amount and orientation of windows, overall building energy reduction can total as much as 10 to 20 percent. Such windows also improve radiant comfort (lower interior air temperatures in winter without discomfort) and permit the specification of downsized HVAC equipment while decreasing external noise penetration and reducing maintenance costs. In addition, they provide better daylighting, which, in commercial settings, can increase worker productivity.

Super-window glazing is most effective when it is mounted in frames with thermal breaks or frames manufactured of vinyl, wood, or fiberglass. Vinyl is the best insulator and costs only slightly more than noninsulating aluminum frames while wood and fiberglass frames are both slightly less effective insulators. Fiberglass, unlike wood, is maintenance-free but costs 20 percent more than vinyl.

Incorporating high-efficiency mechanical equipment. Heating and cooling equipment is available throughout the country with a wide range of system efficiencies. Examples of high-efficiency options include condensing furnaces for residential heating and centrifugal chillers with low kW/ton ratings for commercial cooling. Invariably, the incremental cost of higher-efficiency equipment more than pays for itself on a life-cycle basis, particularly when operations and maintenance (O&M) considerations are taken into account.

From a developer's perspective, the challenge is how to justify any first-cost increase when tenants are responsible for future utility costs. There is no easy answer to this question. However, it has been repeatedly demonstrated that reducing loads through conservation and integrated design can lead to savings in the size and first cost of HVAC equipment; cost savings can then be applied to efficiency upgrades. And some developers, such as the Durst Organization, which is responsible for the highly publicized Four Times Square building in New York City, report that sensitivity to energy and environmental concerns has attracted renters and led to accelerated rates of leasing.

In utility districts with high-demand rate schedules, reducing peak kilowatt electrical demand is as important as reducing annual kilowatt consumption. In these cases, consideration should be given to incorporating peak reduction and peak shifting strategies. Strategies

may be as simple as flushing the building in the evening with cool night air in climates with high diurnal temperature swings (the Southwest) to the development of a full-scale off-peak "coolth" storage plant in the Northeast. A facility of this type takes advantage of inexpensive nighttime electric rates to produce an ice slurry in the evening that is used as a source of cooling when electric rates are high the following afternoon.

In all parts of the country, it is essential to consider other system optimization strategies such as the use of energy recovery and economizer equipment. Energy recovery hardware preconditions outside air by using the exhaust air stream of a building; economizer equipment makes use of unconditioned air directly for ventilation when air temperature and humidity are within the comfort range.

Optimizing distribution and delivery strategies and systems. In commercial and institutional buildings, the energy consumed by fans to distribute hot and cold air throughout a structure often accounts for a surprisingly high share of overall energy consumption. Depending on building type and climate, a wide range of delivery systems such as variable air volume (VAV) fan boxes and raised-floor access plenums for HVAC and network distribution can save energy and improve local comfort conditions. Properly installed access floor systems also provide greater flexibility, improved indoor air quality (IAQ), and reduced O&M costs.

As a rule, it is essential to encourage the use of variable-speed motors and fans throughout a project as well as to encourage the installation of easy-to-use central energy management systems that integrate the operation of all equipment within the building.

Consider Renewable and Alternative Fuel Options. For all developments regardless of building type and climate,

Off-peak energy storage. This off-peak energy storage facility on the University of Pennsylvania campus in Philadelphia takes advantage of low off-peak electric power rates to produce an ice slurry at night that is used as a source of cooling the next day.

it is important to consider renewable and alternative fuel sources. A new generation of decentralized generation equipment is gaining popularity. Examples include small-scale cogeneration equipment for on-site electric production, the use of geothermal heat pumps that rely on the earth as a heat source and sink, and gas-fired, CFC-free absorption chillers. The economic viability of these systems varies on a project-by-project basis.

The use of solar energy in its various forms should be considered for all projects. For example, passive solar heating with south-facing windows is an excellent strategy for application to skin-load dominated buildings in cold climates. And solar hot-water heating (also called solar thermal) can be an excellent choice for domestic hot-water heating in sunny climates, particularly as an alternative to high-cost electric resistance heat.

It is essential to investigate the use of building-integrated photovoltaics (BIPV) in all projects. With photovoltaic (PV) technology (also called solar cells), sunlight is converted directly into electricity. In particular, a new generation of amorphous silicon PV material can be deposed in vacuum chambers in very thin films on traditional building substrates such as glass, plastic, and roofing materials and used as part of conventional building assemblies. Active solar hot-water systems can provide half to all hot water needs but are typically more expensive to install than conventional systems. Nonetheless, they can be much less expensive to operate and extremely cost effective as a supplement to conventional systems, especially when an energy-efficient building envelope lowers heating loads and allows downsizing of conventional systems. In addition, production solar water heaters such as the Copper Cricket and similar systems have no moving parts and are highly reliable. Similar systems are stan-

Access Floors. Access floors permit easy distribution of conduit, cables, and air supply. This example viewed through a transparent panel in the South Central Office Building of the Pennsylvania Department of Environmental Protection outside Harrisburg increases flexibility of service, provides local climate control, and saves energy through reduced fan power and air temperature.

Use of photovoltaic technology. A small PV panel sits atop a metal roofing panel. Under full sunlight, a PV panel of this size is capable of producing about 60 watts of electricity per hour.

dard equipment in new homes and offices in many countries, yet the technology remains virtually ignored in the United States.

PV technology is rapidly becoming more efficient and lower in cost. Homes, office buildings, and retail stores will soon be able to generate more power during the day than they consume at night. In fact, PV power generation costs are approaching a level that is competitive with conventional sources and far lower than that of nuclear power. Greater use of PV cells will make it more feasible to go "off the grid" for electric heating, cooling, and lighting.

Already, the homes in Village Green (see figures 7-1 and 7-2), an 18-acre, 186-unit development of low- to moderate-priced homes in Los Angeles, offer PV solar power as an option. Village Green is being built under the

Partnership for Advancing Technology in Housing (PATH) program—a public/private partnership supported by the U.S. Department of Energy and other groups to speed the creation and use of advanced technologies in making housing more energy-efficient and affordable.

Developed under a joint venture of the Lee Group and Braemar Urban Ventures, Village Green is designed according to new urbanism principles at an overall density of slightly more than ten units per acre. Of the 186 homes, 131 are equipped with PV cells that are expected to generate up to 60 percent of electric power needs. Costs will be partially written down by the Los Angeles Water and Power Company. Each solar system is projected to produce 3,000 kilowatt hours per year—up to 90 percent of a home's electrical demand. In addition, home designs

call for upgraded insulation, spectrally selective glass windows, natural-gas air conditioning and water heating, fluorescent light fixtures and bulbs, and horizontal-axis washing machines. To add to its sustainability features, Village Green is located just across the street from a rail station.

Bring a "Whole-Building Approach" to Design. Integrated, or whole-building design, balances the impact of architectural decisions on heating, cooling, and lighting energy consumption. For example, in a cold climate, adding south-facing windows to a medium-sized office building might reduce winter daytime heating requirements, increase winter nighttime heating requirements, increase summer cooling loads, and reduce electric lighting energy consumption. The extent of the lighting energy savings depends critically on the type of

Village Green, Los Angeles, California 7-1

A section of the site plan indicates the small lots, narrow streets, and outward-looking home sitting next to the transit station.

electric lighting controls in place, the efficiency of the artificial lighting system, and the degree to which the building was already benefiting from daylighting. Given these energy tradeoffs, how does the designer determine if the decision to add windows is a good one?

For complex structures, the emerging answer is that quantitative, computer-based analyses of building energy consumption should be performed as a continuing aspect of the design process. Even if a project cannot justify comprehensive computer analysis, it is advisable to select architects and engineers intuitively familiar and experienced with the relative energy implications of design decisions. Many of the most cost-effective energy strategies, such as the extent and orientation of glazing and the relationship between building envelope design and building interior systems, must be addressed early in the design process. As a proj-

ect progresses, more and more opportunities are lost.

As an illustration of the variety of energy-efficiency choices and trade-offs, the developers of Four Times Square in New York City considered a wide range of energy-saving options during development of the high-rise office building depicted in figure 7-3. Ultimately, they chose large windows that provide daylighting but minimize solar heat gain; electrical-generation fuel cells for the late-night base load and photovoltaic cells integrated into the building's southern and eastern façades; the introduction of filtered outside air from ducts in higher floors for indoor air quality; use of natural gas as the cleanest-burning fossil fuel for heating and cooling; and an absorption chiller for energy-efficient cooling. The developers rejected light shelves as too risky for implementation by tenants; wholesale use of fuel

cells as inefficient for the given building height and mass; roof-top photovoltaic cells as unsuited to the weight of window-washing rigs; greater reliance on photovoltaic cells on the façade as financially unacceptable because of the cost risks of an untested application; and operable windows for indoor air as impractical because of the building's height.[4]

Unquestionably, the greatest energy savings associated with any structure comes from an integrated approach to design, as illustrated by the experience at Prairie Crossing near Chicago. At Prairie Crossing, Shaw Homes worked with the U.S. Department of Energy (DOE) and the Building Science Corporation under DOE's Building America Initiative to develop and test an integrated residential design. By incorporating an advanced framing system, high-efficiency windows, increased insulation, extensive sealing

Energy-Saving Features in Village Green Homes 7-2

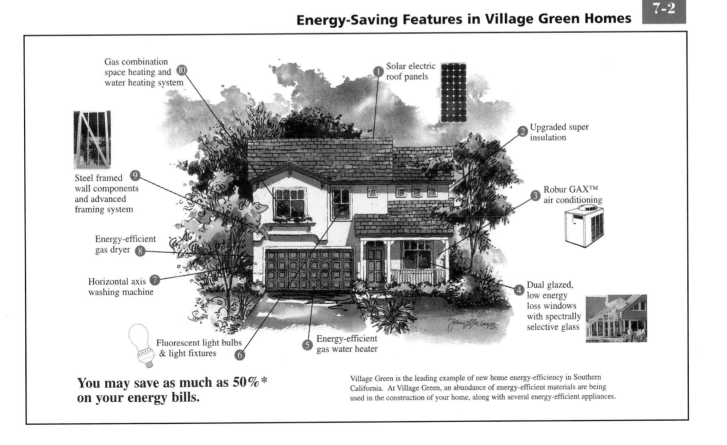

Gas combination space heating and water heating system ⑩

Solar electric roof panels ①

② Upgraded super insulation

Steel framed wall components and advanced framing system ⑨

③ Robur GAX™ air conditioning

Energy-efficient gas dryer ⑧

Horizontal axis washing machine ⑦

④ Dual glazed, low energy loss windows with spectrally selective glass

Fluorescent light bulbs & light fixtures ⑥

Energy-efficient gas water heater ⑤

You may save as much as 50%* on your energy bills.

Village Green is the leading example of new home energy-efficiency in Southern California. At Village Green, an abundance of energy-efficient materials are being used in the construction of your home, along with several energy-efficient appliances.

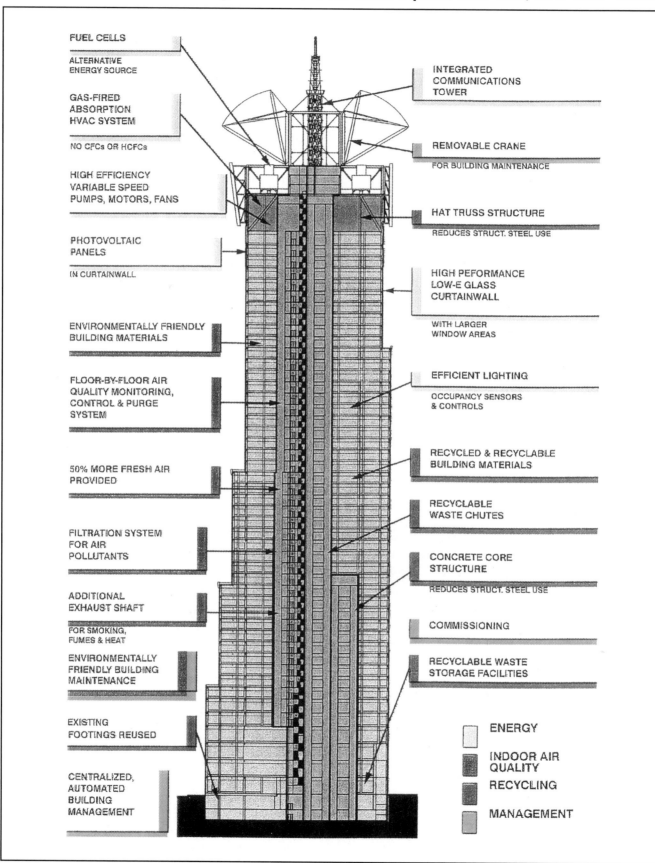

FUEL CELLS

ALTERNATIVE ENERGY SOURCE

GAS-FIRED ABSORPTION HVAC SYSTEM

NO CFCs OR HCFCs

HIGH EFFICIENCY VARIABLE SPEED PUMPS, MOTORS, FANS

PHOTOVOLTAIC PANELS

IN CURTAINWALL

ENVIRONMENTALLY FRIENDLY BUILDING MATERIALS

FLOOR-BY-FLOOR AIR QUALITY MONITORING, CONTROL & PURGE SYSTEM

50% MORE FRESH AIR PROVIDED

FILTRATION SYSTEM FOR AIR POLLUTANTS

ADDITIONAL EXHAUST SHAFT

FOR SMOKING, FUMES & HEAT

ENVIRONMENTALLY FRIENDLY BUILDING MAINTENANCE

EXISTING FOOTINGS REUSED

CENTRALIZED, AUTOMATED BUILDING MANAGEMENT

INTEGRATED COMMUNICATIONS TOWER

REMOVABLE CRANE

FOR BUILDING MAINTENANCE

HAT TRUSS STRUCTURE

REDUCES STRUCT. STEEL USE

HIGH PEFORMANCE LOW-E GLASS CURTAINWALL

WITH LARGER WINDOW AREAS

EFFICIENT LIGHTING

OCCUPANCY SENSORS & CONTROLS

RECYCLED & RECYCLABLE BUILDING MATERIALS

RECYCLABLE WASTE CHUTES

CONCRETE CORE STRUCTURE

REDUCES STRUCT. STEEL USE

COMMISSIONING

RECYCLABLE WASTE STORAGE FACILITIES

ENERGY

INDOOR AIR QUALITY

RECYCLING

MANAGEMENT

and caulking of the building envelope, high-efficiency (and downsized) mechanical systems, and a controlled ventilating system, Shaw Homes was able to reduce home energy consumption for heating and cooling by 48 to 65 percent compared with typical Chicago-area new homes. In addition, construction waste was lowered by 20 percent. On the basis of the success at Prairie Crossing, Lake County, Illinois, adopted a new Advanced Energy-Efficient and Resource-Efficient Single-Family Residence Code, which is the first voluntary code in the United States to incorporate the principles of the Building America Initiative.

The Bottom Line. Many of the strategies employed to reduce energy consumption, such as tighter envelopes, reduced infiltration, and controlled daylighting, also contribute to improved building durability and increased user productivity. For example, based on a daylight demonstration project outside Kansas City, Wal-Mart has reported that natural light contributes to retail sales. While it is often difficult to quantify nonenergy benefits, they are real and in many developments can offer critical marketing advantages.

This message has not been lost on consumers. Over the last decade, several surveys confirm that consumers are willing to pay a modest premium for buildings that do not pollute and that contribute to rather than detract from the environment. Low-energy development is good building and good business.

Construction Materials

Building components (walls, roofs, floors, and so forth) are composed of an extraordinary number of materials (wood, concrete, metal, rubber, and so forth) and natural and synthetic substances. Materials consume resources and energy and generate indoor and outdoor pollution through manufacture, extraction, or collection; assembly into building components and transportation to the construction site; installation in or on the building; and even eventual removal. A sustainable design approach to choices of materials strives to reduce the several environmental effects of building construction. Buildings designed for resource efficiency minimize the use of nonrenewable resources, eliminate toxics, use recycled and recyclable components, recycle construction waste, and plan for long-term durability, adaptability, and low-cost maintenance.

Strategies for optimizing choices of materials for new buildings fall into three categories:

▪ Use less. Finding ways to use less of any material will reduce any negative impacts associated with the material's production and installation.

▪ Reuse materials. Using salvaged or recycled-content materials can reduce the amount of "new" energy and resources required to produce a material.

▪ Choose wisely. Evaluating and balancing environmental performance criteria such as long-term durability, embodied energy, toxicity, and pollution against conventional criteria such as cost, appearance, code compliance, ease of use, and resistance to fire, pests, storms, earthquakes, and so forth can guide the selection of new building materials.

Use Less. A sustainable design approach suggests using only as much material as needed, i.e., build the smallest building that will accommodate the proposed use. The single most important step in designing resource-efficient buildings is to make structures space-efficient by reducing their size and thus reducing the use of materials and overall environmental impacts while lowering land and construction costs. The current interest in the "small house" is a recognition of both environmental and cost concerns in the residential market, although such interest is being counteracted in many areas by trends toward building "monster" houses.[5]

Designing to use materials more efficiently can also help reduce overall material use. Modular design that uses the familiar two-, four-, and eight-foot sizes common to many building products in the United States can reduce construction waste from cut-offs and trimming. Here, the manufactured housing industry stands as a model. The manufacturing process generates little waste by using full sheets of materials such as plywood, wallboard, and flooring. A recent publication by the Natural Resources Defense Council describes framing techniques for more efficient use of wood.[6]

Reuse Materials. Reuse of salvaged building products and materials extends the life of products/materials and eliminates the impacts related to the production of new goods. When a product is "reused," the product or material is used in substantially the same condition as its previous installation, capturing the benefit of desirable materials, such as old timbers, as well as the processes that created it. Recycling, by comparison, involves some form of processing and remanufacturing the material into a new item. Recycling usually downgrades the characteristics of the product in the remanufacturing process; it also requires energy and sometimes produces pollution or waste. Nevertheless, recycling means less demand for new resources.

Active markets in salvaged timber, flooring, and other wood products provide materials that can be less expensive than, and provide unique qualities not available in, virgin materials. In addition to salvaged materials, a wide range of building products is available with varying percents of recycled content—from wallboard, flooring, and ceiling tiles to structural steel, roofing, and decking. Several resource guides list recycled building products.[7] For the Norm Thompson Outfitters building in Portland, Oregon, hardwood flooring was created from salvaged railroad cars; interior walls and floors were finished with Milestone, an aggregate of cement and crushed windshield and bottle glass; and restroom partitions were fabricated of 90 percent recycled plastic bottles. At the Cusano Environmental Education Center in Philadelphia, the exposed timber structure is made from 60-year-old salvaged Douglas Fir logs, the rubber flooring from recycled truck tires, the ceramic tiles from recycled glass, and wall insulation from recycled newsprint.[8]

Recycling waste from construction sites is becoming more common and accepted in many parts of the country. Due to rising tipping fees at landfills, recycling materials can often be less expensive than disposal. It is estimated that between 15 and 20 percent of the solid waste in the United States is construction and demolition debris.[9] According to the National Association of Home Builders Research Center, construction of a 2,600-square-foot house today generates more than 10,000 pounds of scrap material, about 50 cubic yards in volume. That represents a material cost of $1,274 and a disposal cost averaging $511. Some 40 to 50 percent of the waste is wood and wood-based products that could be recycled for mulch or other building products.[10]

The advantages and costs of jobsite recycling have been studied by the NAHB Research Center, which found that savings on disposal costs could range from 25 to 50 percent.[11] Several local government agencies have developed specifications and recommendations for recycling materials, including

Salvaged timber. Wood for the timber frames at the Cusano Environmental Education Center in Philadelphia was salvaged from the Columbia River. Fifty-year-old Douglas Fir logs had been abandoned after logging operations ceased.

Construction site recycling in Philadelphia. A truck unloads scrap wood at a facility dedicated to recycling construction and demolition materials.

the Triangle J Council of Governments in North Carolina, Alameda County (California) Waste Management Authority, Metro (Portland, Oregon), and King County (Washington).

"Deconstruction" is a term that describes piecemeal demolition of

buildings to allow reuse of materials. In some communities, deconstruction has provided opportunities for training and employment of people otherwise unemployed.[12] The ability to dismantle a building or its parts to permit salvage for reuse and recycling is thus a consideration for sustainable design.

During renovations or demolition, it is much more likely that materials will be recycled if they are easily separated from each other. Composite products made of dissimilar materials permanently bonded together are often used in buildings because of their complementary qualities (such as steel-reinforced concrete and carpet with backing). These qualities must be weighed against the difficulty of separating the materials for recycling after their removal from a structure.

Choose Wisely. The selection of building materials requires several traditional criteria, including cost, appearance, and performance, to be balanced against one another. A sustainable design approach, however, requires environmental performance to be balanced against the range of traditional criteria. Life-cycle analysis (LCA) of building materials was developed to assist in the evaluation process. LCA is a formalized method to assess the economic and environmental costs of production, use, and disposal of a given material. The *AIA Environmental Resource Guide* includes LCAs for several but not all construction materials. In the absence of a national database of information on building materials and assemblies, designers and builders should take into account durability, resource efficiency, use of renewable resources, embodied energy, and avoidance of materials generating toxic gases—in addition to availability and ease of use.

Durable materials have two advantages. First, although their initial cost might be greater, durable materials' longer life provides lower operating and maintenance costs. Second, durable materials over their lifetime consume fewer resources and generate less waste than that associated with replacement or reconstruction. If necessary, durable materials can be more easily reused in other buildings.

Resource-efficient construction makes efficient use of limited resources and nonrenewable materials. In addition to salvaged and recycled goods, resource-efficient materials include engineered wood, sustainably harvested lumber, and products made from renewable resources.

There has been much discussion during the past decade over the appropriate use of wood in construction. Lumber from old-growth forests, for example, is valuable and will have a long life if it is cut from high-quality trees into large-dimension units. Yet, North America's remaining old-growth forests are increasingly valued as habitat for endangered and other species. In fact, environmentalists strongly discourage the use of wood from these forests. At the same time, though, the dimensional framing lumber (2 x 4s and 2 x 6s) so popular for residential and light-commercial construction is increasingly cut from fast-growing softwood trees; it has a relatively short life and is subject to warping and splitting, leading to installation and maintenance problems. As a result, many residential builders are

switching to engineered wood products and alternative materials despite the products' higher material costs.

Engineered wood products are also made from fast-growing species but are processed and shaped to provide efficient structural members and panel products. Engineered wood products include plywood, oriented strand board (OSB), laminated veneer lumber, and engineered I-beams. The environmental benefits of engineered lumber lie chiefly in the fact that a higher percent of the tree is used; moreover, the fiber comes from younger, smaller species, thus reducing pressure to log the remaining older, more ecologically sensitive forests. Some manufacturers are also beginning to incorporate wood from "certified well-managed" forests. Other environmental considerations are the type of binder or glue used in the manufacture. Most products use a phenol formaldehyde binder that offgasses small amounts of formaldehyde, but some producers are using safer non-formaldehyde binders.

The widespread adoption of engineered wood products is attributable to the

Engineered wood products. These laminated veneer lumber and wood I-beams are examples of structural members made of engineered lumber that make use of fast-growing tree species.

products' other attributes. They are stronger, straighter, and easier to work with than sawn lumber. The Cusano Environmental Education Center, described above, uses a wide variety of engineered lumber—laminated veneer lumber for girders, wood I-joists for the floor structure, parallel strand lumber for headers and beams and, even white-washed OSB for exposed paneling. Engineered wood products cannot, however, replace dimensional sawn lumber for all framing needs; some-times a component must be specifically engineered for a given project.

A related product is structural insulated panel systems (SIPS) made of foam insulation sandwiched between sheets of OSB. SIPS offer high insulation values, minimal waste, and rapid assembly of walls and roofs, albeit with some loss of flexibility in design. Expanded poly-styrene insulation is currently the best choice for foam board, thus avoiding some of the toxic foams and glues that can cause indoor air pollution. The interior surfaces can be finished with drywall or wood panels.

Embodied energy defines the amount of energy a material requires for extraction, refining, shaping, and transportation to a building site. Because burning fossil fuels to make energy is the largest source of air pollution, embodied energy is an important factor in assessing the environmental impact of a particular material. For example, steel has high embodied energy since it involves mining and manufacturing and then transport usually across considerable distances. Concrete also has a relatively high embodied energy content due mainly to the presence of cement, a particularly energy-intensive compound to produce. Wood products, by contrast, consume a relatively small amount of humanmade energy but often require transport to the building site from great distances.

Despite its high embodied energy, concrete offers unique qualities that make it hard to replace as a building material, and there are ways today to reduce its embodied energy. Concrete is now available in new forms, such as autoclaved cellular concrete, which can be fabricated as lightweight blocks made from low-density formulas. Fly ash, the residue of coal-fired power plants, and pozzolanic materials (volcanic ash and pumice) replace some of the conventional Portland cement, thus reducing embodied energy while improving workability and reducing water demand.

Alternatives to concrete, such as earth and straw construction, have been used for centuries. Earthen walls last hundreds of years and eliminate the need for paint. Rammed earth has been used to build structural walls since the construction of the Great Wall of China. It was used by Thomas Jefferson at Monticello after he discovered its use in the French châteaux of the period. Industrialized countries have been developing methods

The National Audubon Society Reception Area. The reception area and interior stair receive daylight from a skylight and south facing windows. The reception desk is constructed of certified mahogany and maple.

Source: Jeff Goldberg/Esto.

for producing rammed earth walls at low cost and with high strength and great durability. Modern variants of rammed earth use high-strength binders and are gaining popularity in places such as France and Australia because of their beauty and practicality. New production methods such as pneumatically impacted stabilized earth have been developed in the United States to meet California's strict energy and seismic codes. The new methods incorporate steel reinforcement and can be produced quickly at costs competitive with wood-frame construction. According to the Worldwatch Institute, earthen materials have an ecological price only one-fortieth that of concrete.[13] Rammed earth, straw bales, and other alternative construction materials have met some resistance with building code officials. Once building code and distribution questions have been resolved, the various methods of rammed earth construction will undoubtedly become more popular.

Roofing materials are one of the most important and expensive elements of a building and therefore pose a major challenge for green building. Because roofing is usually replaced several times during the life of a building, its most important environmental aspect is longevity. A durable roof is long-lasting and thus produces less waste and requires less energy and fewer resources than new roofing. About 75 percent of roofs on new homes and small commercial buildings are covered with asphalt shingles, which are energy- and resource-intensive to produce and offer only limited durability. Old asphalt shingles also contribute substantially to landfills when they are finally discarded. Other commonly available roofing materials such as clay tile, fiber-cement tiles, and metal roofing are more durable and can sometimes achieve energy savings by reflecting heat. Fiber-cement roofing is emerging as a highly resource-efficient, durable alternative, although some products have performed poorly in northern climates

where freeze-thaw cycles are prevalent. Metal roofing, common in commercial and retail construction, is gaining market share in the residential market due to its durability and fire resistance.

Avoid Toxic Materials. The EPA estimates that over 1.3 million office buildings in the United States have indoor air quality problems. Many chemical and bacterial pollutants have been identified, including bacteria in air-handling systems, ozone from fax machines, and hydrocarbons and particulates from printers. Symptoms of exposure to toxics in the indoor environment include headache; eye, nose, and throat irritation; sinus congestion; sleeping difficulties; and fatigue.

Building materials, particularly interior finishes, have also been identified as potential sources of indoor air pollution. For this reason, building designers should avoid specifying products that include or produce toxic materials such as formaldehyde, volatile organic compounds (VOCs), and certain wood preservatives. VOCs, such as solvents and thinners found in paints, finishes, and glues, contribute to photochemical smog and ground-level ozone pollution. They are also the major source of indoor air pollution and cause toxic or allergic reactions in many people. Recent research by Lawrence Berkeley National Laboratory indicates that indoor VOCs from water-based paints and solvents may be directly responsible for eye and skin irritations.[14] One of the most effective practices for good indoor air quality is to specify low– or no–VOC adhesives and glues for carpet, flooring, wall coverings, and other finishes. Petroleum distillates, dyes, and formaldehyde-based adhesives and backings generate gases for years.

CFCs and HCFCs are volatile chlorine compounds that decrease the ozone layer in the stratosphere. The stratosphere protects us from excessive

exposure to ultraviolet rays, which can cause skin cancer and eye disease. Excessive exposure to rays also affects wildlife and ecosystems. Freon is a CFC, as are many other refrigerants. CFCs are also used in the manufacture of many types of rigid foam insulation (such as Styrofoam). HCFC refrigerants are less harmful than CFCs; in fact, in a properly maintained system, they are benign. The use of HCFCs in manufacturing foam board, however, releases a great deal of gas into the atmosphere. Foam insulation board made without these compounds should be specified when possible.

Nearly all pressure-treated wood contains toxic substances such as inorganic arsenic, copper, naphtha, and pentachlorophenol that cause damage to ecosystems, especially aquatic life, and pose a health hazard for construction workers. The substances can contaminate soil long after construction. Alternative treatment methods such as borate are becoming more widely available, but building codes do not always recognize the alternatives as equivalent. Although more expensive than conventional products, recycled or synthetic materials used for decking, posts, and pilings are safer and more durable than pressure-treated lumber for applications requiring resistance to dampness and soil organisms.

An environmentally sensitive approach to building requires the consideration of several factors—in addition to cost, appearance, and function—in the selection of materials. "Green" factors include the effects of the materials on building energy consumption and durability as well as the environmental implications of the material itself. The selection process is rarely easy and requires the designer to balance numerous factors at the local, regional, and global scales that are often difficult to compare. However, given the tremendous impact of construction materials on the natural environment, it is impera-

The Thoreau Center for Sustainability, the Presidio, San Francisco, California. Environmentally sensitive materials included acoustical ceiling tiles from Armstrong World Industries, medium-density fiberboard (MDF) from Medite, panels made of wood from sustainably harvested forests from Architectural Forest Enterprises, wall panels from Homasote, cellulose insulation from GreenStone Industries, low-VOC carpeting from Collins & Aikman, linoleum (a product derived from natural materials) from DLW Linoleum, ceramic tile from Terra Green, and low-VOC paint from American Formulating and Manufacturing (AFM).

tive that we do the best with the information we have and strive to select materials with the optimum combination of desired characteristics and least ecological impact.

As an example, many insulation materials are energy-intensive in their manufacture, use toxic chemicals during production, and irritate the skin in the case of direct contact. On first appearance, the materials might be discounted for these reasons. However, when the impact of insulation on the energy use of the building is considered, the overall energy savings over the life of the building far outweighs the embodied energy of the insulation material; the pollution prevented from the associated power generation offsets the effects of the toxic chemicals used in the manufacture of the insulation; and building occupants will never come in contact with the insulation if the product is properly installed.

Adaptive Use of Buildings

The reuse of existing buildings, whether through restoration, renovation, or adaptation, presents a great opportunity for resource conservation and sustainability while meeting future needs for human shelter. From a sustainability perspective, the resource efficiency achieved through the embodied energy of existing building materials—the amount of energy required to produce, transport, construct, install, maintain, and dispose of a material—makes reuse the preferred alternative over new construction. Similar benefits arise from the infusion of new activities into business centers and neighborhoods seeking revitalization. Reuse of existing buildings also helps support existing infrastructure, including public transportation, saving millions of dollars in facility costs and further enhancing the economic and environmental benefits of rehabilitation. The timeless beauty, high-quality construction, and

durable materials of historic architecture that have allowed structures to withstand the ravages of time can continue to enrich our built environment.

Developers attracted by expanding consumer interest in in-town living and distinctive architecture, the availability of historic preservation and low-income tax credits, and active support from city agencies and community groups have generated a wave of adaptable use projects, especially over the past decade or two. Recycling old buildings has become a respectable market niche in almost every city and many older suburbs across the nation. Indeed, the abandoned industrial quarters of large cities offer good opportunities for reuse of existing structures. Many old industrial buildings, built of solid materials to withstand heavy loads and uses, provide wide-open floors and large expanses of glass. The flexibility inherent in their original design makes them adaptable for any number of uses.

In Tucson's old warehouse district, threaded along the Southern Pacific (now Union Pacific) railroad tracks that slice diagonally across the city's downtown, many of the old food depots,

lumber yards, icehouses, bottling plants, and commercial dry cleaners are being converted into artists' studios and art galleries. Previously slated for demolition to allow construction of a six-lane elevated highway, these buildings are being redeveloped through a combination of federal community redevelopment block grants, low-interest city loans targeted at the warehouse district, and federal and state tax incentives available for the rehabilitation of historic structures.[15] In older-city industrial districts, similar adaptive use is taking place: in Wichita's railroad industrial corridor, Denver's Lowertown, Portland's (Oregon) River District, "the Flats" along the Cuyahoga River in Cleveland, and Philadelphia's Old City. These former manufacturing and warehouse districts are finding new lives as old industrial structures are converted to apartments, offices, galleries, restaurants, and nightclubs.

Two interesting small-scale examples of industrial building reuse are Knickerbocker Lofts in New Rochelle, New York, and West Village in Durham, North Carolina. The Knickerbocker Press Building, built in 1890 in New Rochelle, was a three- and four-story

West Village, Durham, North Carolina. This nicely designed tobacco warehouse is one of five being refitted for loft aparments.

135

brick structure. It was renovated to provide 46 rental loft apartments, exercise and community rooms, and a small retail shop. It attracted middle-income tenants in a market known for its expensive homes. Financing was privately arranged but was supported in part by Fannie Mae's American Communities Fund, which purchased the historic tax credits generated by the project.

West Village in Durham is being developed near the successful Brightleaf Square, which opened in 1981 as an upscale retail project in two restored ornate brick warehouses. Brightleaf's performance in a declining industrial location prompted the developers of West Village to renovate five old tobacco warehouses for a mix of apartments, offices, and, possibly, stores. Planned to open in late 2000, the $36 million development will include 243 market-rate, loft-style apartments and about 31,500 square feet of commercial space. The largest private investment ever in Durham's downtown and the first apartment project in more than a decade, West Village is one of a number of projects underway that promises to revitalize downtown Durham. It, too, benefited from the purchase of federal historic preservation tax credits by Fannie Mae's American Communities Fund.[16]

Adaptive use is occurring in other urban locations as well, frequently in downtown centers and environs but increasingly in outlying locations such as neighborhood commercial centers. The Belmont Dairy project in Portland, Oregon, offers a premier example of reusing old structures and developing them to meet a broad array of sustainability principles. The Belmont Dairy, located in a mature residential neighborhood, had been abandoned for several years and was a neighborhood eyesore and a magnet for vandals. It was rehabilitated to house 19 market-rate loft units and 66 affordable, energy-efficient rental apart-

The Belmont Dairy Building, Portland, Oregon. The former industrial building has been adapted by using green building techniques to produce loft housing, retail shops, and offices. Photo provided by Shiels, Obletz Johnsen, Inc., Portland, Oregon.

Bethesda Row, Bethesda, Maryland. Federal Realty Investment Trust transformed several blocks of former light-industrial buildings and vacant lots near Metro Center to create pleasant shopping streets.

ments plus 26,000 square feet of retail space. The retail shops include a food market, restaurants, and other neighborhood-serving businesses.

Before construction, developers mitigated site contamination and removed asbestos-wrapped pipe, asbestos-packed boilers, lead paint, and transformer PCBs. During construction (half the original structure was reused), 90 percent of construction waste was recycled, including 612 tons of metal, 1,560 tons of concrete, and 52 tons of wood. The building's renovations called for maximizing insulation and weatherization, incorporating natural lighting and ventilation, and installing energy-efficient appliances and lighting, thereby saving about $3,000 annually in energy costs for the apartments. In addition, materials selected for the building included carpets made from recycled soda and catsup bottles, insulation made from recycled newspapers, and composite wood floor joists containing 40 percent less wood than sawn lumber. Native plants and a water-conserving irrigation system cut landscaping costs. A number of public and private financing sources funded the project, including city and state loans, federal grants, and low-income housing tax credits. The Belmont Dairy is viewed as a valuable addition to the neighborhood and has been applauded for spurring restoration in the area.

The EPA's retrofitted 600,000-square-foot office building in downtown Philadelphia includes the reuse of many building materials, lighting enhancements, improved indoor air quality, and proximity to a major commuter rail system. And the design and renovation of the National Audubon Society Headquarters in New York City involved innovative material specifications and measures designed to improve energy efficiency, resource conservation, and indoor air quality. The energy features alone have resulted in savings of

$100,000 per year with a five-year payback. A recycling system that added $185,000 to renovation costs will significantly reduce trash hauling fees, which averaged $12,000 annually. Altogether, Audubon estimates that renovation of its new headquarters will save $1 million a year in operations and maintenance costs.

Other examples are as diverse as two mixed-use projects developed in former department stores in downtown Newark, New Jersey; rebuilding an old Ford manufacturing plant in Richmond, California, for 246 live/work housing units, 49 of them affordable, as well as 185,000 square feet of office and retail space; converting a 21-story office building built in 1896 in New York City into 345 rental units; restoring and developing the mixed-use Tower City Center in Cleveland over the city's central rail station; and transforming a 20-story office building in downtown Seattle into a hotel. Although these projects may incorporate relatively few of the green measures described above, the use of the embodied energy of the existing buildings and the likelihood of spillover revitalization effects make the projects part of the sustainability story.

Another opportunity for reuse of existing structures is the wealth of existing construction on the many military bases and installations now abandoned by the federal government. As an example, at the Presidio near San Francisco, the wards of a former military hospital have been converted into the Thoreau Center for Sustainability. This $4.1 million project transformed a 75,000-square-foot complex into office space for 20 nonprofit organizations. While it includes a number of environmentally sensitive features, such as natural ventilation, energy-efficient building systems, sustainable or recycled materials, superior indoor air quality, indigenous low-maintenance landscaping and minimal

paving, and the reuse of an existing structure, the project remained within a tight construction budget of $55 per square foot. At the former Philadelphia Navy Yard, now the Philadelphia Naval Business Center, existing industrial structures are undergoing rehabilitation for office, educational, and light-industrial uses.

One hindrance to rehabilitation and reuse of existing buildings has been local and national building codes. Focused on new construction, the codes often make rehabilitation costs appear prohibitive. However, innovative code compliance alternatives, such as the BOCA National Building Code's Chapter 34 for Existing Structures and the New Jersey Uniform Construction Code's Rehabilitation Subcode, are now being used to encourage reuse of the existing building stock while maintaining the health, safety, and welfare of the public. In addition, recent efforts to create performance measures for green buildings are beginning to bear fruit, as discussed in the next section.

Finally, although the reuse of existing buildings offers great opportunities to conserve resources and encourage the redevelopment of urban centers, perhaps the most important legacy of reused structures is the example the structures set for new construction. Buildings designed and built to endure and be adaptable can be preserved for future uses. Flexible building systems, including moveable walls and raised-access floors, allow frequent and efficient changes in use with little to no waste. Buildings that are built to meet short-term needs, that are poorly designed, and that use materials of limited life spans result in excessive waste, loss of embodied energy, and destruction of natural resources. Although the lesson is simple, it is one that we have forgotten all too often, at great cost to our natural environment, our communities, and our quality of life.

Quality Assurance and Building Operation

Oceangoing ships undergo a prolonged series of sequential tests called sea trials before they are commissioned for service. Sea trials are a process in which every aspect of a ship's design is tested in real-world operation and adjusted until it works properly. New buildings, on the other hand, rarely get so much as a test drive.

Building Commissioning. As the construction process becomes more and more fragmented with construction managers, cost consultants, and client representatives vying with architects and engineers for control of a building site, it is important to ensure overall building performance through an aggressive program of quality assurance. Sometimes quality assurance involves a relatively new field called building commissioning. Commissioning is a systematic process for verifying adherence to design specifications and intent. It is usually accomplished through continuous adherence to a written program of testing, approvals, and acceptances throughout the design and construction process.

Preoccupancy commissioning should be commonplace for all buildings: single-family homes, renovated buildings, high-rise office buildings, and the rest. More complex systems require a structured approach to operations. A new or renovated building should be inspected and tuned before delivery to its users. Proper set up and balancing of HVAC systems is critical, as is ensuring that computerized thermostats and controllers are properly set for the specific building.

Maintenance and Operation. Even when buildings are properly commissioned, improper operation and neglected maintenance can turn structures into energy hogs and undo everything that was done right in design and construction. Once a building is occupied, it is essential to monitor performance of the facility and equipment over time. An essential part of ensuring the sustainability of green building features is to establish procedures for managing and monitoring building operations. To optimize performance, a comprehensive operations manual should be provided to occupants to detail the design and operation, maintenance, and trouble-shooting procedures for all significant systems and components, including measures such as calibration of sensing devices and operation of shading devices. A planned and integrated maintenance program helps realize the full potential of energy-efficiency measures as well as prevent problems that can lead to sick building syndrome.

Endnotes

1 Nicholas Lenssmen and David Malin Roodman, "Making Buildings Better," *State of the World 1995* (Washington, DC: Worldwatch Institute, 1995).

2 Lawrence Berkeley National Laboratory, *Center for Building Science News,* Winter 1996.

3 Rocky Mountain Institute, *Green Development* (New York: John Wiley & Sons, 1998), p. 166.

4 "Lessons Learned: Four Times Square." published by Earth Day New York, 1999, pp. 19-23.

5 See, for example, Sarah Susanka and Kira Obolensky, *The Not So Big House* (Taunton, MA: The Taunton Press, 1998).

6 Ann Edminster and Sami Yassa, *Efficient Wood Use in Residential Construction: A Practical Guide to Saving Wood, Money, and Forests* (Washington, DC: Natural Resources Defense Council, 1998).

7 One example is the *Guide to Resource Efficient Building Elements*, 6th Edition (Missoula, MO: The Center for Resourceful Building Technology, 1997).

8 Architect Susan Maxman & Partners.

9 Triangle J Council of Governments, *WasteSpec: Model Specifications for Construction Waste Reduction, Reuse, and Recycling* (Research Triangle Park, NC: author, 1995), p. 1.

10 Peter Yost and Eric Lund, *Residential Construction Waste Management: A Builder's Field Guide* (Upper Marlboro, MD: NAHB Research Center, 1997).

11 Ibid.

12 See the newsletter of the National Neighborhood Coalition, August/September 1998, p. 5, for information about programs of the Institute for Local Self-Reliance, based in Washington, DC, which promotes such programs.

13 Worldwatch Institute, *State of the World 1995*, p. 120.

14 Lawrence Berkeley National Laboratory, *Center for Building Science News*, Fall 1995.

15 Margaret Regan, "The Arts Give New Life to Tucson's Warehouse District," *New Village*, Issue 1, 1999, pp. 65-67.

16 For more information on this and other Durham projects, see David Salvesen, "A Catalyst for Redevelopment," *Urban Land*, November/December 1999, pp. 77-81.

ACHIEVING SUSTAINABLE DEVELOPMENT

chapter 8

Douglas R. Porter with George Brewster

The previous two chapters outlined development and design approaches and building construction techniques that can advance the cause of sustainable development. The "what, where, and how" of these approaches and techniques recognize that market, location, site, technological, and regulatory variables influence the sustainability of specific projects. Given the wide range of variables, it is not surprising that few if any developments completely satisfy all the principles of sustainable development. Furthermore, it is understood that the "science" and knowledge of sustainable practices are and will be continually evolving. Today's financially infeasible technology may well become tomorrow's profitable technology. Our capabilities for tracing the effects of development on natural resources will expand; and the intricate interrelationships between nature and human settlements will be better understood.

That said, the information and examples in this book make it clear that every development can make important contributions to furthering sustainability. In

other words, every developer can choose to move beyond conventional practices to think and work in ways that will make his or her next development more sustainable in terms of environmental, economic, and social concerns.

This chapter suggests ways in which developers can apply sustainable practices. It pulls together the aims and tools of sustainable development discussed in previous chapters to identify specific thought processes, design concepts, and technological measures that can preserve the environment and promote economically and socially viable communities. The chapter demonstrates that these approaches can gain recognition as feasible—even preferred—options to today's conventional forms of development. The first section summarizes from the previous chapters the range of techniques and technologies that can be considered "best practices" in sustainable development. The chapter then describes the obstacles or hurdles, both in public regulatory regimes and the business of private development, that must be overcome to put

ideals into practice. Finally, the chapter offers some solutions or opportunities that demonstrate capabilities for applying principles of sustainability in today's and tomorrow's marketplace.

A Summary of Best Practices in Sustainable Development

To move toward more sustainable development, what must developers, builders, and their consultants consider? What alternatives to conventional development practices respond constructively to the principles of sustainable development? Drawing from chapters 6 and 7 in particular, we can summarize sustainability practices in all phases of the development process, including initial project conceptualization and choice of site, protection of on-site natural resources, overall design of a development, and building design and construction.

The Project Concept and Site. Developers' initial decisions concerning their "next" project determine the "what" and "where" of the project, two of the most fundamental contributions to sustainability. These decisions are influenced, of course, by the developer's interests and particular expertise as well as by his or her perceptions of market and regulatory opportunities and constraints. Development firms tend to cultivate a focus on certain types of development—high-income residential projects, or neighborhood shopping centers, or large-scale planned communities, or downtown mixed-use complexes, for example. Each type of development requires expertise in particular market segments, construction processes, financial backing, and other aspects of development. Development firms also tend to establish a presence in and develop a knowledge of certain locales wherein their networks of business and government contacts can help smooth the development approval process. Thus, developers frequently are predisposed to formulate ideas for prospective developments similar to those just completed or already in the pipeline. However, developers interested in working to further sustainability principles can venture beyond their established practice by considering the following possibilities when planning and executing development projects.

Build more compactly. Land-saving, resource-saving goals require a stronger emphasis on compact building patterns, which can also reduce the automobile's adverse impact on energy resources and air and water quality. Building compactly need not require highly intensive development. It can mean laying out a single-family residential subdivision on smaller lots—say, a quarter of an acre versus a conventional half-acre lot, or 8,000 square feet compared with a local average of 12,000 square feet. It can also mean building higher—two-story houses and multilevel shopping centers. It can mean inserting well-designed townhomes on infield lots in existing neighborhoods. In the right places, of course, building

compactly can also mean high-density apartment and office buildings.

Robert Burchell, director of the Rutgers Center for Urban Policy Research, holds that development density in most areas can be increased by 30 percent without noticeably altering the scale and quality of development, assuming reasonable quality of design. Even higher density increases can be acceptable if they are offset by special amenities or visible open space, as demonstrated by many of the examples of cluster development throughout this book. In all cases, density is a relative determination. The "right" degree of compactness can be ascertained only by consideration of the prevailing norms, the locational context, and the site constraints on the type of development contemplated. In addition, it should recognize that a contingent consequence of building more compactly is exporting some elements of sustainability, such as protection of natural features, to other locations in the region or watershed.

Mix uses. Mixing uses within relatively small areas is essential in providing a range of travel choices for residents and workers and increasing opportunities for economic and social interaction. Developing a variety of significant destinations within walking distance of one another promotes walking, cycling, and use of public transit as alternatives to the automobile. By multiplying the types of activities taking place within a business center or neighborhood, mixing uses helps generate mutually supportive economic growth.

Mixing uses can be as simple (conceptually, at least) as adding an apartment building to a shopping center, or lofts over shops, or a small commercial and community center within a residential neighborhood or business park. Or mixing uses can take the form of promoting housing in central business districts and developing major complexes

to include offices, shopping, hotels, entertainment centers, and housing, all of which encourage interactive functions. Even within single types of uses, greater variety is achievable; for example, many developers are creating mixed-income residential developments as a means of promoting long-term neighborhood stability and value. For purposes of sustainable development, the main feature is clustering a variety of activities within easy reach of each other.

Conserve natural systems. Sustainable development calls for respecting the natural systems on a site or within the area of a site. In considering development options, developers should take into account potential opportunities for conserving environmental features and qualities at both the regional and local scales. If developing on greenfield sites at the urban fringe, developers can frame a design concept that retains and restores significant natural landscape features, vegetation and habitats, and hydrologic processes. In most cases, preservation of these natural qualities can be capitalized in the value they add to project marketing and profits. If redeveloping or adapting sites or buildings in built-up areas, developers may lack options for preserving natural systems; instead, though, they can contribute to sustainability goals by reducing conversion of natural landscapes and limiting demand for long-distance travel. In making choices about development forms and locations, developers should weigh the compensating factors that can determine constructive movement toward environmentally responsible development.

Recycle land and buildings. One way to practice resource conservation is to develop infield sites by undertaking infill and redevelopment projects, brownfield cleanup, and adaptive use of historic or architecturally distinctive buildings and areas. Recycling sites and buildings reduces the demand for development of natural landscapes elsewhere and makes efficient use of resources already committed to development. Developers can be rewarded by heightened consumer and community interest in revitalized inner-city locations and special places.

The increasing amount of development activity focused on "recycling" projects has produced a class of developers, designers, and builders with special expertise in identifying opportunities for and implementing profitable projects that involve the reuse of land and buildings. At the same time, though, the small scale and relatively greater risk usually attending such ventures has dissuaded involvement by development firms accustomed to creating large-scale projects in greenfield areas. Still, infield development could benefit from large firms' marketing and construction savvy and access to financial resources. As potential markets within urbanized areas continue to evolve, the development industry is likely to pay increased attention to investments in infield locations and forms of development.

Connect to adjoining development. In determining the type and location of their next project, developers should consider a project's potential relationship to what already exists, particularly with respect to the scale and appearance of the built environment, community economic structure, community facility and infrastructure systems, social networks, and natural features such as terrain, vegetation, and drainage that extend to surrounding areas and watersheds. Connections among and between natural and human systems keep systems alive and healthy. Extending existing roads, sewers, and school systems to contiguous developing areas, for example, helps contain costs and maintain a compact development pattern. Making connections with already available commercial,

community, and transportation services enhances the efficiency of both new and existing development. Linking on-site natural features to communitywide and even regional ecologic systems is also important for opening opportunities for greenways, trails, and other recreational uses of extended open-space networks.

Attempts to extend connections into the surrounding community may be at odds with forces in some communities that are pressing for more, not less, exclusivity. "NIMBYist" neighbors may object to linking streets and greenways that permit easy access between adjoining subdivisions. At the same time, developers know that protective walls and gateways add significant value to homes within gated communities. Somehow, the long-term community-wide benefits of connected communities must be factored into the regulatory and financial equation of project feasibility—perhaps through the use of public incentives for linking natural and built systems.

Contribute to local economic and social advancement. The selection of a desirable site should consider the potential function of the prospective project in the economic and social life of the development's future occupants as well as in the life of the larger community. Developments that offer residents convenient access to jobs, social and cultural amenities, affordable housing, and expanded opportunities for education and personal advancement make important contributions to project sustainability. Developers can enhance their projects at the outset by incorporating these elements into the overall development plan.

Be mindful of successive uses. The conceptualization of a development should take into account possibilities and opportunities for an evolution in uses within the development itself and its

component buildings and features. Twenty years is a short time frame in development terms; attitudes toward development change, markets mature, new technologies emerge, and new uses evolve. Developers cannot hope to predict all eventualities, but they can take care to plan and design projects that can be adapted to new uses, or "infilled" with more development, or retrofitted for different functions. Developers of large-scale, multiphase projects know that their initial master plans must be sufficiently flexible to accommodate new realities. Other developers should think ahead about future opportunities that might emerge and plan accordingly.

Care of On-Site Natural Resources. Early proponents of sustainable development tended to emphasize the conservation of natural resources. They called for "environmentally responsible" development that would maintain and restore natural systems within a development site while minimizing the export of waste from that site. For many project designers and environmentalists, the best development is one that least disturbs natural systems. This dictum appears most achievable in the design of alternatives to conventional suburban-style development. Instead of spreading relatively low-density development evenly over the landscape, site planners now espouse cluster development within a conserved natural environment. The shift from conventional subdivision design is still evolving; however, it is held back in some instances by professional and regulatory resistance to innovation.

Developers of large-scale planned residential developments have embraced many of the resource-saving principles of sustainability. Projects such as Coffee Creek and Hidden Springs have been designed to conserve and restore large areas of open space while still meeting development and profitability goals. Even developments aiming for moderate to middle densities can preserve significant proportions of open space through the design of multistory buildings and tighter clusters of housing units. At some point on the density scale, however, the tradeoff between conserved and developed land on a given site challenges the conservation of natural systems and requires technological "fixes" such as drainage and sewer pipes. Nevertheless, even in these circumstances, development can be designed to retain important natural assets, maintain some connections between on- and off-site natural systems, and respect particular features that contribute to the place-making aspects of a development even as they add amenity value to a project. The following aspects of natural systems should be considered in designing and developing all projects.

Respect geography. A site's terrain, vegetation, and drainage systems should be viewed as assets, or natural capital, to be valued in guiding site design and development. Most sites will have been touched by human activity—even farming and second-growth woodlands alter the natural landscape—but site planners should identify the significant attributes that constitute the natural resource base for a site and its area. Features such as hills, rock outcrops, woodlands, stream valleys, and wetlands can become attractive elements in a planned development. However, conserving and restoring these natural elements requires technical knowledge of the evolution and current balance of a site's natural assets as evidenced by factors such as soil quality, groundwater recharge zones, and phases of vegetative succession. Looking beyond the site to understand how the assets function within the larger ecosystem is likewise important. The objective is to maintain the natural systems to the fullest extent possible, recognizing

constraints imposed by the magnitude and intensity of a proposed development.

Restore native vegetation and habitat. Restoring vegetation native to a site and locale can contribute to long-term sustainability. Cultivation on the site and in nearby development may have introduced so-called "exotic" species of plants that in turn support nonnative birds and other wildlife. Frequently, invasive species outcompete and displace native vegetation and wildlife, leading to the decline of the region's biodiversity. In this respect, the large lawns and ornamental shrubbery and trees so typical of suburban development are not necessarily beneficial to the environment.

To the extent that native vegetation can be reintroduced and maintained within part or all of a development, developers can help endow a more sustainable future for their projects and surrounding areas. Saving significant natural areas by clustering development can provide opportunities for revegetation and habitat conservation. Some developers have even written requirements into covenants for the use of native plants in developed areas.

Preservation or restoration of habitat areas must also consider the range of habitat necessary to sustain wildlife, whether flora or fauna. Most species will not flourish in isolation; they require nurturing environments that may stretch over large areas. In particular, the natural movements of animals and birds depend on connective corridors. Therefore, restoring and maintaining native vegetation and habitats is most effective when efforts are part of a community- or regionwide conservation program. Lacking that, developers can still make a difference with the land under their control.

Retain and restore streams and wetlands. Streams once thought of as

dumping grounds and wetlands once considered useful only when filled are now protected by public policies and regulations and valued as natural amenities by many developers and their constituents. The section on hydrology in chapter 6 describes the essential role of streams and wetlands in maintaining the cycle of water flows into aquifers and across the landscape. Wetlands also act as temporary storage basins for stormwater and as natural filters for pollutants that might otherwise find their way to water bodies. And both streams and wetlands provide significant habitats for flora and fauna.

Conservation of streams and wetlands may require protection of erodible banks and shorelines, setbacks of development from stream and wetlands edges, and even restoration of riparian functions, including replanting of appropriate native vegetation. Once conserved, these resources can become valuable amenities for site occupants, although they may need some protection from human intrusion.

Where a site's locational attributes generate opportunities for intensive development that meets community objectives, it may be appropriate to achieve conservation goals outside the site—elsewhere in either the community or region. Indeed, shifting implementation of conservation goals to other locations might require actions by public agencies rather than by individual developers—for example, to establish regional conservation and/or wetlands mitigation areas. Further, as discussed in an earlier section on tradeoffs between development and conservation goals, building compactly may necessitate construction close to a stream or along its edge and may even benefit from filling a wetlands.

Consider on-site stormwater management. Site planners are increasingly concerned about the consequences of developing extensive impermeable surfaces—rooftops, roads and driveways, parking lots—that generate large volumes of stormwater runoff. Conventional drainage systems collect stormwater runoff and transport it by pipe to nearby streams and rivers where storm surges promote erosion and downstream flooding and dump large amounts of pollutants into water bodies. Once stormwater has been carried away, water must be imported, often over great distances, for human consumption and maintenance of the landscape.

A less resource-consumptive approach is to retain most stormwater on site to recharge underground aquifers and reduce peak downstream flows. For many forms of development, on-site stormwater retention can be accomplished through the reduction of impervious surfaces and the use of various methods to induce seepage into the ground. Permeable materials now available for roads, sidewalks, and parking lots allow penetration of water into the ground. Detention ponds, wetlands, and shallow pipe systems can provide temporary storage of stormwater to expedite groundwater recharge.

Consider construction of wetlands to treat wastewater. Several examples of sustainable development mentioned in chapter 6 have adopted natural methods for treating wastewater. The most common alternative to expensive community or regional sewage treatment systems or to individual septic tanks is construction of wetlands that allow organisms and plants to remove harmful bacteria and nutrients. The effluent can then be used for landscape irrigation while settled sludge may be pumped out for agricultural use. Designed correctly, constructed wetlands are odor-free and can serve as visual amenities for adjoining development. Several dozen such wetlands systems are now in operation.

Overall Design of Development.
Besides incorporating more on-site sustainable uses of natural resources, developers can design a project's physical development, transportation systems, and other community facilities to function in sustainable ways. An earlier section described the virtues of compact and mixed-use development. In addition, the following practices can help create a sustainable built environment.

Design for walking, cycling, and transit use. Most conventional forms of development are designed to encourage automobile use and discourage other modes of travel. Indeed, in most locations, developers can reasonably expect that 90 percent or more of travelers to, from, and within a development will drive cars. Overdependence on automobile travel, however, is consuming land and nonrenewable resources at unsustainable rates. For purposes of achieving more sustainable development, every development should incorporate features that encourage other forms of travel. Such features include efficient, connected street networks, convenient and attractive pathways for walking and cycling, and access to public transit service—either now or in the future. Forms of development as varied as single-family residential subdivisions, regional shopping centers, and mixed-use complexes can expand the range of travel options—at little additional cost but with a substantial increase in convenience for occupants and visitors.

Incorporate facilities and amenities that build community. Developments do not simply provide human shelter; they also provide space for many types of activities that collectively form the economic, social, and cultural fabric of communities. At a larger scale, we call this civilization. The most sustainable developments are those that meet most needs for daily life and work. Large-scale planned communities are designed to accommodate a wide range of

human activities over time. Typically, they incorporate community and recreational centers as well as various types of open spaces for passive and active recreation. Frequently, they also include arts and other cultural facilities and child care and adult education facilities in addition to the usual array of schools. Some of these facilities and amenities can be provided in smaller-scale developments, but many or most must be available in the surrounding community. Almost every development depends to some degree on specialized facilities available in other parts of the community and region, a factor that should be considered in designing connections to adjoining developed areas.

Make distinctive places. In site and building design, developments should aim to create distinctive places that make them memorable for occupants and visitors alike. The progression of open spaces and streets and the location of major buildings and building complexes should establish a hospitable environment and singular identity for every development. While a development's layout and appearance should be compatible with surrounding areas, its design can mark a community as a special place. Experienced designers know how to use the attributes of a site and its surroundings—terrain and water courses and native trees and other vegetation—to heighten the character of the development. Increasingly, too, streets and pathways are designed to function as pleasant public realms rather than simply as traffic conduits. Such placemaking adds value in the initial marketing of developments but, more important, helps sustain long-term value as developments mature and gain respect as distinguishing elements of the larger community.

Building Design and Construction.
Compared with conventional buildings, green buildings that consume less energy and other resources were once viewed as

unprofitable for developers and unappealing to consumers. However, with the emergence of new technologies, increasing knowledge among designers and builders of those technologies, and growing consumer concern over environmental issues, green buildings are understood to be cost-efficient and marketable and, in many cases, are even preferable to traditional structures. Today, developers and builders can easily turn to designs and technologies that make buildings more energy-efficient and less consumptive of nonrenewable materials. These approaches can be applied to the construction of individual homes as well as to the development of large office structures and mixed-use complexes. And green structures are at least as comfortable and appealing as conventional buildings. Although initial costs may be higher in some cases, experience has shown that lower operations and maintenance costs quickly repay initial costs. Developers and builders should consider the following practices, drawn from chapter 7, that can produce more environmentally responsible buildings.

Design a low-energy building shell. Walls, windows, and roofs should be designed to optimize a building's energy efficiency. Downsizing the building to shrink its perimeter lowers energy use. Energy consumption also can be decreased through the use of additional wall and roof insulation, appropriate window orientation and careful glazing selection, tight construction to minimize air infiltration, and the specification of sun-reflective roofs.

Use energy-efficient mechanical systems. Heating, ventilating, and cooling equipment and lighting, appliances, plumbing, and related mechanical and electrical systems all can be designed to reduce energy consumption. High-efficiency options include, as examples, condensing furnaces for residential heating, centrifugal chillers for commercial cooling, off-peak coolth storage

plants, energy recovery and economizer equipment, variable-speed motors and fans, gas-fired water and air heating, advanced controls for managing energy use, and home appliances such as horizontal-axis washing machines. Manufacturers and distributors are making such equipment readily available, and designers and consumers are becoming more knowledgeable about its reliability and advantages.

Tap solar energy. Increasingly, buildings are relying on passive solar design and active solar energy production. In part, the growing acceptance of solar energy systems is the result of government and utility energy-savings programs that publicize and create incentives for the use of such systems. Building designers can take advantage of passive solar energy by correctly orienting buildings relative to the sun, maximizing the amount of south-facing glass in relation to a building's thermal mass, and specifying high-performance super windows selected either to transmit or reflect heat. Depending on an area's climate and the designer's skill, passive solar energy can supply up to 75 percent of home heating requirements and meet nearly all office building heating and cooling needs.

Employ low-energy lighting. Lighting can account for a substantial share of energy costs—up to half of all such costs in older commercial and institutional buildings. However, the use of compact fluorescent lighting, task-oriented ambient lighting, and controls such as occupancy sensors and on/off scheduling can cut energy consumption and costs by 50 to 75 percent. Today, building designers are rediscovering natural daylighting, which can cut energy use even further. Large, high-performance windows, reflected light, and skylights bring sunlight into buildings and not only save on energy use for lighting but also on cooling energy required to overcome heat generated by incandescent lighting.

Reduce and reuse construction materials. Construction requires a tremendous amount of material plus energy to transport the materials to building sites. Buildings designed for resource efficiency minimize the quantity of needed materials, especially nonrenewable materials and materials that must be transported great distances. In particular, building smaller structures and using "standard" material sizes can reduce the demand for materials. In addition, salvaging or recycling existing building materials and construction waste can diminish the energy and resources needed to produce and dispose of materials. Active markets exist for salvaged materials, and many building products made of recycled materials are available.

Select environmentally friendly materials. Designers should select new materials only after weighing their long-term durability, particularly with respect to resistance to fire, pests, storms, and earthquakes and other properties such as energy efficiency, nontoxicity, ease of use, and the potential for future recycling. Given that these properties differ for each material type, building designers need to strike a balance in terms of a given location, climate, and type of building. In addition, the selection of materials should consider both initial and life-cycle costs. In pursuing ideal materials, some building designers have turned to traditional materials such as stone, adobe, and rammed earth, all environmentally pleasing but requiring intensive labor. Various new types of concrete are also available. In working toward sustainability, developers and builders should not simply assume that the obvious materials are necessarily the best.

Making It Happen: Challenges and Principles

Chapter 2 identified several obstacles to sustainable development. Some problems stem from the operation of the private development industry, which, like other industries, has evolved relatively standard approaches to producing a variety of relatively standard products. Developers, builders, lenders, project designers, construction contractors, and other participants in the development process have gained experience in and knowledge of conventional projects, their risks, and likely success. In chapters 4 and 5, Leinberger and Blakely detail some of the approaches that make it difficult to apply principles of sustainability to development, including developers' and lenders' fixations with, first, short-term profitability rather than long-term value and, second, the development of new rather than the adaptation of existing buildings and areas.

Other problems arise from public policies and regulations, most of which are geared to encouraging developers and builders to develop conventional projects. Outmoded zoning and subdivision regulations discourage clustering, compact growth, and mixed-use projects. Out-of-the-ordinary developments are subject to exhaustive discretionary reviews, making them highly vulnerable to NIMBY opposition. Fractionated jurisdictions compete for revenue-generating development with little regard for resulting fiscal disparities or rational patterns of development.

Still other obstacles are associated with consumers' knowledge and perceptions of "desirable" development. Consumers are suspicious of unfamiliar and, to them, untried and unproven forms, designs, and equipage of development. Frequently, they favor short-term pricing over long-term value, leading developers to continue producing development types that recover costs quickly. Often, consumers are not aware of the environmental and other consequences of their choices of living and working spaces.

Overcoming business-as-usual approaches in favor of introducing principles of sustainability into the development process is a challenge for all involved. Yet, practical steps and technologies can encourage the use of best practices to achieve more sustainable development, as described in the final sections of this chapter. First, however, it may be useful to define two guiding principles for applying sustainable practices to development:

- *Redirecting development practices to meet sustainability goals will take time.* Progress toward sustainable development will evolve as we learn more about what to do and how to do it. It is unreasonable to expect developers and builders to alter development practices overnight and unilaterally, but it *is* reasonable to initiate new concepts and techniques as they become feasible in the marketplace.

- *Achieving a perfect score on the sustainability scale is unnecessary and probably impossible.* Few if any developments can achieve all the goals of sustainability, especially given the inevitable tradeoffs among goals. Still, taking *some* steps toward sustainability is preferable to taking none while waiting to reach perfection.

Making It Happen: Industry Support for Best Practices

All developers can shape their development practices to respond to the concept of sustainability if they change the shape and tilt of the playing field to make such practices more profitable in the marketplace, more attractive to consumers, and more desirable as components of community development. The following sections suggest some aids to achieving sustainability in the development process.

Recognizing Needs for Sustainable Practices. The business of development is always evaluating and adjusting to emerging trends in the marketplace—whether related to demographics and demand, public policies, financial markets and credit sources, or new technologies. Calls for more sustainable development ask development firms to add another factor to these considerations. They are urged to reassess their decisions about development to recognize responsibilities and opportunities for sustaining the environment while advancing economic growth and social equity.

Developers whose minds are open to new ideas and concepts will understand how the growing diversity of American households calls for rethinking and reformulating options for the location and design of development. Developers who find feasible ways to apply sustainable practices in their projects will develop compelling explanations of the benefits of those practices for the enlightenment of consumers and, for that matter, financial backers.

The last point merits further discussion. At a regional conference on smart growth in Maryland last year, a builder relayed a comment often heard from developers and builders that "builders build what the market wants." He went on, though, to suggest that someone needs to educate the general public about sustainable development and thereby begin to create a sustainability-conscious market for builders. As discussed in chapter 2, it appears that a market that values sustainability is emerging. The real estate industry could support expansion of this market by continuing to generate compelling evidence about the benefits of and opportunities for designing and building sustainable developments.

Developers of the 48-story Four Times Square building in New York City confronted the market issue head on during the design and marketing of the building. The first speculative office tower to be built in Manhattan since 1988, Four Times Square was also the first project of its size in New York City to adopt standards for energy efficiency, indoor ecology, sustainable materials and responsible construction, and operations and maintenance procedures. According to the developers' report entitled "Lessons Learned: Four Times Square," the design and construction process for a speculative building "is contractually divided into two camps: the 'core and shell' (or 'base building') under the developer's purview and the 'tenant work' (or 'tenant improvements') directed by the tenants."[1] This functional and contractual separation presents constraints in building design, construction, and occupancy that affect the integration and coordination of building systems for efficiency and comfort.

To overcome these constraints, the architects made informational presentations to tenants' senior executives and their design and construction teams to highlight the new building's environmental requirements and potential economic benefits. Presentations focused on the sample DOE-2 evaluations of the energy savings achievable with various designs of individual tenant space. The "Lessons Learned" report concluded, "While leading, cajoling, educating and pushing the tenants goes a long way, there is no substitute for concrete economic analyses."[2] In addition, the building designers published a set of guidelines that both illustrated how tenant work could take advantage of the building's infrastructure and outlined opportunities for extending energy efficiency and other sustainable features in the tenant work. Admittedly, developers and consumers are still low on the learning curve about sustainable development, but informational efforts such as that carried out by the developers of Four Times Square will prove extremely productive.

Reformulating the Financing Paradigm.
Current financing approaches are designed to shun innovation and reward conventional practices. In chapter 4, Christopher Leinberger makes a strong case for changing the valuation process for financing development. "Conventional financing puts a significant hurdle in front of innovative developments," he observes, "and ignores a rich source of financial return that would be highly valued by appropriate investors." Reliance on discounted cash flow and related analytic methods to compare alternative investments, Leinberger states, tends to emphasize the value of immediate returns from short-term investments. This bias, in turn, provides an incentive for building inexpensively for short-term gain. Contrast that incentive with sustainable practices that encourage building durable structures and often require a multiphase process to develop fully functioning mixed-use projects.

Leinberger suggests that many investors are interested in mid- to long-term returns from real estate investments. They would benefit from dividing project financing into several pieces (termed tranches) that could be sold to different investors. Part of a project loan, for example, would be paid off last and therefore would be more risky but generate a higher yield. Despite some difficulty in evaluating returns on such investments, Leinberger notes that real estate investors before the mid-20th century typically expected to gain most from long-term holdings.

Other possible arrangements that could assist in financing sustainable projects are creation of a secondary mortgage market for nonstandard loans and the development of location-efficient mortgages. At present, conventional financing allows securitization of packages of loans of similar types and quality while residential mortgages and rated commercial mortgages are currently the only types of real estate loans considered for securitization. Thus, the federal government could directly encourage sustainable development by creating a secondary market for nonstandard loans.

Several nonprofit groups as well as the U.S. Department of Energy and the U.S. Environmental Protection Agency have promoted the concept of a location-efficient mortgage. Such a mortgage is based on revising loan qualification calculations to account for transportation savings in location-efficient neighborhoods situated near public transit routes or within walking distance of neighborhood shopping centers. The premise is that home-buyers who spend less on automobiles and automobile travel can devote more income to housing. (It remains to be seen whether market forces will adjust the prices of location-efficient properties upwards to account for their greater value, thus wiping out the benefits of higher loan ratios.)

Lenders should consider supporting the concept of sustainability through the above actions and by changing underwriting practices to take into account today's increasing diversity of housing and lifestyle choices. The importance of changing current financing criteria to underwrite sustainable development cannot be overstated.

Setting Standards and Measuring Performance.
It is always important to understand how a development will mature—how it will continue to function and hold its value. In the case of sustainable development, which involves many innovative designs and technologies, it is doubly important to ensure that developments will perform according to expectations for efficient use of resources and proper operation of economic and social functions. Several techniques have been formulated to help developers, designers, and public officials measure the performance of proposed and completed projects. Examples of such techniques, described below, include performance standards

developed for Civano in Tucson, Playa Vista in Los Angeles, Dewees Island in South Carolina, and Hidden Springs near Boise; the Conservation Development Evaluation System (CeDES) for measuring the environmental friendliness of proposed developments; and the Leadership in Energy and Environmental Design (LEED)™ rating system for green buildings.

The various systems of performance measures are valuable in several ways: as prompts for identifying opportunities for incorporating sustainable features into projects in the conceptualization stage; as devices for determining contributions to the sustainability of proposed designs and features; as measures of progress once development is underway and completed; and as definers of the community and global benefits of sustainable development. Much work remains in defining desirable outcomes and measurable standards for sustainable development, but the existing approaches provide useful pathways to understanding.

Sustainable development performance standards. Many development projects in the United States have adopted covenants, conditions, and restrictions (CC&Rs) to ensure the quality of future development. In particular, developers like to use CC&Rs for large-scale, multiphase residential and business park developments in order to maintain long-term property values. CC&Rs, which function like "private zoning," lay out standards and criteria for building siting, landscaping, and other elements in projects involving a variety of builders over time. Several developments rely on CC&Rs to establish performance guidelines intended to promote sustainable development qualities.

The master plan for the 1,145-acre Civano development on former state lands in Tucson, Arizona, includes performance targets for seven aspects of

sustainable development. In accordance with a development agreement with the city of Tucson, Civano's developer committed to sustainable community design and building construction. Proposed as a mixed-use project of 2,500 homes and apartments and retail, office, and light industry uses, Civano's development began in 1996 and will extend over 12 years. As shown in figure 8-1, performance targets include both initial and long-term targets. In addition, the master plan identified developer/builder actions for first-phase action to meet the initial targets.

The targets and requirements are to be reached through a variety of developer and builder actions such as efficient street and lot layouts, building designs that accommodate solar equipment, use of reclaimed water for irrigation, land setasides for a recycling and composting center, commercial services located near residences to reduce automobile travel, and other innovative approaches.

The Playa Vista sustainable performance guidelines for residential development are somewhat more detailed. They respond to state and city laws regarding energy efficiency, waste man-

8-1

Summary of Civano Performance Targets

Master Plan Performance Targets	Initial Minimum Requirements
Energy demand—reduce by 75 percent	Single-family residential—reduce by 65 percent
	Multifamily residential—reduce by 65 percent
	Commercial—reduce by 55 percent
Energy supply—increase innovation	Initial photovoltaic/solar thermal demonstrations (later, wider photovoltaic/solar thermal use, other innovations)
Water use—reduce by 65 percent	Residential—reduce by 54 percent (to 53 gallons per day)
	Commercial—reduce by 62 percent (to 15 gallons per day) (for interior potable water)
Solid waste—reduce by 90 percent	Reduce by 30 percent through recycling
	Reduce by 60 percent after project half built
Air pollution—reduce by 40 percent	Reduce by 40 percent over project life
Job creation—one job for two homes	Construct 300 square feet of non-residential space for every two housing units, with credit for home offices
Affordability—enable workers to live in Civano	Provide 20 percent of units (all types) for households under 80 percent of median income

Source: Handout at presentation by John Laswick, city of Tucson, Urban Land Institute 1999 fall meeting, Washington, DC, October 23, 1999.

agement, and landscaping as well as to agreements on additional targets and requirements worked out as part of the project approval process, including a development agreement with the city of Los Angeles. The guidelines are meant to guide the plans, designs, and construction management practices of the many builders who will develop various parts of the site.

The performance guidelines establish about 100 sustainability measures in 9 categories, as shown in figure 8-2. Most measures affect all residential buildings in the project, but some apply specifically to high-density structures (stacked units of 25 or more dwelling units per acre) or low-density structures built at less than 25 units per acre. The guidelines describe principles, specific guidelines, performance measures, and potential techniques for meeting the 100 sustainability measures.

For building materials, for example, the stated principle is that materials should "save energy, improve indoor air quality, last longer, and require less labor than traditional materials." The specific guideline requires the use of materials that embody some or all of a list of characteristics, including, for example, zero or low volatile organic compounds, no or low toxicity, durability, and high recycled content. Mandatory performance measures require fiberglass insulation to have at least 30 percent recycled content, cellulose 85 percent, and gypsum board 25 percent (with facing paper 100 percent recycled); cabinets made of sustainably harvested lumber and plywood (as certified by the Forest Stewardship Council) or non-formaldehyde medium-density fiber board or particle board; and paint, finishes, and adhesives with less than 250 grams of volatile organic compounds per liter. In addition, discretionary measures include, for example, materials manufactured or reprocessed within a 300-mile radius to reduce shipping

costs, pressure relief wall systems and flashing details, and flooring made of renewable materials such as bamboo or cork-based linoleum. Discretionary measures are recommended whenever the builder controls the selection of materials or offers packages to purchasers. The discussion of applications describes the purposes and advantages of recommended materials.

The performance measures are subject to ongoing evaluation and revision. Originally prepared to require awards of points for "base case" measures and discretionary actions, the measures have been simplified by dropping points in favor of required and optional actions.

The Presidio Trust, which is redeveloping the historic Presidio site in San Francisco, has taken one step beyond Playa Vista's residential design guidelines by developing draft guidelines for the rehabilitation of historic and non-historic buildings, based in part on the

Green Building Council's LEED™ system described on page 150.

At the other end of the nation from Playa Vista and the Presidio, the Dewees Island resort development in South Carolina adopted rigorous restrictions on the form of development in order to protect the island's natural features and qualities. Planned for 150 home lots on 1,200 acres, Dewees Island carefully preserves extensive salt marsh estuaries, freshwater lagoons, and forests—all rich in wildlife—and substitutes nature for golf courses as the focus of development. Some of the restrictions include no building on the shoreline, prohibiting gasoline-powered cars, limiting building sizes to 5,000 square feet per lot, and requiring rainwater irrigation for plantings and native landscaping instead of conventional lawns. To minimize energy consumption, homes are to be sited to take advantage of the winter sun, summer shade, prevailing breezes, and natural

Playa Vista Categories of Performance Guidelines 8-2

Construction Waste
Building Materials
Energy, Including:

Building envelope
Space conditioning
Interior and exterior lighting
Water heating
Renewable and alternative energy sources
Controls and feedback
Appliances

Domestic Water
Recycling and Solid Waste
Power Signal and Control
Adaptability
Landscape
Transportation

Source: *Playa Vista Residential Sustainable Performance Guidelines,* prepared by Zinner Consultants, Constructive Technologies Group, Environmental Problem Solving Enterprises, IBACOS and the National Renewable Energy Laboratory for the Playa Vista Capital Company, March 1999.

lighting. Roads and driveways are paved with porous materials to allow rainwater drainage into the aquifer.

The "Residential Design Guidelines" for Hidden Springs, Idaho, conform more closely to traditional CC&Rs but are fashioned to promote sustainable treatment of the natural landscape, which, in contrast to Dewees Island, is hilly and dry. The guidelines include a list of principles that guided formulation of the development plan (e.g., "We will maintain the 135-year-old farm and rural traditions of the area"); a description of the site plan and its rationale; site development, landscape, and architectural guidelines; the design review and approval process; and construction regulations. On pages 1 through 5, the plan describes as its major goals "(a) preserving and protecting large tracts of land in open space or as farmland and (b) clustering appropriately scaled development in areas that are less visually or environmentally sensitive." It proposes to preserve the more visually sensitive foothill slopes as open space and to cluster homes in a "traditional" village on the valley floor or within hidden side valleys where they will not dominate the landscape.

Site design requirements include, as examples, the protection of natural drainage courses, grading that minimizes site disruption, the use of retaining walls that blend with the existing topography, and plantings that emphasize native, drought-tolerant vegetation. The architectural guidelines encourage diverse designs suited to the surrounding landscape as well as the use of certain materials, massing, and colors. Supplementing these guidelines is a transportation management plan described in chapter 6.

For the communities discussed above, the guidelines for sustainable development have been prepared by the projects' respective developers who, in many cases, worked closely with community groups to create special places. The guidelines promote distinctive developments that respond to widespread concerns for sustainability and, in so doing, add long-term value to the development and the larger community.

Conservation Development Evaluation System (CeDES). The CeDES evaluation system is a project rating system that evaluates the water quality and landscape impacts of a conservation-oriented residential development over the project's lifetime.[3] Developed by the Conservation Fund's Great Lakes Office in cooperation with members of the Conservation Development Alliance[4] and several professional planners and site designers, the CeDES is intended to encourage developers of environmentally responsible residential subdivisions to analyze environmental concerns early in the site planning process. It is also useful to consumers and community agencies as a means of assessing the impacts of site design practices. The system is intended primarily for application in the eastern and midwestern United States rather than in the arid West because of differences in water resources and land cover. In addition, it does not evaluate other types of development such as commercial and industrial uses, infill and redevelopment sites, and mixed-use, transit-oriented design, although the concept could possibly be expanded to evaluate these development types.

In accordance with specified criteria, the CeDES system rates 11 environmental criteria as they apply to residential developments (see figure 8-3). The criteria are quantifiable and measurable and eliminate subjective judgment as much as possible. (The system recognizes site limitations on planning and design by allowing the elimination of criteria that are irrelevant to a given site.) For each criterion, points are awarded (from –2 to +2) for the extent to which the criterion is met. For example, for impervious surfaces relative to conventional development (Criterion 1a), developments are awarded –2 for no decrease in impervious surfaces, 0 for a 15 percent decrease, +1 for a 35 percent decrease, and +2 for a 60 percent decrease. Developments are awarded from one to four "leaves" for earning 20 to 50 percent of the points. Thus, the system provides a means of singling out developments that are especially responsive to conservation needs.[5]

CeDES Categories and Criteria 8-3

Site Design and Construction Practices
Percent impervious surfaces relative to conventional development
Preservation of natural features/land form change
Erosion control and sediment control
Stormwater Management
Runoff rate
Runoff volume
Open Space
Management of open space
Environmentally constrained open space
Protection of natural resources
Development of natural resources protection plan
Existing vegetation—tree and plant conservation
Newly planted vegetation; other landscaping

The LEED™ Green Building Rating System. The U.S. Green Buildings Council has prepared the LEED™ Green Building Rating System as a self-certifying system designed for rating the environmental performance of new and existing commercial, institutional, and high-rise residential buildings. It evaluates performance from a "whole-building" perspective for the building's life cycle, providing a clear standard for what constitutes a green building.

LEED™ is meant to offer an alternative to the Building Research Establishment Environmental Assessment Method (BREEAM) rating system that was developed in England in the early 1990s and is now in its second revision. BREEAM is a sophisticated system that requires a high level of professional interpretation and assessment to ascertain the "greenness" of a building. The system assigns points to a set of criteria in accordance with the impact they are understood to have on the planet. The system has been used successfully in England and is beginning to find application in North America.

LEED™ has been under development for four years as a less labor-intensive rating system attuned to the building environment in the United States. The system is undergoing a pilot phase of review and fine-tuning tailored to the U.S. building environment. In the past, owners, designers, and builders had no accurate definition of performance criteria and no thresholds for green buildings. LEED™, however, establishes minimum levels of performance for an environmentally responsible building, with credits earned by adopting practices such as installing sunlight-reflecting roofing, using recycled materials, installing graywater recovery systems, and incorporating other aspects of sustainable building design and construction. Under the system, buildings can earn a maximum 44 credits for performance. Building owners can earn

certificates that identify the performance level achieved by a building: platinum for acquiring at least 81 percent of the credits, gold for 71 percent, silver for 61 percent, and bronze for 50 percent. Obtaining a LEED™ certificate requires substantial contributions to environmentally responsible design and development. LEED™ does not purport to offer a complete definition of green building performance. Nonetheless, without weighting individual criteria, it lays out general criteria in five fundamental areas: energy, water, site sustainability, indoor environmental quality, and resources.

The goal of LEED™ is to help designers and developers understand the tools and techniques readily available to achieve more "greenness" in building development. LEED™ is meant to be a simple, easy-to-use rating system that would be applied by designers to self-evaluate projects. It is hoped that the evaluation system will function as a tool for transforming the market for green building—creating incentives for moving toward more sustainable building. Such a program can also provide a basis for revision of appraisal and underwriting practices. To use LEED™, professional staff reviews documentation provided by building designers to determine the appropriate level of formal certification. After testing was completed during 1999, the LEED™ program for certification was to be officially launched in April 2000. Information about the LEED™ Green Building Rating System can be obtained by visiting www.usgbc.org/programs/leed.htm or from the Green Building Council at 415-445-9500.

The Business of Sustainable Development. Because they deal daily with decisions and issues involving environmental, economic, and social resources, development firms can make tremendous contributions to sustainable development. The best practices identified

at the beginning of this chapter are a starting point. In addition, in *The Ecology of Commerce*, the noted futurist Paul Hawken directs our attention to farther horizons. He outlines six fundamental principles that might well be adopted by developers to guide business activity toward a more sustainable world.

- Replace nationally and internationally produced items with products created locally and regionally.

- Take responsibility for the effects of all products on the natural world.

- Do not require exotic sources of capital in order to develop and grow.

- Engage in production processes that are human, worthy, dignified, and intrinsically satisfying.

- Create objects of durability and long-term utility whose ultimate use or disposition will not harm future generations.

- Change consumers to customers through education.[6]

In sum, Hawken's principles advocate that businesses should take responsibility for their own actions in support of sustainable development.

Making It Happen: Public Support for Best Practices

In every community, government policies and regulations are part and parcel of the development process. Developers have a keen understanding of how public actions can thwart or encourage development. It stands to reason, then, that the best practices for sustainable development will succeed only within a framework of supportive rather than obstructive public policies and incentives. Unfortunately, public policies and regulations too seldom reward innovative behavior by developers. To develop sustainable projects, private development practices and public actions that influence the development process must evolve in tandem to ensure a receptive public context for private development.

Public support for sustainable best practices can be manifested through community plans and zoning that promote elements of sustainable development, subdivision requirements and building codes that provide incentives for green building, redevelopment and infill activities that stimulate recycling of land and buildings, and public attention and investments that focus on creating a sustainable public realm, thereby spurring regional efforts that reduce interjurisdictional disparities and improve delivery of fundamental services and educating the public about the need for sustainable development.

Planning and Zoning to Promote Sustainability. In too many communities, planning and zoning encourage low-density, dispersed development and discourage compact, mixed-use, and infill development. Zoning and subdivision regulations emphasize large lots and wide streets and pay little heed to the clustering, connectivity, and walkability that conserve energy and other natural resources. The move toward sustainability requires public policies that promote a better balance between conventional and sustainable development patterns. Both development types are reasonable responses to current demographic and market trends, but conventional development—development as usual—is the overwhelming favorite of public policies and regulations. Instead, communities should make it easier to obtain public approvals for sustainable projects than for conventional projects.

Local governments and regional agencies should establish a more balanced public context for sustainable development. Local and regional plans should

identify targets and incorporate performance measures, similar in concept to the Civano and Playa Vista systems, for achieving sustainability goals. Commitments to implementing those measures should be incorporated into the requirements and provisions of regulatory instruments such as zoning ordinances and subdivision regulations. Regional and local plans should alert landowners to conservation needs by identifying and assigning priorities to natural areas in need of protection. Local plans and zoning ordinances should identify specific areas where compact, mixed-use development will be permitted and even welcomed by supportive public programs. Growth management techniques such as urban growth boundaries and adequate public facilities requirements should be structured to lend constructive support to sustainable forms of development rather than simply hindering development in certain areas.

To the extent that any of these regulatory provisions is administered through discretionary procedures, such as conditional zoning, design reviews, and special hearings, all requirements and procedures should be simple and straightforward to reflect the community's commitment to sustainable forms of development. To prevent delays and continuous third-party interventions, detailed performance goals should be established to guide approval decisions and procedures.

Establishing Community Sustainability Indicators. To guide public programs for achieving more sustainable development and to provide a supporting policy context for private efforts in sustainable development, communities can define indicators of sustainability and periodically gauge progress toward meeting their sustainability targets. Indicators are short-hand, measurable data points that identify important conditions and qualities of sustainabili-

ty, such as energy use, transit ridership, wastewater flows, and the number of affordable housing units. Programs in Seattle, Santa Monica, and other cities have demonstrated the value of identifying indicators for measuring the environmental, economic, and social health of the community. By tracking changes in the indicator statistics, community leaders can determine which programs are working well to meet sustainability goals and which need strengthening or redirection.[7]

Building Regulations and Incentives that Promote Green Building. Zoning and subdivision provisions should encourage energy-efficient, land-conserving design of lots and buildings, including land- and travel-saving clustering and flexibility in siting for solar orientation. Building codes should encourage green building as a preferred alternative to conventional building designs and practices. As more and more developers become interested in green buildings, it is becoming clearer that current hurdles for green design should be removed to permit new approaches to the design process and a reworking of current building codes to recognize the innovative features needed for green building. Rewarding designers of mechanical and electrical systems for what they save rather than what they spend is a new concept that is beginning to attract attention. According to Amory Lovins, "Fragmented and commoditized design, false price signals, and substitution of obsolete rules-of-thumb for true engineering optimization have yielded buildings that cost more to build, are less comfortable, and use more energy than they should." Model building codes such as the Uniform Building Code have simplified code requirements in most states and encouraged nationwide distribution of materials and hardware that comply with the uniform standards, but we have yet to formulate a model green building code that specifies the use of environmentally responsible materials. Such a code could overlay existing codes and exempt builders from conventional code requirements if their buildings meet green building standards for energy conservation, water conservation, and resource efficiency. The BREEAM and LEED™ building rating systems are a step in this direction but fall short of a national or state model code.

Many municipalities and communities have adopted building energy codes. In the case of commercial and institutional buildings, most of the codes are based on language contained in the American Society of Heating Refrigeration and Air-conditioning Engineers (ASHRAE) Standard 90.1. The standard is soon to be tightened and revised by ASHRAE into a code that is likely to be adopted on a widespread basis. Even in its revised and upgraded form, ASHRAE 90.1 is a low hurdle to clear in the quest for energy-efficient buildings. As is often noted, to boast that a building meets the local energy code is actually to admit that if the building were built to a lower standard, it would be illegal. So for what energy target should a "sustainable" developer aim?

As discussed, the amount of energy a building consumes depends on many factors, including local climate, square footage, functional use profile, architectural design, and the selection of mechanical systems. Therefore, it is extremely difficult to establish a single, absolute, annual energy consumption target for all buildings. However, when selecting design professionals for a project, developers should challenge the design team to create buildings that are in the lower quartile of energy consumption—whether measured in BTUs or dollars—for new buildings of the same use type in the same region. In most cases, this means achieving an annual energy performance between 10 and 30 percent better than a base-case reference building

constructed to the standards in the latest version of ASHRAE 90.1.

In addition, public programs should aid builders and developers interested in developing green buildings by providing information about feasible options, assistance in overcoming regulatory obstacles, and financial incentives for innovative practices. In fact, several local jurisdictions have instituted such programs. In 1991, Austin, Texas, established the Green Builder Program to move energy-efficient, environmentally responsible design and construction practices into the mainstream development process. The program's rating system awards points to builders who incorporate energy-, water-, and resource-efficient practices into their buildings. The program also assists designers working on commercial projects in applying sustainable concepts and conducts research to test new equipment and materials. The small city of Ashland, Oregon, enacted a solar access ordinance in 1980 and has offered housing density bonuses since 1982 for use of energy- and water-efficient features in new homes.[8] Portland, Oregon, conducts a BEST program (Businesses for an Environmentally Sustainable Tomorrow) to help businesses learn about pollution prevention, energy efficiency, waste reduction, transportation alternatives, and water efficiency. Each year since 1993 the program has recognized local businesses that have successfully adopted innovative techniques in these areas. It publishes case studies of award winners to provide information to other businesses.[9]

In 1997, Boulder, Colorado, revised its Energy Option Points program, which allows builders to earn points toward approval of building permits by adopting various green building measures. Well-known for its restrictive standards for development and building, Boulder now requires, under the new Green Points Program, a minimum number of green measures for new homes and

additions. Points are awarded for an approved permit for eight categories of energy- and resource-efficient features, including HVAC equipment and solar energy. Applicants for new-home permits must, however, earn a minimum of two points for use of sustainable building materials and methods and two points for measures related to indoor air quality.[10]

The Energy Star program promoted by a voluntary partnership of public agencies and private corporations rates energy-efficient household and business products and provides a store locater for the products. Initiated by the U.S. Environmental Protection Agency and the U.S. Department of Energy, Energy Star lists products such as household applicances, lighting, office equipment, heating and cooling systems, and insulation. The program can be accessed through the Web at www.energystar.gov or a hotline at 1-888-STAR-YES.

A little-known program that could benefit many homebuyers—and hence homebuilders—is the energy-efficient mortgage, known as an EEM. Many lenders, especially those using government-sponsored home mortgage programs, offer energy-efficient mortage programs for home purchases and upgrades. For homes incorporating energy-efficient features or equipment, buyers can quality for a larger mortgage due to the lowered utility costs. Owners of existing homes can include the cost of eligible improvements in refinancing their mortgages. The most complete explanation of such mortgages can be accessed at the Pacific Gas and Electric Company's Web site (www.pge.com/customer_services/ residential/saving_energy).

Conducting Redevelopment and Infill Programs. Retrofitting and restoring existing neighborhoods and business centers is a critical part of any community program to promote sustainable development, but it is far more difficult than developing open lands on the edge of the urbanizing area. Typically, the first obstacle is the perception that many older parts of cities and suburbs are undesirable places to work and live. As noted earlier, that perception is changing, but inserting new development in already developed areas, no matter how marketable it may be, often runs afoul of restrictive codes and ordinances and unhappy neighbors. Public agencies can help entice developers to consider development of underused or vacant properties, including brownfields, by reducing the associated risks or compensating developers through other measures such as land assembly and provision of needed infrastructure.

Developers of the Bethesda Row retail commercial project described earlier in this chapter claim that the project was feasible only because Montgomery County had adopted firm policies promoting developments of that type in that location and, through a parking authority, had constructed a 1,000-car parking structure to support business development.

Increasingly, many communities have been engaging in redevelopment activities with heartening results. Doing so, however, requires vision and leadership on the part of community officials. Often, the public sector must make commitments for advance funding of land acquisition and planning as well as for other investments for improving roads, streetscapes, parks, parking garages, and the like. Sometimes city officials receive the wholehearted support and involvement of community residents, but sometimes they meet with caution or outright antagonism. In either case, public leaders must be willing to take chances to overcome obstacles to recycling declining areas.

An example, one of many that could be cited, is the leadership of the Metropolitan King County (Washington) Coun-

cil in helping form the Duwamish Coalition, which is charged with preserving and reclaiming an 8,500-acre industrial area near downtown Seattle. Specifically, "[t]he Coalition will further address regulatory, infrastructure, and institutional barriers to economic growth and environmental protection in the corridor" through a multijurisdictional public/private partnership.[11] Almost 87,000 employees now work in the area, with another 25,000 projected to be employed there over the next 20 years. In addition to promoting industrial revitalization, the coalition is mounting campaigns to expand access to new jobs in the corridor for minorities, women, and economically disadvantaged individuals and to ensure that the economic well-being of the corridor remains compatible with the needs and desirability of neighborhoods within and adjoining the area.

Promoting Sustainability in the Public Realm. Communities can make meaningful contributions toward sustainable development by developing significant public places and siting and designing public buildings to meet sustainable goals. Since ancient times, public places—dramatic gathering places, pleasant green spaces, clusters of distinctive buildings, attractive streetscapes—have hosted civic interaction and established a unique civic identity. In chapter 3, Rutherford Platt described the evolution of public places in America from colonial times onward, observing that the outward spread of suburban growth has been accompanied by relatively little concern for creating such places. Over the last decade, however urban designers have reasserted the importance of the public realm as a critical element in sustainable social and economic development. Urban planners have promoted central places to encourage walking and use of transit. Environmentalists have emphasized the significance of green spaces in sustaining fundamental environmental qualities and adding value to

the built environment. Most important, perhaps, community attention to creating and maintaining public places signals a civic consciousness of the value of sustainable development. Says Nancy Graham, former mayor of West Palm Beach, Florida, who almost singlehandedly spurred revitalization of that city's downtown, "The public realm is the connective tissue of our everyday world. The task will be to make our cities worthy, to reconstruct them in a physical design form that is worth caring about, and to reinhabit them."[12]

Cities such as the Portlands in Oregon and Maine; Cleveland, Ohio; and Long Beach, California, have been establishing distinctive places as focal points of urban activity, some by recreating waterfronts as public places, others by siting sports and cultural centers in downtown areas, and still others by supporting concentrations of development around new transit stations. Suburban towns such as Smyrna, Georgia, have been investing heavily in creating clusters of civic buildings and spaces to spur revitalization of their town centers. Many small towns and large cities alike have redesigned their streetscapes in central places as a way to maintain their long-term stability and value and to enhance the urban fabric.

Public agencies are also investing in more environmentally responsible public buildings.

Oakland, California, for example, when contracting for the design of two office buildings totaling 450,000 square feet, required designers to achieve a 25 percent reduction in energy use over the level established by California's strict energy-efficiency requirements. The Port of Portland (Oregon) Building, a 350,000-square-foot office building owned by Pacific Development, Inc., was upgraded in 1992 to become one of the most energy-efficient buildings in the city. Highly efficient parabolic light fixtures and lighting controls, a variable air volume heating and cooling system, and high-performance window glass cut energy use by 40 percent; 90 percent of waste is recycled.

Other communities are improving environmental sustainability in public open spaces. Olympia, Washington, example, has focused considerable effort on water quality and habitat protection in three watershed basins most affected by development. To reduce the effects of stormwater runoff, the city is introducing permeable paving for streets and sidewalks and intensifying the tree canopy along streets and streams as a means of absorbing and softening rainfall.

Pricing Public Services to Promote Sustainability. In chapter 4, Christopher Leinberger points out that basic public services are often priced in ways that reward unsustainable practices. He cites water supplies as one example. In most communities, water users are charged a standard rate for the amount of water they use, regardless of whether a user is located in an area served easily or with difficulty and without significant cost incentives to install water-conserving devices. Subsidizing water costs for users who have little incentive to reduce water use supports consumption rather than conservation. The same is true for other services such as police and fire protection, which in most communities is funded through a general operating budget that does not charge higher costs for providing protection in more remote locations. Instead, political pressures usually favor "equal treatment" rather than "true costs" for all consumers. Implementing a pricing policy in stages over several years that differentiates between high- and low-cost users would immediately introduce more sustainable consumption of the environmental resources affected by public services.

Targeting Public Investments to Promote Sustainable Development. In the same way that Smyrna, Georgia, decided to focus investments in new community facilities to strengthen its downtown, public agencies can direct funding for infrastructure and public buildings to areas most suitable for sustainable development. In downtown Los Angeles, for example, the historic building that once housed the Broadway Department Store was rescued from demolition through a complete retrofitting for use as a state office complex—what, it is hoped, will be a harbinger of revitalization in a rundown area. West Palm Beach, Florida, following a master plan developed in 1993, has invested $10 million in revitalizing the old downtown area, improving Centennial Square as the city's activity center, helping to fund façade improvements, adding traffic-calming measures to local streets, and hosting weekly "block parties" at the square. The city's investment has generated $350 million in private reinvestment in new and rehabilitated buildings.

One of the most significant efforts to target public investments is taking place in Maryland, where the state's smart growth program is two years into implementation. Legislation called for the state to direct capital funding to municipalities, empowerment and enterprise zones, the areas within the Baltimore and Washington beltways, and growth areas designated by counties. Only under extraordinary circumstances can state funding for capital projects be used in rural areas not designated for growth. By the end of 1999, the act had prompted relocation of a state university branch and a police training facility from proposed sites outside cities to sites within cities. In addition, several highway bypasses scheduled for construction were either dropped or allowed to proceed under negotiated restrictions on adjoining land uses. Not surprisingly, Maryland's

smart growth policy is attracting great interest from many other states.

Regional, Interjurisdictional Efforts to Develop Sustainably. The fragmented government structure in nearly all metropolitan areas poses a roadblock to sustainability, leading to sharp disagreements among jurisdictions about how and where to stimulate development, creating heightened fiscal and social disparities between jurisdictions, and resulting in inefficient delivery of many essential public services. Fragmentation is antithetical to the collaborative problem solving required to move toward more sustainable development. Americans traditionally have downplayed regional powers in favor of local independence, but growing frustration over inadequate transportation and other interjurisdictional services, concerns over taxation and other fiscal issues, and recognition of the significance of watershed and ecologic systems that cross jurisdictional boundaries are spurring interest in regionwide planning and selective management of regional systems. In several metropolitan areas, for example, regional wastewater collection and treatment, public transit, and park and open-space systems are now planned and managed by regional authorities. In addition, some jurisdictions are cooperating to initiate cross-jurisdictional programs such as economic development and access to work.

Public Education about Sustainable Development. If the principles of sustainability are to form the basis for a new development paradigm, the public—all consumers—must understand and embrace those principles. They need to know how their individual decisions about where and how they live and work can either help or harm both natural and built environments. The discussions of long-term versus short-term costs of development in chapters 5 and 6 pointed out that homebuyers and office tenants alike must understand the tradeoffs involved. Greater investment now in environmentally responsible development and buildings will pay off in lower operations and maintenance costs in the years to come, not to mention the benefits associated with conserved resources. Developers and builders can help make the case for cost-effective sustainable development, but public agencies and nonprofit organizations should take primary responsibility for spreading the word in ways that make immediate as well as long-lasting impressions.

Conclusion: What Developers Can Do

This chapter has summarized a range of best practices that, applied to everyday development projects, can help contribute to rather than detract from the long-term sustainability of developments and communities. The chapter has also identified some ways that both the private real estate industry and government entities, with the participation of nonprofit groups, can encourage the use of best practices. Activities in support of sustainable development can be most effective if pursued through collaborative working relationships and whole-systems thinking.

In Western civilization, we have developed a system of decision making that tends to focus narrowly on certain goals that can be widely understood and for which progress can be easily measured. While we lament the unintended consequences of such systems of thought and action (in this context, sprawling development and polluted water), we pay little attention to the underlying frameworks of public and private powers and communications that generate them. Yet, the concept of sustainable development reminds us that we cannot continue to disregard the fundamental motivations in our approach to private and community development without grave damage to our global and community environment. Sustainability calls for us to mobilize the entire constituency of interests to participate in making choices for more environmentally responsible development. To move in this direction, developers should work collaboratively with the public affected by their developments, with public agencies that guide their projects, and with nongovernmental groups that can help clarify issues and implement solutions. As stated earlier, public and private efforts must move in tandem to be most effective.

Whole-systems thinking, discussed briefly in chapters 6 and 7, requires a broad understanding of the multiple relationships among the components of development as well as a recognition of how to use those relationships to raise the level of sustainability (and often profitability) attained by development. Most of the building designs of the past few generations have ignored common-sense relationships to nature, actually separating us from the benefits of nature. Whole-systems design considers integration of building systems with environmentally responsible design and construction. Chapter 7, for example, pointed out that marginal cost increases for energy-efficient windows and lighting can be repaid in a few years. At the project level, as discussed in chapter 6, conservation of natural features generates long-term increases in development value, adding to conservation objectives and profit goals.

Both collaboration and whole-systems thinking in approaching development will allow developers to realize more sustainable relationships with their constituent public officials and consumer markets, more sustainable support from environmental and other interest groups, and more sustainable returns, in monetary and fulfillment terms, from their professional pursuits.

Endnotes

1. "Lessons Learned: Four Times Square," published by Earth Day New York, 1999, p. 19. The report describes the evolution of ideas and techniques applied to the design and construction of office buildings, plus a number of informative articles by experts in green building.

2. Ibid, p. 23.

3. All information was drawn from Sarah Bennett Nerenberg and Kevin Friel, "The Conservation Development Evaluation System (CeDES): Evaluating Environmentally Friendly Developments," *Land Development*, Fall 1999, pp. 22-25.

4. The alliance included the U.S. Environmental Protection Agency, Center for Watershed Protection, National Association of Home Builders, Natural Lands Trust, Wisconsin Department of Natural Resources, Ohio Environmental Protection Agency, and Countryside Program.

5. For more information or a copy of CeDES, contact The Conservation Fund, 53 W. Jackson Boulevard, Suite 1332, Chicago, Illinois 60604; telephone 312-913-9065; E-mail SarahTCF@aol.com.

6. Paul Hawken, *The Ecology of Commerce* (New York: HarperCollins Publishers, Inc., 1993), p. 144.

7. Information about indicators and examples of programs can be found in Kevin J. Krizek and Joe Power, *A Planners Guide to Sustainable Development*, Planning Advisory Service Report No. 467 (Chicago: American Planning Association, 1996); and Virginia W. Maclaren, "Urban Sustainability Reporting," *Journal of the American Planning Association*, Vol. 62, No. 2, Spring 1996, pp. 184-202.

8. More information on this program can be found in Alex Wilson et al., *Green Development: Integrating Ecology and Real Estate* (New York: John Wiley & Sons, 1998), pp. 220-221.

9. The BEST program description and case studies can be found on the net at www.ci.portland.or.us/energy/bestmain.

10. "Boulder at Forefront with Green Points Program," *Environmental Building News*, Vol. 7, No. 3, March 1998, p. 3.

11. *Report of Duwamish Coalition Accomplishments*. Prepared by the King County Office of Budget and Strategic Planning for the Duwamish Coalition, March 1997.

12. Cynthia Pollock Shea, "West Palm Beach: The Resurrection." News Services of the Florida Sustainable Communities Center, http://sustainable.state.fl.us/fed/fscc/news, posted October 28, 1998.

AFTERWORD

Douglas R. Porter

The authors and ULI project staff associated with this publication were aware before, during, and after writing the book that the practice of sustainable development is very much a work in progress. Our understanding of sustainability in all its manifestations continues to evolve as we learn more about natural and human systems and how they interrelate. Our knowledge about practical applications of the goals of sustainable development is also unfolding as we find ways to adapt technologies, behaviors, and ways of thinking to come closer to achieving sustainability goals. One of the expected outcomes of this publication was to identify areas for undertaking further research and understanding and for working out practical applications to promote sustainable development.

At the most fundamental level of sustainable development, we still lack operational definitions of sustainable economies and social systems to guide best development practices. Most discussions of economic and social sustainability are concerned with environmental effects but pay little attention to fashioning economies and societies that can sustain, for example, life, wealth, justice, and civilization. The overarching question is: How can community development and real estate development promote sustainable local economies and societies that *also* reduce waste and consumption of natural resources? Presumably, the answer requires actions and practices more profound than typical public programs for economic development and social welfare.

Focusing more on the subject of this book, the next question is, How can real estate development contribute to sustainable economic and social systems? In chapter 4, Christopher Leinberger provides one answer to this question when he proposes reconfiguring the real estate financing paradigm to serve more diverse social and economic needs and more environmentally sustainable forms of development. Edward Blakely in chapter 5 makes a case for more socially responsible development—development that begins to build bridges rather than walls between people. But, without question, we have only begun to work out paradigms that satisfy the aims of sustainability.

As for the day-to-day practice of real estate development, we have identified some innovative techniques and approaches that move in the direction of sustainability. In the environmental arena in particular, a considerable amount of inventive thinking has generated good ideas about environmentally friendly alternatives to conventional suburban development projects, including treatments of landscapes, vegetation, habitats, wetlands, stream valleys, and other aspects of the natural world. Relatively new approaches to stormwater retention and wetlands restoration, for example, are becoming well known and are now frequently used in low-density fringe-area developments, as are Randall Arendt's "conservation design" ideas for subdivisions. We also know a great deal about conserving energy through technologies such as solar cells, coated glass, and energy-efficient heating and cooling equipment, although applications of this knowledge still come up against marketplace and regulatory obstacles.

But, as the authors are uncomfortably aware, our current knowledge of best practices leaves some distinct gaps, raises unresolved issues, or falls well short of promoting truly sustainable development. The following are a few—not all, by any means—of the areas in need of better data or fresh approaches.

Reconciling Environmental Conservation with Compact Development. To what extent can our knowledge of sustainable environmental practices in low-density suburban projects be adapted for more compact forms of development? Most conservation design projects that cluster development to retain sizable amounts of open space basically reconfigure the sprawl patterns of conventional suburban subdivisions. As a recent reviewer of Arendt's newest book puts it, "Conservation design is a formula for decentralizing settlements in a more tasteful and ecologically sound way. It does nothing to increase the overall density of human settlement. . . ."[1] How realistic or desirable is it to expect to retain natural landscape and hydrologic conditions on sites proposed for overall densities of more than one or two units an acre? In chapter 6, we suggest that every effort be made to preserve unique natural qualities of every site, but we recognize that intensive development will inevitably obliterate most natural features. Presumably, by reducing demands for land, compact development reduces impacts on natural areas elsewhere. On-site features such as working farms and constructed wetlands for wastewater treatment, however, are most likely infeasible while methods for accommodating aquifer recharge in densely built areas, for example, are still being developed. More attention to this issue is needed if we are to promote compact yet environmentally friendly development.

Creating Processes for Off-Site Mitigation. If part of the answer to the above issue is to compensate for environmental damage on densely built sites by conserving large natural areas elsewhere, what financing or regulatory mechanisms could be instituted to achieve that tradeoff? And to what extent do such tradeoffs actually assist in achieving sustainable development? Increasingly, programs are acquiring and preserving open space around many metropolitan areas, but so far they appear disconnected from commitments for achieving compact development. Furthermore, off-site mitigation of environmental harms frequently runs into regulatory obstacles and generates controversy in the environmental community. As discussed in chapter 2, environmentalists' divergent views on the extent to which urban development should be allowed to disrupt natural land and water functions need to be reconciled.

Establishing Long-Term Viability of New Technologies. Many of the technologies and approaches proposed today to achieve more sustainable development are relatively new; in other words, experience with them over time is limited. Using constructed wetlands for wastewater treatment, for example, has been thoroughly tested in new installations, but requirements for maintaining water quality standards in wetlands 20 to 30 years ahead are perilously close to guesswork at this point. We know that argon gas enclosed in high-performance windows eventually leaks and must be refreshed to maintain windows' light- and heat-transmission capabilities, but when and whether that happens depends on management standards and financial resources available at the time. And even solar panels need occasional cleaning to function efficiently. These types of management issues are similar to experience with so-called package sewage treatment plants. They may be engineered to function effectively for many years, but too often maintenance lags and systems fail. The long-term maintenance involved in using innovative technologies needs more attention.

Building Adaptable Communities. People trained in environmental sciences understand succession—the ways forests and wetlands and other natural features evolve through multiple stages. Somehow, although we can observe it occurring every day, we pay too little attention to the parallel process that communities experience over time. The ways we use our built environment change in response to new circumstances and technologies. At the neighborhood level, school officials understand that schools empty when neighborhoods age but then become overcrowded as the elderly population is replaced with new families, often within a few years. At the regional scale, over the past 50 years, we have seen centers of commerce and industry wane as new technologies allowed evolution of a service-driven economy located in multiple nodes of activity. How can these types of evolutionary changes be accommodated in the sustainability paradigm? How can we introduce new activities and more sustainable patterns of development in the aging suburbs found in every metropolitan area? How and when do the scattered agglomerations of economic activity typical of today's metropolitan form reach a sustainable critical mass? What scale and mix of activities in communities and neighborhoods truly sustain social interaction and satisfaction? Which parts of our communities should be built for all time, and which ones should we expect periodically to replace and rebuild? All these are questions for which we have few answers.

Overcoming the Builder/User Benefit Disconnection. By their nature, innovative technologies often cost more at the outset than over the long haul. Viewed with a life-cycle lens, they may prove much less costly than conventional technologies. But life cycles often involve different "owners" of the technology and therefore different financial stakes. Developers and builders understandably shy away from higher-priced basic equipment and appliances unless the ultimate consumer understands and accepts their long-term financial benefits. Unfortunately, many consumers are unwilling to pay more now in order to spend less ten years from now; the time horizon is too long and the uncertainties—in terms of operational efficiencies and value added to the property—are too great. This reluctance will be cured in time as more and better information based on empirical experience demonstrates benefits; in the meantime, however, developers, builders, and the public sector must do everything they can to identify and internalize the current benefits of long-term financial returns from the use of innovative technologies. Part of that effort should focus on educating consumers about the external costs of conventional development.

In conclusion, the task of developing more sustainable buildings, projects, and communities is worth the effort of spreading knowledge, trying out new technologies, and changing the institutional norms and processes that underwrite nonsustainable forms of development. Each of us can play an important part in seeking and applying practices that promote sustainable development.

Endnote

[1] Harold Henderson, "Planners Library," *Planning*, March 2000, p. 39.

160

PROJECT INDEX